September 1978

Happy Birthday
to Betsy

With love,
Aunt Ruth, Uncle Rudy and Karen

A Time of Growing

Eighteen stories . . . funny, sad, and bittersweet . . .
about girls on the threshold of womanhood

A Time of Growing

edited by Jean Van Leeuwen

Random House • New York

Library of Congress Catalog Card Number: 67-24689
Manufactured in the United States of America
Designed by Jackie Corner Mabli

Acknowledgments

"Between the Dark and the Daylight" by Nancy Hale. Copyright 1940 by Nancy Hale. Reprinted by permission of Harold Ober Associates, Inc.

"Sixteen" from *Sixteen And Other Stories* by Maureen Daly. Copyright 1938 by Scholastic Magazines, Inc. Copyright renewed 1966 by Maureen Daly. Reprinted by permission.

"A Very Continental Weekend" from *The Beautiful Friend And Other Stories* by Mary Stolz. ©Copyright 1960 by Mary Stolz. Reprinted by permission of Harper & Row, Inc. Four lines from the poem "To the Not Impossible Him" from *Collected Poems* by Edna St. Vincent Millay. Copyright 1922, 1950 by Edna St. Vincent Millay. Reprinted by permission of Norma Millay Ellis.

"Her First Ball" from *The Short Stories of Katherine Mansfield.* Copyright 1922 by Alfred A. Knopf, Inc. Copyright renewed 1950 by John Middleton Murry. Reprinted by permission of Alfred A. Knopf, Inc. and The Society of Authors, literary representative of the estate of the late Katherine Mansfield.

"Road to the Isles" from *Cress Delahanty* by Jessamyn West. Copyright 1948 by Jessamyn West. Reprinted by permission of Harcourt, Brace & World, Inc.

"The Impossible He" by Rosanne Smith Soffer. ©Copyright 1956 by *Quixote.* This story appeared in *The Best American Short Stories of 1957* edited by Martha Foley. Reprinted by permission of the author.

"Rebellion" by Ruth Harnden. Copyright 1953 by The Hearst Corporation. Reprinted by permission of the author.

"A Chain of Love" from *The Names and Faces of Heroes* by Reynolds Price. ©Copyright 1962, 1963 by Reynolds Price. This story has appeared in *Encounter* and *The Critic.* Reprinted by permission of Atheneum Publishers.

"The Lovely Night" by Shirley Jackson. Copyright 1950 by Shirley Jackson. Reprinted by permission of Brandt & Brandt.

"The Strange Thing" by Emily Hahn. Copyright 1935 by Emily Hahn. Copyright renewed 1963 by Emily Hahn. Reprinted by permission of Brandt & Brandt.

"Little Baseball World" from *Happy New Year, Kamerades!* by Robert Lowry. Copyright 1946 by Street & Smith Publications, Inc. This story originally appeared in *Mademoiselle.* Reprinted by permission of the author and Doubleday & Company, Inc.

"The First Prom's the Hardest" from *We Shook the Family Tree* by Hildegarde Dolson. Copyright 1941, 1942, 1946 by Hildegarde Dolson. Reprinted by permission of Random House, Inc.

"Party at the Williamsons'" by Astrid Peters. Copyright 1946 by Astrid Peters. Reprinted by permission of *The New Yorker* and Russell & Volkening, Inc.

"Sunday Afternoon" by Lucile Vaughan Payne. Copyright 1951 by Lucile Vaughan Payne. This story originally appeared in *Seventeen.* Reprinted by permission of McIntosh & Otis, Inc.

"A Hundred Years from Now" by Nancy Cardozo. Copyright 1951 by Nancy Cardozo. Reprinted by permission of the author and her agent, James Brown Associates, Inc.

"The Legacy" from *The Blue Cup and Other Stories* by B. J. Chute. ©Copyright 1957 by B. J. Chute. Reprinted by permission of E. P. Dutton & Company, Inc.

"Down in the Reeds by the River" by Victoria Lincoln. Copyright 1946 by Victoria Lincoln. This story originally appeared in *The New Yorker.* Reprinted by permission of Harold Ober Associates, Inc.

"Bottle Night" by Jean Fritz. ©Copyright 1958 by Triangle Publications. Reprinted by permission of Triangle Publications and Russell & Volkening, Inc.

Contents

Introduction

To live is to grow. From the moment of birth a child grows, in body and mind and understanding. And when the body is as tall as it will ever be, still the mind continues to expand. An eighty-year-old man who learns to play the violin is growing.

But there is a time, when a girl is thirteen or fourteen or fifteen, when growing seems to happen all at once. And the girl who was a child becomes a woman.

The moment when it happens cannot be pinpointed exactly, just as we can never be sure at what instant a bud blossoms into a flower. And perhaps the transformation is never really total for, as there is a glimpse of the woman-to-be in the youngest child, so there is a remembrance of the girl in all grandmothers. But a turning point is passed, and after that nothing is ever quite the same again.

This book is a collection of such turning points. The events that lead up to them are different, as are the girls who experience them. Some, like Cress Delahanty in "Road to the Isles," are secure in happy families. Others, like Lucy in "A Hundred Years from Now," are adrift, waiting to be grown up so their lives can begin. Some, like Catherine in "The Strange Thing," are surrounded by material wealth. And others, like Rosacoke in "A Chain of Life," have only the wealth of the mind and heart. They live in the suburbs, the city, the North Carolina hills, in China, New Zealand, New England. But inside, their geography is the same. Each inhabits that never-never land between childhood and womanhood. And each is a little bit frightened, a little unsure of what happens next.

The turning point for Cress in "Road to the Isles" is the surprising discovery that her parents worry about her performance in public, just as she does about theirs. For the heroine of "Sixteen" it is the realization that love stories don't necessarily have happy endings. For Catherine in "The Strange Thing" it is simply the dawning awareness of herself as a separate person: "It was amazing. He was old, he knew all about things, and yet he had recognized her. He had said to himself: Here is a girl, Catherine. You are Catherine; I am Bud and in the same world with you..."

So they move into the adult world, a little frightened but eager for the wonderful things that surely lie just ahead. With the heroine of "Bottle Night" they shout, "Here's to Life!" And under their breath they add, "And how!"

J.V.L

A Time of Growing

BETWEEN THE DARK AND THE DAYLIGHT

Nancy Hale

This was the bed where Sara had always been put when she was sick. Not her own bed, narrow and tidy against the wall of her room, among her own books, her own furniture, so well known to her that she did not see them any more. This bed was different. This was the guest-room bed, a double bed with white-painted iron from head to foot. All her fifteen years she had been put here when she had a cold, or tonsillitis, or measles. It was higher, and broader, and softer than her own bed, and being here pulled her back to the books she had read when she had been sick, or that had been read to her; to the long, unlabored trains of fantasy that had swung in her mind like slow, engrossing ocean swells.

Within the enchantment of the bed in the guest room her mind was released over centuries and into palaces and into the future, and she could alter her person from small to tall, from quiet to commanding. In this bed she had been by turns a queen, a Roman, a man during the Massacre of St. Bartholomew. Here she had imagined herself grown up and having five children, had given them names and learned their separate faces and spoken to them and punished them. She had always dreamed in this bed of new things and new feelings. She had never reached backward for anything within her own experience.

She had not been sick in several months, but she had bronchitis now, and since she had been sick last something had dropped away from her. She had changed. Without questioning what was happening to her, or even being conscious of it, she had stopped playing in brooks and running fast in sneakers and wearing her hair in two pigtails. In these autumn months the girls she played with had changed too. They bought sodas in the drugstore. They walked slowly, eternally, along the tarred New England sidewalks, with their arms around each other's waists. Suddenly they would laugh together helplessly for a moment; at what, they did not know. They cut their hair and curled it, or brushed it out smooth and tied a hair ribbon around it. They watched themselves pass in the shop windows of the town. And all of it had come like a natural change and occupied her fully.

It was not that she turned her head away from one side and looked toward the other. The old things she had known so many years now stood still without a sound to call her as they used, and until she took sick she did not think of them. But as she lay in the guest-room bed she resented more and more what was happening to her. She had no pleasure in remembering the shop windows, the drugstore, the boys—only a sort of weariness and distaste. She did not want to go that way. It all began when she read the Indian book.

After three days her fever went down and she stopped coughing so much and was allowed to go from the guest room into her own room, in her nightgown and wrapper, and take books out of the shelves and bring them back to bed. The first day she brought a book of Poe's short stories that she loved, and two of the Little Colonel books, and a book about English history, and an old book that she had not read for years, about Indians and wood lore. Her Uncle Lyman had sent it to her one autumn after he had been at their house for a visit. That was when she was eleven.

He belonged to a mountain-climbing club and took long walks in the woods behind their house and she used to go with him. She felt something wonderful in the way he walked without noise along the smooth brown paths, and liked to walk behind, watching him. When it grew dark early in those fall afternoons he would still follow the path without hesitation.

One afternoon when it was cold and frosty and the sun was setting, they came out on a hillside that ran down to the road. There was a clump of birches at the top and he took a knife out of his pocket and showed her how to cut away a strip of birch bark and then to pare its delicate, pale-pink paper from within. That was Indian paper, he said. He took up a rock with big spots of mica and held it up into the shining of the late sun. "If there was someone over on that far hill, I could signal to him with this," he said, "if we were Indians."

What he had said about the Indians filled her mind after he was gone. Through the winter and through the spring she went to the woods. In the winter it was only in the afternoons that she could go, late, after she got home from school. But when the spring came there was more time; it didn't get dark so early. She found a pool beside a rock, covered with green slime, and at the edges the ice-cold water was full of the blobs of transparent jelly that held a million black spots: frogs' eggs. She took them home with her in a tin lard pail and put them in a glass bowl, to watch the polliwogs hatch out. They turned from eggs to tadpoles, to strange creatures with a tail and two legs. And one morning they jumped out of the bowl and hopped about the dining room floor and had to be thrown out in the garden.

When it was summer she could go all day. She asked for Indian clothes and was given them for her birthday: a fringed coat and skirt, and a leather band for her head, with a feather in it. The skirt had a pocket in the side, where she carried her lunch, done up in waxed paper. When she was alone, on the long paths that had been there for a hundred years and led, if you could follow them, to other states, to other woods and meadows miles away, she was satisfied and at home. She lived within her own private world—this world with a pine-needle floor, peopled by the shadow shapes of men who moved without noise, surmounted by tall plumes. This world was beautiful and intricate and still. The ground pine ran along under the dead leaves in secret; the shallows of the little ponds were filled with a minute and busy life, tiny fish and frogs and "rowboats" that skittered across the slimy surface into the shade. The grouse hid in the underbrush, and the small animals, the rabbits and the sudden moles, ran at intervals across the path, into the sunlight and out of it.

When she went home late in the afternoons it was walking out of one world into another. It required a readjustment of the hearing. From the minute sounds of the woods to which she was acute all day, she walked down along the road past the cultivated meadows, where the sounds were bolder—loud crickets and the long squeal of the cicada—past the hunting dogs that were penned up behind their neighbor's house and barked at all passers, past the hired man putting his tools away in the barn.

Finally there was the house, and she would have supper with her mother and father. In a cotton dress and socks and sneakers, she would sit at the round table and talk and eat and watch the sun going down at last through the west window. The door stood open on the garden and the smell of early-evening grass, the sound of birds, came in as they finished supper. Much later, when she was going to bed, she would kneel down on the floor in her room and crane her head far out of the window to smell the smell that came across the fields, to see through the light summer night the dark, irregular silhouette against the sky; that was the smell and the shape of the woods.

But somehow it had sifted away, melted into the next year of her life, and become like a streak of old color in the long stream of being alive. Now, as she read that book, which had been a Bible to her, everything she had been doing for months seemed dingy and dull and unbeautiful. The Indian book awoke in her the recollection of the woods and being in the woods. For the first time in her life, now in this bed, she thought longingly of something that she had already experienced. She felt her mind entering the woods and inhabiting them again. She had never finished with the woods, she decided. She had left them for no reason, and when she was well again she would go back to them. That was what she wanted. She did not know why she had penetrated that other world, the new, sharp, bright-lit life that she had begun lately, but it was not what she wanted. She did not want to grow up and be with people. It was not suited to her, and she rejected it now, lying free to choose in bed.

She lay with her legs spread comfortably beneath the smooth, cool sheet and stared sightless at the bare yellow-and-white buttonwood branches outside her window. Trays were brought to her and she ate thin soup with lemon in it, and hot buns, and scrambled eggs, and ice cream. The sunshine moved regularly across the floor of the guest room, from beside her bed in the morning to the farthest corner by the window at sunset. Then it disappeared and twilight filled the room. In the house across the road the lights went on for supper and the lights went out for sleep. And there were stars in the black square of her window.

She was in bed six days and at the end of that time she got up. She saw things again vertically and shook herself like a dog and went outside on the side porch, where the November sunshine lay in pale, lemon-colored stripes. The outdoors smelled sharp and sunny, and her muscles came to life and itched to move. She ran down through the garden to the apple tree and climbed it as she had always done for years, up through its round, rough, pinky-gray branches to a crotch high up, where she sat and surveyed the land. The swamp lay beyond, all still and golden. The apple trees round her were not as high as this one, and she could look down into them. Across the fields the white farmhouse let a thin stream of smoke up through its chimney, where it wavered and turned blue and vanished into the chilly blue sky. The air smelled of late autumn; the air smelled of dead leaves; the air was sharp and lively and wishful. Sara sat in the tree and swung her legs and thought about nothing until somebody called her and she looked down. It was her friend Catherine, who lived in the farmhouse. She stood under the tree and squinted her eyes up at Sara.

"Hi!" Sara said.

"You all well?"

"Sure!"

"Let's go for a walk."

"O.K."

She clambered down the tree and they left the orchard and started to walk down the road to the town, along the lumpy sidewalk made of tar and pebbles. The trees beside the road were bare and clean, and the sky was bluc, and the cars drove by gaily. In this November day there was a feeling of activity and of happiness, the brisk, anticipatory feeling of winter coming. Sara and Catherine put their arms around each other's waists and strolled, smiling and talking about what had been happening in school, and about boys.

It was exciting to talk about school. Talking about it, Sara smelled the smell of the classroom, of new, freshly sharpened lead pencils. The impetus of living took hold of her and she was eager and ready for it. She looked at Catherine's plaid wool skirt switching beside her own blue one, casting a thin, swaying shadow on the sidewalk. They strolled on into the town. All the plate-glass windows of the stores glittered in the sun and there was a busy air about the town, of things to be done, of putting on storm doors, of settling down to wait for winter. They passed Tracey's newsstand, where the boys stood in a group looking around. Catherine waved and Sara looked over her shoulder.

"Ha ya?" the Tracey boy said.

"Ha ya doing?" Sara said. She and Catherine laughed lightly, meaningfully, and walked on down the street to the drugstore. They went inside and sat at one of the black glass-topped tables with triangular seats. The store smelled of soda and drugs and candy. The soda clerk walked over to their table.

"What are you having?" he asked.

"Chocolate float," Catherine said.

"Chocolate float, too," Sara said.

It was somehow delightful in the drugstore, full of promise and undisclosed things. To sit, elbows on the damp black glass, and watch the solid glass door and the people who went in and out was somehow exciting. Sara looked at the other customers out of the corner of her eye, wisely, with poise, and drank her drink through a straw without looking down at it.

"Gee, I'm glad you're over that old bronchitis," Catherine said.

"Gee, so am I."

"I thought you'd never be out. You must have been in the house a whole week."

"Pretty near."

"Don't you just *hate* being sick?"

"I certainly do. Just lying there in bed."

"My mother's going to buy me four new dresses for school. She said I could pick them out myself."

"That's keen. My mother says . . ."

Sara went on talking, eagerly, with satisfaction. She was glad to be well and out and doing things. She felt new vistas opening up before her: school, the girls at school, boys, and beyond that unimaginable things, growing up. For an instant her thought trembled alone, apart from what she was saying.

She thought it was nice to be well and going on with living. It was horrid to be sick and just lie and think. Then her mind switched away from that, the inaction of it, and back into the occupying present, and was happy.

About the Author

The New England of "Between the Dark and the Daylight" has always been part of Nancy Hale's life. She was born there, a descendent of patriot Nathan Hale. Her grandfather was Edward Everett Hale, author of *Man Without a Country,* and among her great-aunts was Harriet Beecher Stowe.

Her parents were both painters, and Nancy Hale was a portrait artist before becoming a writer. Her first novel, *The Good Die Young,* was published in 1932. She has contributed extensively to *Vogue, The New Yorker,* and various other magazines and literary reviews. Among her books are *The Prodigal Woman, A New England Girlhood,* and *Black Summer.* Her latest collection of short stories is *Pattern of Perfection,* published in 1960.

SIXTEEN
Maureen Daly

Now don't get me wrong. I mean, I want you to understand from the beginning that I'm not really dumb. I know what a girl should do and what she shouldn't. I get around. I read. I watch TV. And I have two older sisters. So, you see, I know what the score is. I know that anyone who orders a strawberry sundae in a drugstore instead of a lemon Coke would probably be dumb enough to wear colored ankle socks with high-heeled pumps or use "Evening in Paris" with a tweed suit. But I'm sort of drifting. This isn't what I wanted to tell you. I just wanted to give you the general idea of how I'm not so dumb. It's important that you understand that.

You see, it was funny how I met him. It was a winter night like any other winter night. And I didn't have my Latin done either. But the way the moon made the twigs lash and silver-plated the snowdrifts, I just couldn't stay inside. The skating rink isn't far from our house—you can make it in five minutes if the sidewalks aren't slippery, so I went skating. I remember it took me a long time to get ready that night because I had to darn my skating socks first. I don't know why they always wear out so fast—just in the toes, too. And then I brushed my hair—hard, so hard it clung to my hand and stood up around my head in a hazy halo.

My skates were hanging by the back door all nice and shiny, for I'd just got them for Christmas and they smelled so queer—like fresh-smoked ham. My dog walked with me as far as the corner. She's a red chow, very polite and well mannered. She panted along beside me, and her hot breath made a frosty little balloon bouncing on the end of her nose. My skates thumped me good-naturedly on the back as I walked. The night was breathlessly quiet and the stars winked down like a million flirting eyes. It was all so lovely.

I had to cut across someone's back garden to get to the rink and last summer's grass stuck through the thin ice, brown and discouraged. Not many people came through this way and the crusted snow broke through the little hollows between corn stubbles frozen hard in the ground. I was out of breath when I got to the shanty—out of breath with running and with the loveliness of the night. Shanties are always such friendly places—the floor all hacked to wet splinters from the skate runners and the wooden wall marked with signs of forgotten love affairs. There was a smell of singed wool as someone got too near the iron stove. Girls burst through the door laughing, with snow on their hair, and tripped over shoes scattered on the floor. A pimply-faced boy grabbed the hat from the frizzled head of an eighth-grade blonde and stuffed it into an empty galosh to prove his love and then hastily bent to examine his skate strap with innocent unconcern.

It didn't take me long to get my own skates on and I stuck my shoes under the bench—far back where they wouldn't get knocked around and would be easy to find when I wanted to go home. I walked out on my toes and the shiny runners of my new skates dug deep into the sodden floor.

It was snowing a little outside—quick, eager little Lux-like flakes that melted as soon as they touched your hand. I don't know where the snow came from for there were stars out. Or maybe the stars were in my eyes and I just kept seeing them every time I looked up into the darkness. I waited a moment. You know, to start to skate at a crowded rink is like jumping on a moving merry-go-round. The skaters go skimming round in a colored blur like gaudy painted horses and the shrill musical jabber re-echoes in the night from a hundred human calliopes. Once in, I went all right. At least after I found out exactly where that rough ice was. It was "round, round, jump the rut, round, round, jump the rut, round, round—"

And then he came. All of a sudden his arm was around my waist so warm and tight and he said very casually, "Mind if I skate with you?" and then he took my other hand. That's all there was to it. Just that and then we were skating. It wasn't that I'd never skated with a boy before. Don't be silly. I told you before I get around. But this was different. He was a smoothie. He was a big shot up at school and he went to all the big dances and he was the best dancer in town except Harold Wright who didn't count because he'd been to college in New York for two years. Don't you see? This was different.

At first I can't remember what we talked about. I can't even remember if we talked at all. We just skated and skated and laughed every time we came to that rough spot and pretty soon we were laughing all the time at nothing at all. It was all so lovely.

Then we sat on the big snowbank at the edge of the rink and just watched. It was cold at first even with my skating pants on, sitting on that hard heap of snow, but pretty soon I got warm all over. He threw a handful of snow at me and it fell in a little white shower on my hair and he leaned over to brush it off. I held my breath. The night stood still.

The moon hung just over the warming shanty like a big quarter slice of muskmelon and the smoke from the pipe chimney floated up in a sooty fog. One by one the houses around the rink twinkled out their lights and somebody's hound wailed a mournful apology to a star as he curled up for the night. It was all so lovely.

Then he sat up straight and said, "We'd better start home." Not "Shall I take you home?" or "Do you live far?" but "We'd better start home." See, that's how I know he wanted to take me home. Not because he *had* to but because he *wanted* to. He went to the shanty to get my shoes. "Black ones," I told him. "Same size as your pet movie star's." And he laughed again. He was still smiling when he came back and took off my skates and tied the wet skate strings in a soggy knot and put them over his shoulder. Then he held out his hand and I slid off the snowbank and brushed off the seat of my pants and we were ready.

It was snowing harder now. Big, quiet flakes that clung to twiggy bushes and snuggled in little drifts against the tree trunks. The night was an etching in black and white. It was all so lovely I was sorry I lived only a few blocks away. He talked softly as we walked, as if every little word were a secret. "Did I like band music, and did I plan to go to college next year and had I a cousin who lived in Appleton and knew his brother?" A very respectable Emily Post sort of conversation and then finally—"how nice I looked with snow in my hair and had I ever seen the moon so—close?" For the moon was following us as we walked and ducking playfully behind a chimney every time I turned to look at it. And then we were home.

The porch light was on. My mother always puts the porch light on when I go away at night. And we stood there a moment by the front steps and the snow turned pinkish in the glow of colored light and a few feathery flakes settled on his hair. Then he took my skates and put them over my shoulder and said, "Good night now. I'll call you." "I'll call you," he said.

I went inside then and in a moment he was gone. I watched him from my window as he went down the street. He was whistling softly and I waited until the sound faded away so I couldn't tell if it was he or my heart whistling out there in the night. And then he was gone, completely gone.

I shivered. Somehow the darkness seemed changed. The stars were little hard chips of light far up in the sky and the moon stared down with a sullen yellow glare. The air was tense with sudden cold and a gust of wind swirled his footprints into white oblivion. Everything was quiet.

But he'd said, "I'll call you." That's what he said—"I'll call you." I couldn't sleep all night.

And that was last Thursday. Tonight is Tuesday. Tonight is Tuesday and my homework's done, and I darned some socks that didn't really need it, and I worked a crossword puzzle and I listened to the radio and now I'm just sitting. I'm just sitting because I can't think of anything else to do. I can't think of anything, anything but snowflakes and ice skates and yellow moons and Thursday night. The telephone is sitting on the corner table with its old black face turned to the wall so I can't see its leer. I don't even jump when it rings any more. My heart still prays but my mind just laughs. Outside the night is still, so still I think I'll go crazy and the white snow's all dirtied and smoked into grayness and the wind is blowing the arc light so it throws weird, waving shadows from the trees onto the lawn—like thin, starved arms begging for I don't know what. And so I'm just sitting here and I'm not feeling anything. I'm not even sad because all of a sudden I know. All of a sudden I know. I can sit here now forever and laugh and laugh and laugh while the tears run salty in the corners of my mouth. For all of a sudden I know, I know what the stars knew all the time—he'll never, never call—never.

About the Author

Maureen Daly wrote her perceptive story, "Sixteen," when she herself was sixteen. It placed first in a national short story contest sponsored by Scholastic Magazines, and was selected for the annual O. Henry Memorial Award volume. She has not stopped writing since—stories, articles, and novels. Her novel *Seventeenth Summer* is considered a classic in teen-age fiction.

Born in County Tyrone, Northern Ireland, Maureen Daly grew up in Fond du Lac, Wisconsin. She has been a reporter-columnist for the Chicago *Tribune,* and Associate Editor of *Ladies Home Journal.* Married to novelist-script writer William McGivern and the mother of two children, she now lives in Hollywood, California.

A VERY CONTINENTAL WEEKEND

Mary Stolz

There was no privacy anywhere. Not at home, where her parents watched over her with brooding concern (their fledged but unflown chick) and would say, at any suspicion of withdrawal or detachment, "Betty, darling, what is it? Is something wrong? You can tell *us,* you know."

Could she say, "But I cannot tell you, and you can't help me, and I just want to be alone"?

It was out of the question. She and her elderly parents loved each other with that stiff-necked, nervous, uncomprehending love which so often exists between generations and precludes ease of manner or freedom of expression. Besides, they never wanted to be alone themselves, and would not understand why she did.

Certainly if she explained that it was because Chris Brennan was apparently going to stick to his decision (which she hadn't told them about) and not take her out anymore, she'd never be let alone. They'd exclaim in outrage and indignation. They'd run him down as wholeheartedly as, in the past two months, they'd run him up. They'd tell her there were just as good fish in the sea as ever came out of it. They'd try to be with her every possible minute and they'd call her friends to rally round. They'd offer, in abundance, the sort of consolation they felt the situation called for, and never think that it wasn't acceptable.

How could she say, "Please, please . . . leave me alone. I don't want to be consoled, I just want to be by myself"?

Plainly, she could not.

"How's Chris?" her mother had asked a few nights ago. "You seeing him this weekend? Such a nice young fellow. In some men, you'd say almost too good-looking, but he isn't the sort to get carried away by his own good looks. He's got this modesty, hasn't he?"

Stifling a wish to cry out in protest, Betty agreed that Chris had this modesty. She avoided a direct answer about the weekend. What could she have told them? That after dating her for several successive Saturdays, Chris had said to her last weekend that he found himself getting dangerously fond of her and therefore had decided to stop seeing her (outside the office, where it was frequently unavoidable) .

"Forever?" she'd blurted, hurt and not able to understand what she'd done or not done to cause this. They'd seemed to be having such fun together.

"I don't know," he'd admitted. "I just don't know. You see, Betty, I'm not in a position yet to get too fond of any girl." He thought that over and went on with desperate candor, "I don't even *want* to. I mean, sure, in time . . . only not just yet. You do see, don't you?"

She seized on his tone of anxiety and told herself he couldn't care so much that she understand if he did not care very much for her, that what he was saying was not just a kindly excuse to stop seeing a girl in whom he'd lost interest, but a literal statement of fact. If, indeed, he was dangerously fond of her, would a refusal to see her put an end to it? Rather the reverse, if you could believe books and adages.

While she was still with him that evening, she managed to be controlled, even gracious. She wanted to shriek at him, to ask how he thought he could engage someone's heart this way and walk off with a casual "Sorry," how he presumed to tell her in all but words that she was to wait and hope but he wasn't making any promises. But she kept her voice gentle and said yes, she did understand how a man might feel that way, and for that matter she wasn't entirely sure herself that she wanted to limit her attention to just one man.

Had he pricked up his ears rather sharply at that? Had an expression of doubt entered the stream of self-justification? She couldn't be sure. Wanting to finish the evening and leave with him, intact, the picture of a girl a man might well wish to return to, she had time only for self-observation. It was watch each word, guard each glance, prevent at all costs the emergence of a girl who lay just under the surface quivering with outrage, a girl who felt entitled to a scene and might at any moment, regardless of the consequences, throw it.

She'd made it safely to the door, and, as if fate now and then relented when she'd pushed you to the breaking point, her mother and father had already gone to bed when she let herself in. So she was able to steal to her room unobserved and cry half the night unconsoled. It had done her some good. It left her still with her parents to face morning and evening, the office to face all day from Monday to Friday without, now, the happy feeling rising on Thursday morning that any moment he would come to her and say, "Doing anything Saturday, Betty?" He'd never been more definite than that, had never said, at the close of one Saturday evening, that he'd like to see her the next. He had never suggested a date during the week, and Betty, loving Saturdays, had schooled herself not to ask (though she had to wonder) what he did with the other six evenings.

But twice in the past month she had made up her mind that *this* Thursday when he came to her desk as if by accident and asked, as if only remotely concerned, whether she were busy Saturday, she would say, "Sorry, I've a date that night. How about some other time?" She told herself sternly that she offered no challenge, turning into a happy limpet and saying, "No, no, I'm not busy at all," practically before he'd put his question. You had to pique a man, tempt him with uncertainty, lead him this way and that. Anyone knew that. Certainly Betty Rowan, a girl well dated from the age of fourteen through high school and two years of college, knew it.

Betty Rowan had never been in love before. She was pretty sure she was in love now. It made a terrible difference. Easy enough to pique, tempt and mislead a man if you didn't basically care whether he asked you again or not, but love, it appeared, made you a coward. You simply could not risk having him say indifferently, "Oh, that's too bad," and then not follow it up with any suggestion at all.

Well, her tactics, if tactics you could call them, had been wrong, but if Chris was to be believed, no others would have served her better. He simply wasn't going to get seriously involved with anyone. Betty tried to believe this, but a small sad voice informed her that no man decided when to fall in love. If he'd been going to love her, he wouldn't have been able to make a cool prudent decision to stop before he did.

And that, she told herself, as the intolerable Thursday morning passed with no sign of Chris, who worked in the layout department two floors above, is what I have to face. He was letting me down kindly.

Kindly was a word like a mallet splintering her reserve, and she wanted to cry out against it, as she'd wanted that night to shriek at Chris. It was quite terrifying, this fear that suddenly, in the full view of the office, she would let out a demonic yell or burst into wild sobbing.

And there really was no privacy anywhere.

She went from her desk to the file cabinet with a sheaf of folders and began, with glazed eyes and clumsy fingers, to tuck them away, checking and rechecking for accuracy. I must not make mistakes, she reminded herself over and over. My job is my job, not my love life. Somewhere, sometime, I liked this job, and sometime I'll like it again. I must not let it suffer because I am suffering.

She wished that it were possible to leave it, just for today. Only where would she go if she pleaded sudden illness? Home? That would be worse than staying here. Last night she had told her parents that she and Chris were not seeing one another anymore, trying to make it sound a mutual decision. They knew her too well and had guessed the truth immediately. With a peculiar disregard of what she might be feeling, they'd proceeded to take out their anger for her in abuse of Chris. She did not want Chris abused. She only wanted not to talk about him, and they wouldn't see it. No, she couldn't go home. She supposed she could ride around on a bus or something, but what was to keep her from crying on the bus? The truth was, an alteration in routine was beyond her and she felt physically able only to stay here or go home.

There's nowhere, nowhere, she thought over and over. I'm like that woman in the Katherine Mansfield story, I want to cry and can't think of anywhere to go and get on with it. What she wanted to do was lean her arms on the file cabinet and weep for hours. She wanted not only to weep into the files, she wanted to crawl into them. She wanted to crawl into some corner of her own mind and die there for a while and be aware of nothing.

She filed away the folders as she had to, neatly and correctly and carefully, and then, as she had to, neatly closed the drawer and returned to her desk, which was one of several in the office adjoining the editor's and left her open to the gaze of eyes right, left and behind. Of eyes ahead, too, should anyone care to turn and study her, though everyone seemed intent on his work.

During her absence at the file cabinet, two manuscripts had been left on her desk for reading. Usually this gave her a sense of exhilaration, of moving forward in the wonderful world of publishing. She was, actually, a clerk, but from time to time the editor allowed her to read and comment on manuscripts. In time, with enthusiasm and taste—she had both—she'd get to be a reader. Until Chris Brennan had come down that day from the layout department and spied her and put his casual request for a Saturday-evening date, it was all she'd been concentrating on.

Oh, but I was happy then, she mourned. Just a little over two months ago, and I was so free, so happy, so full of confidence and hopefulness, in such absolutely charming proportions, if I'd only known it. Her father said nobody recognized happiness except in retrospect, but Betty didn't believe him. She didn't believe him even now. How about all those Saturday evenings with Chris? She'd been transcendently happy, and aware of it, and grateful for the awareness. All except the last one. Nobody ever claimed that people didn't recognize unhappiness when they had it. Nobody could. Unhappiness hit you in the eye, hit you in the heart, made itself felt.

She pulled one of the manuscripts toward her, reminding herself that well-bred people did not make scenes of grief in public. What in the world do well-bred people do? she wondered a bit wildly. She caught her lower lip, which breeding could not keep steady, and breathed deeply, and ran some paper into her typewriter.

"Something wrong, Betty?" the woman at the desk to her right, secretary to the editor, inquired softly.

Betty shook her head, frantic at the kindly tone. Kindness now would be her undoing. She took another deep breath, managed to say, "Nothing, really," managed, even, half a smile, though keeping her eyes averted.

The woman either believed her or understood. She nodded and resumed her typing.

That was really the worst part of a next to unendurable morning. Noon came and brought no sign of Chris, but did bring some peculiar sort of letdown that made her emotions more manageable. She was not afraid now that she'd cry, and the afternoon would be somehow got through, and tomorrow would. She'd passed a crisis, and here she was at the other side of it, emptied of hope or pleasure, but repossessed, in a tired way, of her reason.

Reason is not the most dazzling faculty, but its return is reassuring to people who've been badly shaken by emotion. Reason now suggested that she was a grown person, taking her chances in the field of love, and if she'd had a fall, she had a right to be hurt but no right to be outraged.

If I could only be alone, she thought over and over,

I could somehow find a way of believing in my reason rather than my heart, which goes right on being miserable in spite of logic.

It was after lunch, when she was rereading the manuscript she'd read that morning with no comprehension at all, that Lisa Bergholt, a Danish girl who had a position similar to hers, came across the office to sit on the edge of her desk and make the, to Betty, completely astounding proposal that she buy a railroad ticket and a reservation at a New England inn for the weekend.

"Buy them?" Betty said blankly. "Buy them from whom? I mean, what for?"

"From me," said Lisa in what Betty always thought of as her blonde accent. Lisa was the blondest person Betty had ever seen. Not precisely pretty, but rather devastatingly showy. And just as bright as she was blonde. Every time Chris came into the office, Betty wanted to throw a bag over Lisa's head, or a smoke-screen over that end of the room, to keep him from seeing her, though he apparently never had.

Apparently was not a reliable word.

"I was," Lisa explained easily, "going off this weekend for a little time by myself. Sometimes I think that if I don't see a tree or smell some air that doesn't come out of the back of a bus, I'll lose my mind. So off I go. This weekend, this is where I was going, to this little inn in your beautiful New England."

"All by yourself?" Betty said. Lisa was probably her own age, slightly past twenty. The idea of a girl going off all by herself this way was astonishing, and Betty tried to think what her parents would say. Lisa, she'd heard somewhere, was staying here in the United States with an American aunt and uncle. An aunt and uncle, acting *in loco parentis,* would surely find this a questionable, possibly even dangerous venture. She said this to Lisa, who laughed a rich, blonde laugh.

"Certainly not," she said. "They understand that anyone needs privacy sometimes. Even young people. Though here in America one wonders that they need it as little as they do."

Betty stiffened slightly. "Everybody needs privacy." Some people certainly can't find it, she thought. "It isn't a purely European requirement. But going off alone at your—I mean, at our—age. It just seems funny."

"Not in Europe," Lisa said calmly. "We take these things differently, I expect. This is a very Danish—a very continental—thing to do. Young girls in Denmark have to go by themselves once in a while and think. The same as the young men. Don't you think it's odd . . . America is the most youth-conscious country in the world—you find it so, do you not?—and yet here is this tremendously important aspect of human life, of young lives, that you neglect altogether. The need of a person to be alone, to think, to be by *himself* from time to time. Your young people act as if they're scared to be by themselves. Why do you suppose this is?"

"You tell me," Betty said grimly.

"I suppose—" Lisa began, and broke off, as if conscious for the first time that she was on delicate ground. High on brains and vocabulary, Betty thought, but low on sensibility. Yet it was difficult to take offense at Lisa's frequent comments on the American scene. Perhaps because she was so detached. Her remarks were scarcely ever personal, and she never seemed to be discussing herself or yourself. She was concerned with types.

"No, go on," Betty said. "I'm interested."

She was. She'd found that one way to forget—momentarily—a personal hurt was to become involved in an objective interest. The sad truth was that large perspectives rarely won out over subjective preoccupations, but they did provide a sort of delaying time. In the broad daylight of human concern your small private pain was vanquished (though you could rely on it, like a sneak thief, to return with the dark).

"Why do you think we're afraid to be by ourselves?"

"Oh, I don't mean you," Lisa said. "I don't know enough about you to say. But—generally speaking—you know . . . American young people go in clusters. Of course, sometimes it's a cluster of two—can you have a cluster of just two?"

"I don't think so," Betty said. "Two is a brace."

"Well . . . but you see what I mean? Never alone."

"I see what you mean. I'd like to hear what you think is the reason."

Lisa debated. "Well, hoping you won't take offense," she began, in a tone that clearly said she didn't care one way or another, being too interested in the pursuit of knowledge to allow any danger of personal offense to hinder her, "I can't help but think it's because you—not, you comprehend, you yourself, but you collectively—are afraid that if you get alone you won't find anybody there. That is to say, you exist only in relation to other people, and the more people, the more you exist." She looked at Betty happily, as if they'd arrived at a scientific truth.

Betty, torn between laughter, outrage and a lurking suspicion that there was something in this analysis you couldn't entirely discard, cast about in her mind for an answer. As a representative of American youth, she must not allow this Danish challenger to unhorse her at the first thrust. On the other hand, aside from a certain weak protest that generalities were never accurate (the trouble was, they often were), she couldn't think of a ready refutation.

She could not, at the moment, call to mind any young Americans of her acquaintance who wanted to go away and think by themselves. She herself wanted most desperately to be alone for a while, but that was to lick a wound and wasn't what Lisa had in mind at all. When I'm happy, Betty thought, or just not unhappy, I rarely crave privacy. The fact was, she liked being with other people, and so did practically everyone she knew. In college there'd been an odd (really odd) person here and there who demanded privacy. If she remembered correctly, the result was they got nothing but. A genuine nonconformist (not the ubiquitous sort you found nowadays who got together with a huge band of his fellows and followed a rigid pattern of nonconformity) was rare and, for purposes of this argument, useless. Besides, it appeared that in Europe—anyway in Scandinavia—there was nothing in the least unusual in a young person's going off by himself to think it all over, so there'd be no credit in claiming that she knew a few people who did.

But what's the matter with us, she wondered, that we *don't* want the . . . the replenishment that time by ourselves could offer?

Would I like to take this ticket and reservation from Lisa? she asked herself. It would be a very strange, unexpected thing to do, to go off by herself to an unknown place for the weekend. It would give her that time alone she'd been so much needing. What in the world could she tell her parents? To go away for a couple of days with another girl—that they would understand perfectly. They would send her off with their blessing, a bit of extra money and a lot of weatherwise suggestions. But alone?

Maybe she could go without telling them the precise circumstances. This thought entered her mind and flowed right through. She didn't lie to her parents. She didn't, if she could help it, lie to anyone. It tended to upset her stomach. Very well, then, if she took this ticket, etc., she would have to face her parents and confess to them that she wanted, enough to do a very peculiar thing, some time away from them. It would not be at all easy.

"I don't know," she said to Lisa.

"Know what?" said Lisa, who'd picked up the manuscript Betty had been reading. "What part of the conversation are we on? This story has some real graces, don't you think?"

Betty, despite heartache and indecision, was drawn into a discussion of the story. It was a quality that would one day make her a good editor, and only when Lisa glanced at the clock and said she'd better be getting back to her desk did they remember the purpose of her being here to begin with.

"Why aren't you going off for the weekend yourself?" Betty asked.

"Oh, that's because I got invited to a typical American festivity—activity? What would you call a football game?"

"Organized murder, but then I don't have the typical American attitude toward it," Betty said, and smiled at herself for sounding a little proud of being different. Lisa had that effect on people.

"So . . . that's very interesting," Lisa said seriously. "Still, I must experience all that I can. And Christopher Brennan—you know him? From the layout department? —he asked me to go to a football game this weekend up in Yale, which is where he went to school. I think this is a chance I shouldn't miss. To go to a typical American sport with this so very American young man. Don't you agree?"

"I think you're bearing down a bit on that typical."

My face, she told herself, is a mask. Lisa won't guess what I feel. She isn't even responsible, except indirectly. Even Chris isn't responsible. I took my chances in love, the same as everyone else, and I lost, and I honestly don't think I'm complaining—much. I just want to be alone for a while to catch my breath.

"Am I?" said Lisa thoughtfully. "Yes, I guess I am. I get carried away by the investigative process."

I wish you'd get carried away by a disintegrating process, Betty thought, not entirely meaning it. There was that in Lisa which no one, not even a wounded and undeclared rival, could dislike. A sort of openness. Which is not, Betty told herself somewhat aggressively, typically anything. Danish, American or Afro-Swiss. It was just a quality some people had.

"Do Danish girls," she said slowly, "go off on these solo weekends to recover from . . . blighted romance, as it were?"

"Oh, my, yes. It's a specific, practically. At such times you need a bit of everything. A little understanding consolation from your friends, a little standing-by on the part of your family—" Lisa ticked these items off on her fingers in an experienced way "—but mostly and above all you require perspective. You must get away from the round track that constitutes your daily pattern. Now, think it over, Betty," she went on in a spirited way. "You get up every day in the same room, eat with the same morning people, probably the same sort of meal. You come to work by the same route, undoubtedly. Do you alter your route much? Take a different transportation, walk instead of riding?"

Betty shook her head, mesmerized. She came to the office from her home in New Jersey by bus and subway, and it never occurred to her to alter either morning or evening routine.

"So . . . you see?" Lisa said with an air of triumph. "Now then . . . you get to the office, where your desk is always in the same place, and do interesting but similar work—similar, that is, to the work you've done the day before, and the day before that—and you go to lunch with the same people at a choice of the same few places, and then you go home and it all begins again. See what I mean? The result is you can't help but get your perspective narrowed. Not narrow, necessarily. But narrowed. Funneled down. And the person you adore . . . you do adore him?"

"I don't know," Betty said, faintly uncomfortable, but not sufficiently to protect or break up the conversation. It was like talking with a young professor of the heart. Lisa sounded so absolutely competent and sure of her subject. "I guess I wouldn't call it adore. I *think* I love him."

"Even more painful," Lisa said soberly. "This person you love, or think you love—it comes to much the same thing while you're feeling it, except that if you can say *think* it's possible you're getting over it— Where was I? Oh, yes . . . after a while you develop a—what shall I say? What was that good expression I heard the other night? Ah, yes—you develop a sort of *rifle vision* about this person. You know what this is, this rifle vision? It's a straightly directed stare that cannot take into account anything to one side, or above, or below. It concentrates on one object. Now, is it any wonder you get to believing that object to be the only one on the scene? When this happens to me, I go off somewhere to broaden my view. Your own poet, your perfectly glorious Edna Millay, has written a charming verse on the matter. Do you know it?"

"I'm not sure," Betty said, thinking that, compared to this girl, she was like a child. Do people grow up quicker in Denmark, she wondered, or am I retarded?

Lisa, her head back, was reciting with every evidence of delight,

"'The fabric of my faithful love
No power shall dim or ravel
Whilst I stay here,—but oh, my dear,
If I should ever travel!'"

Betty smiled, and Lisa said, "Written to order, is it not? Oh, yes, I have had such lonely, restorative weekends."

"Often?" Betty said diffidently.

"Countless times," said the Danish girl. "I am ruled by the heart. Or some such organ," she added thoughtfully.

Betty could think of no reply to that, but she said, not allowing time for further reflection, "All right. How much will this restorative, broadening weekend set me back?"

"You're laughing at me?" said Lisa cheerfully. "Well, that's all right. You'll find I'm right. I'm not guaranteeing you'll get over the man, mind. But, on my *troth,* you'll see him in a less tortured light. What more could a woman ask? Except the man himself, of course, and in the long run that might not be the best answer, don't you agree?"

Feeling deluged with words, oddly a bit comforted, resentful of Lisa and grateful to her, Betty merely shook her head. Oh, well, she thought, I'm not the first person to be somewhat charmed by the enemy. Look at Queen Elizabeth and Mary of Scotland. Look at Caesar and the treacherous Cleopatra. Look at Louis XIV and the Duchess of Burgundy. He knew she was sending French secrets to her Savoyard father, and still he couldn't resist her. It's not always as simple as saying, That person's on the other side from me and therefore I'll dislike him. With these lofty, far-fetched examples in mind, she looked at Lisa and said, "I really have to thank you. . . ."

After dinner that evening she said to her parents in an overstern voice that she was going away for the weekend.

"Well, darling," said her mother. "You don't have to sound so defensive about it. I think it's an excellent notion. Especially since that . . . since you . . ."

"No point beating about the bush," said Mr. Rowan. "You mean since that Brennan character turned out to have none." He looked pleased with this turn of phrase, and Mrs. Rowan's faint smile congratulated him. "The fact is," he went on with dispassionate interest, "from the outset I was not quite sure of him. I believe you felt the same, did you not?" he inquired of his wife, who nodded thoughtfully and said, all things considered, she had.

Less than a week ago they couldn't praise him too highly, Betty thought, and reminded herself that this was protectiveness on their part.

"On the whole, it's probably for the best," Mr. Rowan went on meditatively, and Betty said to herself, I'm all they have. I mustn't forget that. They just don't know how they sound.

Long ago it had taken a family conclave to decide when and where she should go to camp, who was and who was not suitable as a friend, what was to be her choice of a career. Until recently the three of them had even consulted about her clothes, she and her mother shopping and gravely bringing home a selection for Mr. Rowan to study with them. When she left college—a tripartite decision with a foregone conclusion, since they'd run out of tuition money—Betty had decided it was time to stand out for a few other freedoms. At the cost of several painful discussions, she made them see that her wardrobe, the money she retained after paying the board she insisted on, and her hours were henceforth to be her own responsibility. It had never been a conclusive victory, and spots of mutiny appeared from time to time, in her father's gentle "Do you really think that shade of red is your best color, dear?" or in her mother's "Funny, I thought I heard the clock strike two when you got in last night. . . ." As politely as possible, Betty would try not to answer them.

They live through me and for me, she thought now, and it isn't their fault or mine. It's our misfortune. She looked at them, a spare, immaculate couple, sitting in their accustomed chairs, their eyes bent on her with loving bewildered affection, and wondered for the thousandth time why they didn't find some interest in life besides herself. Her father had a job in a printing house which he'd held for twenty-five years and to which he never referred. For the past four years her mother had worked as a part-time saleslady in a department store. When Betty made any attempt to discuss their jobs with them, they consistently moved the conversation to a discussion of hers, saying with what Betty found sad and convincing honesty that they were only interested in what she did.

They aren't even, she thought with helpless despair, very much interested in each other. Her father seemed to feel that the bulk of his paycheck was about the extent of his responsibility to his wife, and Mrs. Rowan looked after her husband rather like a woman minding the neighbor's plants—adequate attention, but no real concern.

What if I said I was leaving them? Betty asked herself. What if I suddenly announced that I'd taken an apartment with another girl, or even—and this was a new idea, sparked, no doubt, by Lisa—that I was taking one by myself? When in the past the notion of moving out had occurred to her, she'd always dismissed it as impossible. Since she'd never be able to bring the move off, mentioning it at all would be a piece of wanton abuse. But the thought was very strong in her now and would not easily be put aside.

She looked around the room, at the good, sturdy furnishings, the precise draperies, the acceptable ornaments. It was all familiar to a point of being unnoticeable, yet tonight she noticed it sharply. Nothing has changed in years, she thought. This room, this house have survived untouched—except to fade a little—since I was a child. It is the house Mother and Dad made for us three a long time ago. Even her own room was a girl's, last changed when her parents redid it as a sixteenth-birthday present for her.

I should like, she thought with a sense of profound surprise, to have an apartment of my own. I'd like to come home evenings to an untidy place full of brilliant colors, with no curtains, and lots of books, and furniture that the cat could scratch. Because I'd have that, too. A little tigerish sort of cat who'd greet me when I came in but wouldn't insist on knowing why I was half an hour late.

"Betty, dear, I don't believe you're paying attention."

Mrs. Rowan unexpectedly lifted her voice, and Betty started. "We—your father and I—have been speculating as to where you'll be going this weekend, and with whom."

Betty took a deep breath and said, "To New England. With nobody."

In the silence that followed she had a chance to think that what she really wanted was not an apartment of her own and a tiger cat. What she wanted was a sense of herself as a grown person. If she seemed like a child next to Lisa, it was because in so many ways she lived like one.

"If I heard you correctly," her father was saying, "it's out of the question."

At the same time Mrs. Rowan was blinking rapidly and saying that if Betty thought this amusing, if she considered it humor, then their ideas of humor were certainly very, very different. "We know you're hurt about this young man," she pointed out, "but it's hardly an occasion for wild talk. It's a time to draw closer to the people who love and understand you, not a time to make fun of them."

They're alarmed, Betty thought. Maybe they sense a resistance in me that I've scarely had time to feel myself. "Mother, please," she said. "And Dad. I'm not trying to be humorous, and at the moment I don't think anything's funny. I bought this train ticket and a reservation to a perfectly respectable little Massachusetts inn, and I'm going there to . . . to be by myself," she ended on a rising note.

"You can be by yourself here," Mrs. Rowan said stiffly. "I'm sure your father and I never want to interfere with you. Why, I never even go in your room without knocking on your door, now do I?"

"Oh, *Mother*. You just don't understand."

"That's what young people always say when they want to do something wrong."

"I don't want to do something wrong. What do you think I'm planning . . . an assignation with the boss?"

"Elizabeth!" said Mr. Rowan, and if Betty hadn't felt so harried, she'd have laughed inwardly. It was his Barrett of Wimpole Street tone, and she hoped he'd never know that it touched her not with awe but with fondness, sadness and an impulse to giggle. They are a Victorian pair of parents, she thought, but I am not a Victorian daughter, and nobody in this household is ever going to understand anybody else.

"Elizabeth, we'll have no such irresponsible *unladylike* talk," Mr. Rowan said, and Mrs. Rowan said perhaps Betty was a bit excited, but of course she must see that they could not allow her to do any such unheard-of thing as traipsing off to New England by herself, and did she really think Christopher Brennan worthy of such melodramatics?

Goaded out of patience, Betty stamped her foot and said, "Listen to me, I am twenty-one years old!" And then she did laugh, because it was all so ludicrous. You could stamp your foot and say you were ten years old, or maybe even fourteen years old. But to stamp it and announce that you were twenty-one? It was too nonsensical. She dropped into a chair and pushed her hair back and wondered if everybody had this much trouble with parents.

"You aren't twenty-one yet," said Mrs. Rowan. "Not till November."

Mr. Rowan said what did age have to do with it anyway? The question was one of propriety.

Oh, lord, thought Betty. Nothing will ever change. I can hear them saying in years to come, "Betty is a very young thirty-five. Betty is an immature forty-eight," and I'll still be living here and they'll still be living through me, and I just cannot *allow* it.

With a sense of now or never, she leaned forward and said, "Mother and Father, please listen to me, because what I have to say is very important to all of us and you aren't going to agree with any of it and I'm not going to change my mind."

They looked so stunned and apprehensive, so quickly uncertain of themselves, that she almost relented, almost decided nothing was worth the bother and the hurt, not what she had in mind to say, not the weekend, not anything. Let's just let everything go on as before, she was about to say, when Mrs. Rowan said, "I knew that young man was a troublemaker. This is all his fault."

To defend Chris gave Betty a painful sort of comfort and made her resolute where, speaking only for herself, she wouldn't have been.

"Chris isn't at fault anywhere," she said. "Not anywhere. He liked me, and we had some lovely times together, and that was all. If I made . . . something more of it, he's certainly not to blame."

With the rather subtle design of weakening their arguments by arousing their compassion, she let them see more than she'd wanted to how much she had cared for Chris and, even as she did it, felt resentful that she had to. "Look," she said abruptly, "tell me why it is I have to explain myself so thoroughly to my parents at my age. Do you really think that's right? Or dignified?"

The rest of the evening went on like a bad dream, with a good deal of harking back to Betty's childhood when she had loved and trusted and relied on them implicitly, and a lot of protest on her part that she still loved and trusted them but surely even they could see that she wasn't a child any more and must rely on herself.

Her mother wanted to know what she meant by even, and Mr. Rowan reminded her that she was not yet fully of age, and Betty, hardly caring what she said any more, told them that if they didn't stop badgering her she'd move out for good.

This was followed by a long silence. Mrs. Rowan covered her mouth with her hands and stared blindly across the room. Mr. Rowan knocked out his pipe and refilled it with trembling fingers. Betty rested her head against the back of the chair, feeling shaky and a bit sick. It occurred to her in a distant fashion that she was scarcely having a moment to be heartsick over Chris, thanks to Lisa and her peculiar, timely, explosive suggestion. Probably she should be grateful, but she wasn't. The weekend by herself had far less to do with Christopher Brennan, or even with privacy, than with Betty herself and how her life was to be lived. It certainly no longer seemed a good idea or in the least restorative, and she couldn't help wishing she'd never heard a word about it.

When I am a parent, she thought, listening to the voices of her own parents swirling about her in tones alternately pleading, sarcastic, autocratic and frightened, when I am a parent, please let me remember this night and what brought it into being. Let me remember that my children are not my children. They are life's, or God's, or their own, but they are not mine.

"Stop it!" she cried out suddenly, and jumped to her feet.

"See here, young lady," her father began to bluster, but he broke off and turned away. Mrs. Rowan said nothing. Betty, who had a lot to say, ran a hand through her rumpled hair and let her shoulders slump.

"I guess we'd better go to bed," said Mrs. Rowan then, and on this sad, inconclusive note they parted for the night.

Betty lay awake for a long time, thinking about love.

Love, she said to herself. Now, what is love? Love is . . . what?

Love, she thought, as she grew drowsy, is like one of those huge Indian deities—Juggernauts? Vishnu?—who sat on their heavy cars and rolled over the idolatrous population, crushing it. She wondered, falling deeper and deeper into sleep, how she could have conceived of it as tender and vital and warm, as human.

In the morning she packed an overnight bag and carried it past the kitchen into the hall. "I guess I'll leave right from the office this afternoon," she said nervously, sitting across from her father in the breakfast nook.

He patted his lips with a napkin, nodded slightly and pretended that only politeness kept him from picking up the morning paper.

"Go ahead and read, Dad," Betty said. "Don't let me disturb you." He never read the paper at breakfast, but apparently there were to be changes made. Now he picked it up and turned to the second-section summary with a purposeful air.

"How would you like your egg?" said Mrs. Rowan at the stove.

"Mother, please," said Betty. "I'm not an overnight guest. You know how I like my egg."

Instead of replying, Mrs. Rowan walked to the kitchen door, studied the bag in the hall for a long moment, returned and put two pieces of bread in the toaster. There were two stiff lines at the side of her mouth that Betty hadn't known to be so deep.

"Please," she said again. "Do we have to be this way? I'm only trying to—to grow up." It sounded childish, put that away, but she persisted, hoping to disperse this almost solidified misery that lay among them, a thing of their own fashioning. "You grew up, didn't you? Both of you? Why shouldn't I? Why should it make a difference in our—" she wanted to say love, but couldn't use the word "—in our feelings for each other?"

"I don't understand your feelings," said Mrs. Rowan. "I don't understand anything. Not anything."

Mr. Rowan said that reading the morning paper became daily more disheartening. "Corruption everywhere," he said coldly. "I believe I shall write an article on the subject. I shall entitle it, 'Should the Wages of Sin Be Cash?' "

Betty smiled. "That's a good title, Dad. Really. I speak as an embryo editor."

They could usually be drawn into a discussion of her work. But not today. Mr. Rowan put the paper aside and said, "I believe the toast is ready."

Forcing herself to finish the egg and one cup of coffee, Betty was free to rise and say, "Good-bye. Sorry for the fuss. Really I am." What little words we use, she thought. What little words for great, big, painful feelings.

"Good-bye," said her parents in polite unison.

People that unhappy should be left alone, Betty thought. There's nothing else to do about them.

She took a cab instead of the subway when she got to the city, because of the bag. "Do you alter your route much? Take a different transportation?" Lisa, my friend, she thought, you have started up a chain reaction in my life with your continental-Danish ideas, and where I'll fetch up, the dear lord only knows.

It had all, since last night, got beyond, or above, or to one side of Christopher Brennan, who rode up in the same crowded elevator with her and did not stir her pulses. It had become a matter of finding whether she was a herd-oriented American girl who couldn't be by herself. A matter of proving to her parents that she could mature and fall heir to certain adult rights without causing an eternal schism between them. A matter—to put it flatly—of growing up. Perhaps I come to this a little late, she said to herself wryly, but better now than even later.

She got off at her floor, aware that Chris had got off just behind her. Hesitating—ought she to turn and speak, or just keep on walking?—she collided with him and he put a hand on her arm to steady her.

"Sorry," he said, looking surprised and disconcerted.

Betty realized that he hadn't noticed her in the elevator. That was an unexpected and rather bitter dose. Didn't he care for me at all? she wondered. Or is it just that he doesn't have a very good memory?

"What's that?" he said, looking down at the little suitcase in her hand.

"Suitcase," she said, her voice a bit strained.

"Oh. Well, I could take it from you. Carry it someplace."

"Oh, no. I've carried it this far. I'm just going to see it to a corner."

"I see."

They stood deadlocked while morning traffic flowed around them, Chris's eyes embarrassed and uneasy, Betty helplessly remembering when those eyes had looked at her with laughter and affection and perhaps some promise for the future.

She wanted to say, "Don't you remember how you looked at me, and liked to, those nights not so long past? Surely you remember, Chris, how you took me to *The Threepenny Opera,* and held my hand, and when they were singing their daft and raggedy wedding song, you turned toward me in the dark and I knew it and turned to you and we kissed. It was the only time you ever kissed me, and surely you can't have forgotten?"

She wanted to say these things, not because of a hope for the future, but because of some loyalty to the past, and while these thoughts went through her mind, and perhaps across her face, Chris's constrained eyes were fixed on hers, asking for release.

What did he come to this floor for? she wondered. To see Lisa, probably. And now he doesn't know how to extricate himself from me, because he's a kind person and feels some responsibility for me that he can avoid as long as he doesn't actually see me.

This realization formed itself and was followed by another, cold perception. Because it was so fresh in her mind, she recalled her parents saying to her in voices raw with pain and appeal, "Don't you remember, Betty . . . ? Oh, Betty, don't you remember how when you were a little girl you loved and needed us? Surely you can't have forgotten what it was like when you needed us so?"

They had thought that by putting it into words they could make her know that need again, could summon up a feeling among them that was part of the past.

This is what people do to each other, she thought. They do it out of need and call it love. Parents, lovers, friends . . .

"Chris," she said abruptly, "I'm willing to stand here all morning, if we have a conversation. But dumb show has never been my strong point."

He looked almost exaggeratedly relieved, gave her a frightening broad grin and went through the exit door on his way upstairs, forgetful, apparently, of anything he'd come for.

Betty walked slowly to her desk and sat down to muse.

So far as getting perspective on Chris was concerned, she might just as well go home tonight. She'd got it. She'd no longer bend the glare of her rifle vision upon him, because it was not kind. Because—more truthfully—she no longer found him that absorbing. She felt an almost absent-minded twinge of sadness for something lost that might have been lovely, but she had no doubt that something just as lovely would take its place in time.

No, the defection of Christopher Brennan was not the problem. He had just served to bring it into focus. The problem was how to grow up and away from her parents, without hurting them. Well, without hurting them too much. Going away for one weekend wouldn't do it, though as a first flight it might prepare them for another, longer flight. *Anything fledged, flies,* she said to herself. It's a law of nature. She could only hope her mother and father would see that in leaving their house she did not necessarily leave them. Perhaps without her to concentrate on they'd begin to concentrate on one another. It was the sort of thing you were allowed to hope.

How peculiar life was—how sad, how exciting, how unfair, how delicious, how mysterious, how—how many contradictory things all at once. She thought she ought to feel sorry, but the truth was she felt sort of exhilarated. Half closing her eyes, she said without asking herself what she meant, "I'm ready—"

Lisa Bergholt, going by, said in a tone almost reproachful, "For a lovelorn girl, you're looking pretty well self-satisfied."

Betty's eyes flew open. "Am I?" she said, and then, "Well . . . I guess I decided I wasn't in love with him, after all."

"American girls," said Lisa, in her most sweeping fashion, "*never* know what they want. Not ever."

Betty, about to protest, decided she owed Lisa a never-to-be-acknowledged debt, so she smiled and let that pass, thereby proving, in one instance anyway, to be a good deal more grown-up than she knew.

About the Author

Mary Stolz has published seventeen novels for teen-agers, as well as a number of books for younger readers. She is also the author of books and short stories for adults, but she prefers to write for young people. She says, "I don't believe young people are more interesting than other people, but their time of life, their climate, is. To me as a writer, anyway."

Born in Boston, Mary Stolz grew up in New York City, where she attended Birch Wathen School and Columbia University. Her first teen-age novel, *To Tell Your Love,* was published in 1950 and she has been busy writing ever since. She now lives in Stamford, Connecticut, with her husband, Dr. Thomas Jaleski.

HER FIRST BALL

Katherine Mansfield

Exactly when the ball began Leila would have found it hard to say. Perhaps her first real partner was the cab. It did not matter that she shared the cab with the Sheridan girls and their brother. She sat back in her own little corner of it, and the bolster on which her hand rested felt like the sleeve of an unknown young man's dress suit; and away they bowled, past waltzing lamp posts and houses and fences and trees.

"Have you really never been to a ball before, Leila? But, my child, how too weird—" cried the Sheridan girls.

"Our nearest neighbor was fifteen miles," said Leila softly, gently opening and shutting her fan.

Oh, dear, how hard it was to be indifferent like the others! She tried not to smile too much; she tried not to care. But every single thing was so new and exciting . . . Meg's tuberoses, Jose's long loop of amber, Laura's little dark head, pushing above her white fur like a flower through snow. She would remember forever. It even gave her a pang to see her cousin Laurie throw away the wisps of tissue paper he pulled from the fastenings of his new gloves. She would like to have kept those wisps as a keepsake, as a remembrance. Laurie leaned forward and put his hand on Laura's knee.

"Look here, darling," he said. "The third and the ninth as usual. Twig?"

Oh, how marvelous to have a brother! In her excitement Leila felt that if there had been time, if it hadn't been impossible, she couldn't have helped crying because she was an only child, and no brother had ever said "Twig?" to her; no sister would ever say, as Meg said to Jose that moment, "I've never known your hair go up more successfully than it has tonight!"

But, of course, there was no time. They were at the drill hall already; there were cabs in front of them and cabs behind. The road was bright on either side with moving fanlike lights, and on the pavement gay couples seemed to float through the air; little satin shoes chased each other like birds.

"Hold on to me, Leila; you'll get lost," said Laura.

"Come on, girls, let's make a dash for it," said Laurie.

Leila put two fingers on Laura's pink velvet cloak, and they were somehow lifted past the big golden lantern, carried along the passage, and pushed into the little room marked "Ladies." Here the crowd was so great there was hardly space to take off their things; the noise was deafening. Two benches on either side were stacked high with wraps. Two old women in white aprons ran up and down tossing fresh armfuls. And everybody was pressing forward trying to get at the little dressing table and mirror at the far end.

A great quivering jet of gas lighted the ladies' room.

It couldn't wait; it was dancing already. When the door opened again and there came a burst of tuning from the drill hall, it leaped almost to the ceiling.

Dark girls, fair girls were patting their hair, tying ribbons again, tucking handkerchiefs down the fronts of their bodices, smoothing marble-white gloves. And because they were all laughing it seemed to Leila that they were all lovely.

"Aren't there any invisible hairpins?" cried a voice. "How most extraordinary! I can't see a single invisible hairpin."

"Powder my back, there's a darling," cried someone else.

"But I must have a needle and cotton. I've torn simply miles and miles of the frill," wailed a third.

Then, "Pass them along, pass them along!" The straw basket of programs was tossed from arm to arm. Darling little pink-and-silver programs, with pink pencils and fluffy tassels. Leila's fingers shook as she took one out of the basket. She wanted to ask some one, "Am I meant to have one too?" but she had just time to read: "Waltz 3. *Two, Two in a Canoe*. Polka 4. *Making the Feathers Fly,*" when Meg cried, "Ready, Leila?" and they pressed their way through the crush in the passage toward the big double doors of the drill hall.

Dancing had not begun yet, but the band had stopped tuning, and the noise was so great it seemed that when it did begin to play it would never be heard. Leila, pressing close to Meg, looking over Meg's shoulder, felt that even the little quivering colored flags strung across the ceiling were talking. She quite forgot to be shy; she forgot how in the middle of dressing she had sat down on the bed with one shoe off and one shoe on and begged her mother to ring up her cousins and say she couldn't go after all. And the rush of longing she had had to be sitting on the veranda of their forsaken up-country home, listening to the baby owls crying "More pork" in the moonlight, was changed to a rush of joy so sweet that it was hard to bear alone. She clutched her fan, and, gazing at the gleaming, golden floor, the azaleas, the lanterns, the stage at one end with its red carpet and gilt chairs and the band in a corner, she thought breathlessly, "How heavenly; how simply heavenly!"

All the girls stood grouped together at one side of the doors, the men at the other, and the chaperones in dark dresses, smiling rather foolishly, walked with little careful steps over the polished floor toward the stage.

"This is my little country cousin Leila. Be nice to her. Find her partners; she's under my wing," said Meg, going up to one girl after another.

Strange faces smiled at Leila—sweetly, vaguely. Strange voices answered, "Of course, my dear." But Leila felt the girls didn't really see her. They were looking toward the men. Why didn't the men begin? What were they waiting for? There they stood, smoothing their gloves, patting their glossy hair and smiling among themselves. Then, quite suddenly, as if they had only just made up their minds that that was what they had to do, the men came gliding over the parquet. There was a joyful flutter among the girls. A tall, fair man flew up to Meg, seized her program, scribbled something; Meg passed him on to Leila. "May I have the pleasure?" He ducked and smiled. There came a dark man wearing an eyeglass, then cousin Laurie with a friend, and Laura with a little freckled fellow whose tie was crooked. Then quite an old man—fat, with a big bald patch on his head—took her program and murmured, "Let me see, let me see!" And he was a long time comparing his program which looked black with names, with hers. It seemed to give him so much trouble that Leila was ashamed. "Oh, please don't bother," she said eagerly. But instead of replying the fat man wrote something, glanced at her again. "Do I remember this bright little face?" he said softly. "Is it known to me of yore?" At that moment the band began playing; the fat man disappeared. He was tossed away on a great wave of music that came flying over the gleaming floor, breaking the groups up into couples, scattering them, sending them spinning. . . .

Leila had learned to dance at boarding school. Every Saturday afternoon the boarders were hurried off to a little corrugated iron mission hall where Miss Eccles (of London) held her "select" classes. But the difference between that dusty-smelling hall—with calico texts on the walls, the poor terrified little woman in a brown velvet toque with rabbit's ears thumping the cold piano, Miss Eccles poking the girls' feet with her long white wand —and this was so tremendous that Leila was sure if her partner didn't come and she had to listen to that marvelous music and to watch the others sliding, gliding over the golden floor, she would die at least, or faint, or lift her arms and fly out of one of those dark windows that showed the stars.

"Ours, I think—" Someone bowed, smiled, and offered her his arm; she hadn't to die after all. Someone's hand pressed her waist, and she floated away like a flower that is tossed into a pool.

"Quite a good floor, isn't it?" drawled a faint voice close to her ear.

"I think it's most beautifully slippery," said Leila.

"Pardon!" The faint voice sounded surprised. Leila said it again. And there was a tiny pause before the voice echoed, "Oh, quite!" and she was swung round again.

He steered so beautifully. That was the great difference between dancing with girls and men, Leila decided. Girls banged into each other, and stamped on each other's feet; the girl who was gentleman always clutched you so.

The azaleas were separate flowers no longer; they were pink and white flags streaming by.

"Were you at the Bells' last week?" the voice came again. It sounded tired. Leila wondered whether she ought to ask him if he would like to stop.

"No, this is my first dance," said she.

Her partner gave a little gasping laugh. "Oh, I say," he protested.

"Yes, it is really the first dance I've ever been to." Leila was most fervent. It was such a relief to be able to tell somebody. "You see, I've lived in the country all my life up until now. . . ."

At that moment the music stopped, and they went to sit on two chairs against the wall. Leila tucked her pink satin feet under and fanned herself, while she blissfully watched the other couples passing and disappearing through the swing doors.

"Enjoying yourself, Leila?" asked Jose, nodding her golden head.

Laura passed and gave her the faintest little wink; it made Leila wonder for a moment whether she was quite grown up after all. Certainly her partner did not say very much. He coughed, tucked his handkerchief away, pulled down his waistcoat, took a minute thread off his sleeve. But it didn't matter. Almost immediately the band started, and her second partner seemed to spring from the ceiling.

"Floor's not bad," said the new voice. Did one always begin with the floor? And then, "Were you at the Neaves' on Tuesday?" And again Leila explained. Perhaps it was a little strange that her partners were not more interested. For it was thrilling. Her first ball! She was only at the beginning of everything. It seemed to her that she had never known what the night was like before. Up till now it had been dark, silent, beautiful very often —oh, yes—but mournful somehow. Solemn. And now it would never be like that again—it had opened dazzling bright.

"Care for an ice?" said her partner. And they went through the swing doors, down the passage, to the supper room. Her cheeks burned, she was fearfully thirsty. How sweet the ices looked on little glass plates, and how cold the frosted spoon was, iced too! And when they came back to the hall there was the fat man waiting for her by the door. It gave her quite a shock again to see how old he was; he ought to have been on the stage with the fathers and mothers. And when Leila compared him with her other partners he looked shabby. His waistcoat was creased, there was a button off his glove, his coat looked as if it was dusty with French chalk.

"Come along, little lady," said the fat man. He scarcely troubled to clasp her, and they moved away so gently, it was more like walking than dancing. But he said not a word about the floor. "Your first dance, isn't it?" he murmured.

"How *did* you know?"

"Ah," said the fat man, "that's what it is to be old!" He wheezed faintly as he steered her past an awkward couple. "You see, I've been doing this kind of thing for the last thirty years."

"Thirty years?" cried Leila. Twelve years before she was born!

"It hardly bears thinking about, does it?" said the fat

man gloomily. Leila looked at his bald head, and she felt quite sorry for him.

"I think it's marvelous to be still going on," she said kindly.

"Kind little lady," said the fat man, and he pressed her a little closer, and hummed a bar of the waltz. "Of course," he said, "you can't hope to last anything like as long as that. No-o," said the fat man, "long before that you'll be sitting up there on the stage, looking on, in your nice black velvet. And these pretty arms will have turned into little short fat ones, and you'll beat time with such a different kind of fan—a black bony one." The fat man seemed to shudder. "And you'll smile away like the poor old dears up there, and point to your daughter, and tell the elderly lady next to you how some dreadful man tried to kiss her at the club ball. And your heart will ache, ache"—the fat man squeezed her closer still, as if he really was sorry for that poor heart—"because no one wants to kiss you now. And you'll say how unpleasant these polished floors are to walk on, how dangerous they are. Eh, Mademoiselle Twinkletoes?" said the fat man softly.

Leila gave a light little laugh, but she did not feel like laughing. Was it—could it all be true? It sounded terribly true. Was this first ball only the beginning of her last ball after all? At that the music seemed to change; it sounded sad, sad; it rose upon a great sigh. Oh, how quickly things changed! Why didn't happiness last forever? Forever wasn't a bit too long.

"I want to stop," she said in a breathless voice. The fat man led her to the door.

"No," she said, "I won't go outside. I won't sit down. I'll just stand here, thank you." She leaned against the wall, tapping with her foot, pulling up her gloves and trying to smile. But deep inside her a little girl threw her pinafore over her head and sobbed. Why had he spoiled it all?

"I say, you know," said the fat man, "you mustn't take me seriously, little lady."

"As if I should!" said Leila, tossing her small dark head and sucking her underlip. . . .

Again the couples paraded. The swing doors opened and shut. Now new music was given out by the bandmaster. But Leila didn't want to dance any more. She wanted to be home, or sitting on the veranda listening to those baby owls. When she looked through the dark windows at the stars, they had long beams like wings. . . .

But presently a soft, melting, ravishing tune began, and a young man with curly hair bowed before her. She would have to dance, out of politeness, until she could find Meg. Very stiffly she walked into the middle; very haughtily she put her hand on his sleeve. But in one minute, in one turn, her feet glided, glided. The lights, the azaleas, the dresses, the pink faces, the velvet chairs, all became one beautiful flying wheel. And when her next partner bumped her into the fat man and he said, "Par*don,*" she smiled at him more radiantly than ever. She didn't even recognize him again.

About the Author

Katherine Mansfield was born in 1888 in Wellington, New Zealand, and grew up there. But at the age of fourteen, she was sent to Queen's College, London, and after returning to Wellington for two years decided to make London her home. Several years later, she recalled her girlhood in New Zealand in a group of stories including "Her First Ball."

She began her literary career in 1909, publishing short stories in several London literary magazines. In 1911 her first collection of short stories, *In A German Pension,* was published. During the next few years she contributed to several literary magazines edited by John Middleton Murry, whom she married in 1918. With the publication of two more collections of stories, *Bliss and Other Stories* and *The Garden Party,* she became established as an important modern writer.

At the peak of her success, Katherine Mansfield fell ill of tuberculosis. She was thirty-four when she died on January 9, 1923, in France.

ROAD TO THE ISLES
Jessamyn West

It was the last Thursday in January, about nine in the evening, cold and raining. The three Delahantys sat close about the living-room fireplace—Mr. Delahanty at the built-in desk working on his schedule, Mrs. Delahanty on the sofa reading, and between them, crosswise in the wing chair, their daughter.

Cress was apparently studying the program of the folk-dance festival in which she was to appear the next evening. For the most part, however, she did not even see the program. She saw, instead, herself, infinitely graceful, moving through the figures of the dance that had been so difficult for her to master.

The high school folk-dancing class was made up of two kinds of performers—those with natural ability who had themselves elected the class, and those who, in the language of the physical education department, were "remedials." The remedials had been sent into the class willy-nilly in an effort to counteract in them defects ranging from antisocial attitudes to what Miss Ingols, the gym teacher, called "a general lack of grace." Cress had achieved the class under this final classification but now, at midterm, had so far outgrown it as to be the only remedial with a part in the festival.

The first five numbers on the program, "Tsiganotchka," "Ladies' Whim," "Meitschi Putz Di," "Hiawatha," and "Little Man in a Fix," Cress ignored. It was not only that she was not in these but that they were in no way as beautiful as "Road to the Isles," in which Mary Lou Hawkins, Chrystal O'Conor, Zelma Mayberry, Bernadine Deevers, and Crescent Delahanty took part. The mere sight of her name beside that of Bernadine Deevers, Tenant High School's most gifted dancer—most gifted *person,* really—instantly called up to Cress a vision of herself featly footing it in laced kirtle and starched skirts, a vision of herself dancing not only the outward steps of "Road to the Isles" but its inner meaning: what Miss Ingols had called "the achievement of the impossible."

Cress thought that she was particularly adapted to dancing that meaning because she had so recently come that way herself. If she had been given three wishes when school opened in September, two of them would have been that Bernadine be her friend and that she herself succeed in the folk-dancing class. Both had then seemed equally impossible. Now not only did she have a part in the festival but Bernadine was her dear friend and coming to spend the weekend with her. At the minute the evening reached what she considered its peak of mellowness, she intended to speak to her father and mother about the festival and Bernadine's visit. She was exceedingly uncertain about their performances on both these occasions.

The rain suddenly began to fall harder. Cress's father,

hearing it on the roof, watched with gratification as the water streamed across the dark windowpanes. "Just what the oranges have been a-thirsting for," he said.

Mrs. Delahanty closed her book. "How's the schedule coming?" she asked her husband.

"O.K., I guess," said Mr. Delahanty.

Cress looked up from the festival program with embarrassment. The schedule was one of the things she wanted to speak to her father about. She hoped he wouldn't mention it while Bernadine was visiting them. Every winter, as work on the ranch slackened, he drew up a schedule for the better ordering of his life. And every spring, as work picked up, he abandoned it as easily as if it had never been. Last winter, he had made a plan called "A Schedule of Exercises to Ensure Absolute Fitness," which included not only the schedule of exercises and the hours at which he proposed to practice them but a list of the weaknesses they were to counteract. He had even gone so far, last winter, as to put on a pair of peculiar short pants and run six times around the orchard without stopping, arms flailing, chest pumping—a very embarrassing sight, and one that Cress could not possibly have explained to Bernadine.

This winter, the subject of her father's schedule-making was not in itself so unsuitable. He had bought a new encyclopedia set and was mapping out a reading program that would enable him, by a wise use of his spare time, to cover the entire field of human knowledge in a year. The name of the schedule, written at the top of a sheet of Cress's yellow graph paper, was, in fact, "Human Knowledge in a Year." There was nothing about this plan that would call for embarrassing public action, like running around the orchard in shorts, but it was so incredibly naive and dreamy that Cress hoped her father would not speak of it. Bernadine was far too sophisticated for schedules.

"Where are you now on your schedule, John?" Mrs. Delahanty asked.

Mr. Delahanty, who liked to talk about his plans almost as much as he liked to make them, put down his pen and picked up the sheet of paper on which he had been writing. "I've got all the subjects I want to read up about listed, and the times I'll have free *for* reading listed. Nothing left to do now but decide what's the best time for what. For instance, if you were me, Gertrude, would you spend the fifteen minutes before breakfast on art? Or on archaeology, say?"

"You don't ever have fifteen minutes before breakfast," Mrs. Delahanty said.

Mr. Delahanty picked up his pen. "I thought you wanted to discuss this."

"Oh, I do!" said Mrs. Delahanty. "Well, if *I* had fifteen minutes before breakfast, *I'd* read about archaeology."

"Why?" asked Mr. Delahanty.

"It's more orderly that way," Mrs. Delahanty said.

"Orderly?" asked Mr. Delahanty.

"A-r-c," Mrs. Delahanty spelled, "comes before a-r-t."

Mr. Delahanty made an impatient sound. "I'm not going at this alphabetically, Gertrude. Cut and dried. What I'm thinking about is what would make the most interesting morning reading. The most interesting and inspiring."

"Art is supposed to be more inspiring," Mrs. Delahanty told him. "If that's what you're after."

This seemed to decide Mr. Delahanty. "No, I think science should be the morning subject," he said, and wrote something at the top of a sheet—"Science," Cress supposed. "That's better," he said. "That leaves art for the evening, when I'll have time to read aloud to you."

"Don't change your schedule around for my sake, John," said Mrs. Delahanty, who hated being read to about anything.

"I'm not. All personal considerations aside, that's a more logical arrangement. Now the question is, which art?"

This seemed to Cress the moment for which she had been waiting. "Dancing is one of the earliest and most important of the arts," she said quickly.

"Oho!" said her father. "I thought you were in a coma."

"I've been rehearsing," said Cress.

"Rehearsing!" exclaimed Mr. Delahanty.

"In my mind," Cress said.

"So that's what was going on—'Ladies' Whim,' 'Tsiganotchka'—"

"Father," Cress interrupted, "I've told you and told you the T's silent. Why don't you take the program and practice the names? I'll help you." Cress got up and took the program across to her father.

"Practice them," said Mr. Delahanty with surprise, reading through the dances listed. "What do I care how they're pronounced? 'Korbushka,' 'Kohanotchka,' " he said, mispronouncing wildly. "I'm not going to Russia."

"But you're going to the folk-dance festival," Cress reminded him.

"I don't *have* to go. If you don't want—"

"I do, Father. You know I want you to go. Only I don't want you to mispronounce the names."

"Look, Cress," Mr. Delahanty said. "I promise you

I'll keep my mouth shut the whole time I'm there. No one will know you have a father who can't pronounce. Mute I'll come and mute I'll go."

"I don't want you to be mute," Cress protested. "And even if I did, you couldn't very well be mute the whole time Bernadine's here. And Bernadine's the star of the program."

"To Bernadine," said Mr. Delahanty, referring to the program once again, "I shall speak of 'Badger,' and 'The Lumberman's Two Step.' I can pronounce them fine and they ought to hold Bernadine. She's not going to be here long, is she?"

"Friday to Monday," said Mrs. Delahanty.

"In that case," said Mr. Delahanty, "maybe I should find another one. How about 'The Irish Jollity,' Cress? Do I say that all right?"

"Now, John!" Mrs. Delahanty reproved her husband.

"It's all right for him to joke about it to me, Mother. But he mustn't before Bernadine. Bernadine's serious about dancing. She's going to be a great artist."

"A great dancer?" Mrs. Delahanty asked.

"She hasn't decided what kind of an artist yet," Cress said. "Only to be great in something."

"Well, well," said Mr. Delahanty. "I'm beginning to look forward to meeting Bernadine."

"You already have," Cress told him. "Bernadine was one of the girls who rode with us to the basketball game."

Mr. Delahanty squinted his eyes, as if trying to peer backward to the Friday two weeks before when he had provided Cress and four of her friends with transportation to an out-of-town game. He shook his head. "Can't recall any Bernadine," he said.

"She was the one in the front seat with us," Cress reminded him.

"That girl!" exclaimed Mr. Delahanty, remembering. "But her name wasn't Bernadine, was it?"

"No," Cress told him. "That's what I wanted to explain to you, because tomorrow's Friday, too."

Mr. Delahanty left desk and schedule and walked over in front of the fireplace. From this position, he could get a direct view of his daughter.

"What's this you're saying, Cress?" he asked. "Her name isn't Bernadine because tomorrow's Friday. Is that what you said?"

"Yes, it is," Cress told him, seriously. "Only it's not just tomorrow. Her name isn't Bernadine on any Friday."

Mr. Delahanty appealed to his wife. "Do you hear what I hear, Gertrude?"

"Mother," Cress protested, "this isn't anything funny. In fact, it's a complete tragedy."

"Well, Cress dear," her mother said reasonably, "I haven't said a word. And your father's just trying to get things straight."

"He's trying to be funny about a tragedy," Cress insisted obstinately.

"Now, Cress," Mr. Delahanty urged, "you're jumping to conclusions. Though I admit I think it's queer to have a name on Fridays you don't have the rest of the week. And I don't see anything tragic about it."

"That's what I'm trying to tell you, only you keep acting as if it's a joke."

"What is Bernadine's name on Fridays, Cress?" asked her mother.

"Nedra," said Cress solemnly.

Mr. Delahanty snapped his fingers. "Yes, sir," he said, "that's it! That's what they called her, all right."

"Of course," said Cress. "Everyone does on Fridays, out of respect for her sorrow."

"Just what *is* Bernadine's sorrow, Cress?" her mother asked.

"Bernadine never did say—out and out, that is. Once in a while she tries to. But she just can't. It overwhelms her. But we all know what, generally speaking, must have happened."

"What?" asked Mr. Delahanty. "Generally speaking?"

Cress looked at her father suspiciously, but his face was all sympathetic concern.

"On some Friday in the past," she said, "Nedra had to say no to someone. Someone she loved."

"How old is Berna—Nedra?" Mrs. Delahanty asked.

"Sixteen," Cress said. "Almost."

"Well, it couldn't have been too long ago then, could it?" her mother suggested.

"Was this person," Mr. Delahanty ventured, "this person Nedra said no to, a male?"

"Of course," said Cress. "I told you it was a complete tragedy, didn't I? His name was Ned. That much we know."

"Then the Nedra is in honor of—Ned?" asked her mother.

"In honor and loving memory," Cress told her. "On the very next Friday, Ned died."

Mr. Delahanty said nothing. Mrs. Delahanty said, "Poor boy!"

"I think he was probably more than a boy," Cress said. "He owned two drugstores."

After the elder Delahantys had thought about this for a while, Mr. Delahanty asked, "This 'no' Bernadine—Nedra—said, was it to a proposal of marriage?"

"We don't ever ask about that," Cress told her father disapprovingly. "It doesn't seem like good taste to us."

"No, I don't suppose it is," Mr. Delahanty admitted.

"Anyway," Cress said, "that's Bernadine's tragedy and we all respect it and her wish to be called Nedra on Fridays. And tomorrow is a Friday, and it would be pretty awful to have her upset before the festival."

Mr. Delahanty stepped briskly back to his desk. "Don't you worry for a second, Cress," he said. "As far as I'm concerned, the girl's name is Nedra."

"Thank you, Father," Cress said. "I knew you'd understand. Now I'd better go to bed." At the door to the hallway, she turned and spoke once again. "If I were you, Father, I wouldn't say anything about your schedule to Bernadine."

"I hadn't planned on talking to her about it. But what's wrong with it?" Mr. Delahanty sounded a little testy.

"Oh, nothing," Cress assured him. "I think it's dear and sweet of you to make schedules. Only," she explained, "it's so idealistic."

After Cress left the room, Mr. Delahanty said, "What the hell's wrong with being idealistic?"

Cress thought that her friend, in her costume for "Fado Blanquita," the Spanish dance in which she performed the solo part, looked like the queen of grace and beauty. And she said so.

"This does rather suit my type," Bernadine admitted. She was leaning out from the opened casement window of Cress's room into the shimmering, rain-washed air. She tautened her costume's already tight bodice, fluffed up its already bouffant skirt, and extended her hands in one of the appealing gestures of the dance toward the trees of the orange orchard upon which the window opened.

"Is your father a shy man?" she asked.

Mr. Delahanty, who had been working near the driveway to the house when the two girls got off the school bus an hour before, had, instead of lingering to greet them, quickly disappeared behind a row of trees. Now, in rubber boots, carrying a light spade that he was using to test the depth to which the night before's rain had penetrated the soil, he came briefly into sight, waved his spade, and once again disappeared.

"No," said Cress, who thought her father rather bold, if anything. "He's just busy. After the rain, you know."

"Rain, sunshine. Sunshine, rain," Bernadine said understandingly. She moved her hands about in the placid afternoon air as if scooping up samples. "Farming is an awfully elemental life, I expect. My father"—Bernadine's father, J. M. Deevers, was vice-president of the Tenant First National Bank—"probably doesn't know one element from another. I expect your father's rather an elemental type, too, isn't he? Fundamentally, I mean?"

"I don't know, Nedra," Cress said humbly.

"He's black-haired," Bernadine said. "It's been my experience that black-haired men are very elemental." She brought her expressive hands slowly down to her curving red satin bodice. "You must have a good deal of confidence in your family to let them go tonight," she went on briskly.

"Let them!" Cress repeated, amazed at the word.

"Perhaps they're different from my family. Mine always keep me on pins and needles about what they're going to say and do next."

"Mine, too," Cress admitted, though loyalty to her father and mother would not permit her to say how greatly they worried her. She never went anyplace with them that she was not filled with a tremulous concern lest they do or say something that would discredit them all. She stayed with them. She attempted to guide them. She hearkened to every word said to them, so that she could prompt them with the right answers. But *let* them! "They always just take it for granted that where I go, they go," she said. "There's not much question of letting."

"Mine used to be that way," Bernadine confided. "But after what happened at the festival last year, I put my foot down. 'This year,' I told them, 'you're not going.' "

"What happened last year?" asked Cress, who had not then been a dancer.

"After the program was over last year, Miss Ingols asked for parent participation in the dancing. And my father participated. He danced the 'Hopak,' and pretty soon he was lifting Miss Ingols off the floor at every other jump."

"Oh, Nedra," Cress said. "How terrible! What did Ingols do?"

"Nothing," said Bernadine. "That was the disgusting part. As a matter of fact, she seemed to enjoy it. But you can imagine how I suffered."

Cress nodded. She could. She was thinking how she would suffer if her father, in addition to mispronouncing all the dances, went out on the gymnasium floor and, before all her friends, misdanced them.

"Are your parents the participating type?" Bernadine asked.

Cress nodded with sad conviction. "Father is. And Mother is if encouraged."

"You'd better warn them right away," Bernadine said. "Your father just came in the back door. You could warn him now."

Cress walked slowly down the hallway toward the kitchen. Before the evening was over, her father, too, would probably be jouncing Miss Ingols around, and even calling Bernadine Bernadine—then all would be ruined completely, all she had looked forward to for so long. In the kitchen, she noted signs of the special supper her mother was cooking because of Bernadine: the coleslaw salad had shreds of green peppers and red apples mixed through it tonight to make it festive; the party sherbet glasses, with their long, icicle stems, awaited the lemon pudding. But her mother was out of the kitchen—on the back porch telling her father to hurry, because they would have to have dinner early if they were to get to the festival in time.

"Festival!" Cress heard her father say. "I wish I'd never heard of that festival. How did Cress ever come to get mixed up in this dancing business, anyway?" he asked. "She's no dancer. Why, the poor kid can hardly get through a room without knocking something over. Let alone dance!"

"That's *why* she's mixed up with it," her mother explained. "To overcome her awkwardness. And she *is* better."

"But is she good enough?" asked her father. "I'd hate to think of her making a spectacle of herself—to say nothing of having to sit and watch it."

"Now, John," Cress heard her mother say soothingly. "You're always too concerned about Cress. Will she do this right? Will she do that right? Stop worrying. Cress'll probably be fine."

"Maybe fall on her ear, too," her father said morosely. "They oughtn't to put so much responsibility on kids. Performing in public. Doesn't it worry you any?"

"Certainly it worries me. But all parents worry. And remember, we'll have the star of the performance with us. You can concentrate on Nedra if watching Cress is too much for you."

"That Nedra! The only dance I can imagine that girl doing is one in which she would carry somebody's head on a platter."

Cress had started back down the hall before her father finished this sentence, but she had not gone so far as to miss its final word. She stopped in the bathroom to have a drink of water and to see how she looked in the mirror over the washbasin. She looked different. For the first time in her life, she saw herself through other eyes than her own. Through her parents' eyes. Did parents worry about the figures their *children* cut? Were they embarrassed for *them,* and did they wonder if they were behaving suitably, stylishly, well? Cress felt a vacant, hollow space beneath her heart, which another glass of water did nothing to fill. Why, *I'm* all right, Cress thought. *I* know how to behave. I'll get by. *They're* the ones . . . but she looked at her face again and it was wavering, doubtful—not the triumphant face she had imagined, smiling in sureness as she danced the come-and-go figures of "Road to the Isles."

She went back to her room full of thought. Bernadine was changing her costume, and her muffled voice came from under all her skirts. "Did you tell them?" this muffled voice asked.

"No," said Cress, "I didn't."

"Why not? Won't you be worried?"

"They're the ones who are worrying. About me."

"About you?"

"Father thinks I may fall on my ear."

Bernadine, clear of her skirts, nodded in smiling agreement. "It's a possibility that sometimes occurs to *me,*

Cress dear."

Cress gazed at her friend speculatively. "They're worried about you, too," she said.

"Me?" asked Bernadine, her smile fading.

"Father said the only dance he could imagine you doing was one with a head on a platter."

"Salome!" Bernadine exclaimed with pleasure. "Your father's imaginative, isn't he? Sympathetically imaginative?"

"I guess so," Cress said, and in her confusion told everything. "He keeps schedules."

"Schedules?"

"For the better ordering of his life."

Bernadine laughed again. "How precious!" she said.

Then, as if remembering after too long a lapse the day and her bereavement, she said, "Neddy was like that, too."

"Neddy," repeated Cress, pain for the present making Bernadine's past seem not only past but silly. "Oh, shut up about Neddy, *Bernadine!*"

Bernadine gave a little gasp. "Have you forgotten it's Friday?"

"I don't care what day it is," Cress said. She walked over to her bed, picked up the pillow, and lay down. Then she put the pillow over her face.

About the Author

Jessamyn West wrote "Road to the Isles" as one of a group of sketches of a girl growing up in southern California. They were published first in *The New Yorker,* and later appeared in book form as *Cress Delahanty.*

Like her main character, Cress, Jessamyn West grew up in California. She attended Whittier College, where she married one of her classmates. After graduation, she studied for a year in England, and then returned to California, where she still lives.

Her first novel, *The Friendly Persuasion,* was published in 1945. When it was made into a movie, she kept a journal of the transition, which she published under the title *To See The Dream.* Her other books include *Love, Death, and the Ladies' Drill Team,* a collection of stories, and *South of the Angels.* Her most recent novel, published in 1966, is *A Matter of Time.*

THE IMPOSSIBLE HE

Rosanne Smith Soffer

Louisa turned back to the big store plate-glass window and exchanged another placid glance with her own image, and then examined the Madonna-faced dummy resplendent in whipcord jodhpurs and tailored twill riding coat, the tails of which, Louisa knew, would be lined with a silky rubberized fabric. Sighing, she looked up again at the pious plaster face. The body of the dummy was tilted back ever so slightly as though the floor were about to slide away from under it. "You have no one to blame but yourself," Louisa said morosely to the dummy, forever on the edge of a genteel swoon, but the remark was meant for herself. Louisa reached up to push the plait of hair back over her shoulder and withdrew her hand as she remembered, as she had remembered seven or eight times a day, that her hair had been cut two weeks ago for the first time in two years. There were no longer any heavy blond braided ropes of hair to keep check on lest they creep down the collar of her coat or over her shoulder into her plate when she was eating.

Louisa turned her back to the window now and stood as close to it as she could without actually leaning against it. She raised her arm and looked ostentatiously at her wrist as if checking the time, although she had no watch. She knew the gesture gave the definite impression that she was waiting for someone—just in case anyone was looking at her and wondering what she was doing hanging about for such a long time. It felt like fifteen minutes. That meant another five minutes before Patricia was even due and she was always late and she, Louisa, was always early—much too early. That was why Louisa always picked Straus's when she was going to meet Pat. The store had one big window that faced right on the street and behind it ran a corridor shaped like the top half of a hexagon with more windows and the entrance to the store. This way she could stand out of the wind and cold, warmed by the occasional drafts of warm air that came from the store whenever anyone went in or out, and yet she didn't get too hot as she would have inside a store like Ayre's or Block's. But it was her own fault.

Now, thought Louisa, if I had a watch I wouldn't always have to be early because I would know what time it was and I wouldn't have to rush for fear I'd be late. Louisa shifted her Virgil and European History textbook under her arm and opened her pocketbook and took out a slip of paper. She had decided two days ago to be a nurse; nurses led self-reliant lives and made good money even if they had to do a lot of—well, private-type things. Louisa, brave with resolution, had made out a list of the things she wanted and expected and demanded of herself by the age of twenty-four. Unfolding the slip of paper Louisa fondly read the list again:

Acquisitions by age of 24:

Yellow Chevrolet convertible
New pivot tooth without gold
Wrist watch with second sweep hand
Blue cashmere sweater
Fur coat

Well, she had seven years to do it in. The car would be the hardest but maybe her grandmother would have died by then and left her some money that she could use for that. Louisa looked up suddenly to see if anybody had noticed the evil thought she had just had about her grandmother. Across the tile-paved corridor a youngish man in shirtsleeves was standing, his arms wrapped about him for warmth. He had soft brown hair, through which his scalp showed, and his tie was loose enough at the knot to show the top button of his shirt. He was staring at Louisa and there was the merest smile on his face, as though he were remembering something he had done when he was very small. Louisa flushed so strongly that she felt perspiration starting on her upper lip. She put the list back in her bag and snapped it shut. The snap lock made a noise like a glass dish breaking on a hot stove.

Then the young man raised an arm slowly and drew a comma in the air with his thumb. He closed one eye and tilted his face, his tongue caught between his teeth. Louisa felt the back of her head touch the window as she strained away. The young man was wearing crepe-soled shoes and the rubber on the tile made a high squeaky sound as he came over to her.

"Really," he said. "I didn't mean to frighten you. Did I frighten you? Good. It's just that really you should be painted and in just this light. Why it's positively—ah, Renoir. I was going to say Titian but there's not quite enough vibrancy. Perhaps in a few years—when you have matured even more, you know."

Louisa stared at him, conscious now that he was wearing a T-shirt under his regular shirt. "I'm waiting for someone," she said, her eyes on his tie.

"I thought you were," he said cheerfully. "But really I'm not joking, you know. You should be painted. How exciting to try and catch that inner quality," he said, making a little tent with the fingers of his right hand. "I work here," he said, pointing at the door of the store which swung open now against the weight of a short little woman who was breathing heavily and walked away with little choppy steps that set her rocking like a boat at anchor. "Just bread and butter, of course, Really I paint. I do the windows. Of course, I have a girl who helps me. Hands me the stuff."

"Oh," said Louisa and she carefully looked at all the windows, even swiveling around again to look at the Madonna in jodhpurs. "They're nice."

"Nothing really," the young man said, "but a man has to eat. I suppose it would be too much of an imposition to ask you to pose for me sometime."

Louisa swallowed and watched her finger trace its way along the binding of the Virgil.

"Or perhaps you've already been painted?" the young man asked. He touched her arm lightly. He had long fingers and he wore a green stone in a gold setting that glowed like a go light.

"Oh, no," Louisa said. "It's just that I don't think my grandmother would like it. She paints. Strawberries and things."

"Ah, your grandmother," the young man said as though he had just come upon Louisa's grandmother hiding in the bushes. "Well, I'll tell you what we'll do. You give me your name and telephone number and I'll call up and come out and see your grandmother, see. That way it will all be copacetic." He had taken a pencil and notebook from his back pocket and was looking inquiringly at Louisa.

"Aren't you cold?" Louisa asked.

"Used to it," he said. "In and out all day. Let's see if I can guess—ah, now I have it—Linda? No. No—Anna?"

"Louisa," said Louisa. "Louisa Brown. I live at 3318 Central and the number is Talbot 3797."

"Brown," said the young man. "I had an uncle who went to Brown." He closed the pad, tapped it thoughtfully with the tip of his pencil and quickly put it back in his pocket. "You'll be hearing from me, Louisa. Tell you what—maybe we should go out somewhere first so's we can get acquainted. You know, sit around and chat with the—with your grandmother for a while and then go out and take a walk or catch a flick."

"Flick?" said Louisa.

"That's what the English call movies. By the way, my name is Ellery. Nothing I can do about it. Ellery Thomas."

"Ellery Thomas," Louisa repeated dutifully as she stuck her free arm behind her back. She hadn't washed her hands before she left school and she remembered now that they still smelled of the mustard she had smeared on her hot dogs at lunch. Wednesday was the day for barbecue sandwiches at the school cafeteria but they'd had hot dogs instead for some reason.

"And you must promise me something before I go,"

Ellery said, putting his hand lightly again on her shoulder. He was looking straight into her eyes and shivering slightly from the cold.

"What?" Louisa said and her voice came out in an early morning croak.

"Promise me," and his eyes moved now to her hair and then back to her face, "promise me that you'll never wear your hair any other way." He squeezed her arm and smiled and turned on his crepe soles with a squeak and disappeared into the store with its lights in the dusk as orange as a candle flame. Louisa watched as the door slowly closed and then Patricia's voice said, "*Who* was that?" As she turned forward toward her friend, Louisa was conscious that she had started. But it was all right. She could have just been surprised by Pat's creeping up on her like that. "Him?" she said casually. "Oh, he's some friend of that Bill Brewer next door."

"Ugh," said Pat. She had evidently dumped her books with her mother when they got the shoes. Her coat was tightly belted and she had both her hands jammed into her pockets. "Bill Brewer," she said. "Who'd have thought he had any friends."

"Let's move," Louisa said. "We'll be late for the flick."

"The flick?" Pat said.

"What else," said Louisa wearily.

Louisa counted one, two, three, four, and on the fourth tilt the cherry rocker squeaked. Her grandmother sighed, smoothed her dress under her with both hands, looked at the couch seat and then sat down heavily. A series of light belches eased from her throat and made her sunken cheeks puff in and out. Below the hem of her dress Louisa could see the folds of lisle hose neatly pinned with large silver safety pins so they would stay up. Louisa stopped rocking and stared at the old woman. She had no body hair and what there was on her head was brought together in a wretched little knot at the back of her neck. She was frightfully old and so thin that if you looked at her face or neck or her arm or the withered cleavage above the turquoise brooch she wore with all her dresses, you could see her pulse beating. Her very fragility made Louisa dislike her more because, Louisa knew, it scared her; that and the fact that she steamed open every piece of mail that came into the house, even Louisa's letters from her father, which she always offered her anyhow. Her name was Alma but nobody had ever seemed to call her that except her parents maybe and her husband, who had died of acute indigestion after eating something that had been in the icebox too long. "A saint," her grandmother always said, "a saint. Every morning I had to bring him his truss before he could even get out of bed but never a word of complaint ever passed his lips in the forty years the dear Lord allotted us to live together."

Louisa waited while her grandmother poured some lotion from the bottle she kept on the table by the couch and started to rub it into her hands. She never washed the dishes and half the time didn't get down in time to dry them. She always had to go straight upstairs after every meal but she always put the lotion on. "Well," her grandmother said, the skin moving on her hand like a loose cotton glove, "he certainly sounds like a polite young man. Now where did you say you met him?"

"I told you," Louisa said, "he's a friend of Patricia. He knows her brother." It would be awful now if he came in and said something right off about meeting her in front of a store. Louisa looked down at her own hands. The nails were nice and clean from the dishwater, but they still smelt faintly of the onion she had peeled to put in with the boiled chicken. Her grandmother loved onions even though they made her belch. They had boiled chicken for dinner every other Sunday. In between was pot roast. Well, in a few minutes she could go up to her room on the pretense of finishing her homework which she'd really already done and just before it was time for him to get there she'd rub "Quelques Fleurs" on her hands. It was very strong now because a lot of it had evaporated while she was out West for the summer with her father.

"Heavens," her grandmother cried, clasping her hands together and leaning her cheek against them. "It's almost time for 'Music for Your Mood.' My, we are late today. Would you just turn the knob there for your poor old grandmother, that's a love."

Louisa walked over and turned the knob. Her grandmother only listened to one station. She said it was easier that way and you never knew what you were missing because if you didn't know what was on the other stations how could you know what you were missing. Louisa sat down in the rocker again and then said, "Well, I had better go up and do my homework."

"I should say so. I should say so indeed," her grandmother said. She had stood up and sat down again on the middle cushion and now she stretched out full length on the couch and sighed. "If you're going out with a nice young man, you had certainly better have your homework done."

"Well, I'm not sure we're going out," Louisa said. Her grandmother had done all the talking and when she took the phone Ellery had just said, "See you at five. Have you got something blue? Wear something blue, will you? Blue's your color." And then he had hung up without even saying good-bye.

"Why, he said you were going out," her grandmother said. "Would you just pull the throw up over me since you're getting up anyhow, that's a love."

Louisa took the crocheted throw and draped it over her grandmother. As she went up the stairs, she wondered why she didn't feel more excited. She had only had two dates in her whole life, both of them with college men who worked for her father during vacation surveying and things like that. And she knew that they had just taken her out because they felt sorry for her. In her room Louisa sat down in front of the chintz-draped vanity table that had belonged to her mother and stared at herself. It wasn't that she was positively ugly; it was just that—well she looked so sort of bland, like milk and sugar and eggs. Once in a while she had a pimple or two and she could lose five pounds, but there was that fat, dumpy Leona Andrews who had pimples all over her forehead which she positively caked with powder and all the boys ran after her and stood around her locker waiting for her after school and walked all the way home with her. Louisa tried to adjust her face into the kind of bright vivacious twinkly look that Leona Andrews tripped about the halls with but she came out looking as though she were trying not to be sick. It was no use. Whatever was wrong with her was congenital. An old man's darling, that's what she was.

Louisa opened a drawer and took out her good pen and went over to her bed and reached under the mattress and took out the little green book. It opened readily to the frontispiece with its title "Chap Record" and the little verse underneath:

Behold herein, all nice and neat,
A record of the men I meet,

Among them all perhaps, there be,
Who knows, the "not impossible" He.

Sighing, Louisa flipped through the dozens of entries made by her mother. Each page had room for four entries with space for Name, Date, Place, and Opinion. Louisa knew by heart most of the entries her mother had made, but there were two that were her absolute favorites and she always looked at them before she moved on to the page where her two entries were made. "Mr. Shirley O'Connor," one read. "Dec. 5, 1925. Train to St. Louis. Terribly brazen. Fast, fat and forty." Mr. O'Connor exuded the stuff of adventure. Turning two pages she came to "Mr. Fred Smiley. December 8, 1926. Elks Club House. Divine danger. Terribly conceited. Looks like hard drinker." Once again Louisa searched her memory for someone she had seen who looked like a hard drinker. Giving up, she turned to her own page and set herself to making her third entry. There were still lots of empty pages but at the rate she was going it didn't look as though she would be the one to fill them. As she started to print Louisa realized that she had told herself a lie. She had told herself that she didn't really expect Ellery to call, but if she really hadn't she would have made the entry on Wednesday after she had met him. She knew now that she hadn't because she was afraid it would be bad luck. Well, she had been right. It didn't do to be previous about these things. She looked at her entry when she had finished. "Ellery Thomas. February 9, 1966. I.F.O.S. Painter. Not very tall. Middle-aged. Will go bald." The "I.F.O.S." meant In Front of Straus's but with the way her grandmother snooped it wouldn't be wise to write it right out. Later, when she was away studying to be a nurse, she could fill it in.

Well, she thought, it really was time to get dressed and again she marveled at how unexcited she was. Well, after all, what were men in her young life? A career and one's own money were much more important. After she had hung up the phone Louisa had had an immediate vision of herself dressing leisurely for the occasion as her mother always had when as a child Louisa had watched her getting ready to go out for the evening. Stuffing the green book back under the mattress, Louisa began to undress. She tried to do it slowly, dropping her skirt and sweater languidly on the floor, but it was chilly in the room and she soon found herself hurrying as though she were late for school. The water in the tub was only lukewarm. Her grandmother must have turned the heater down when they finished the dishes. She was shivering as she dried herself. She was ready and dressed, hands tingling with "Quelques Fleurs," with half an hour still to go. And then the doorbell rang. He was early.

Louisa forced herself to sit down on the edge of her bed. The bell rang again. Her grandmother never answered until the third ring. Already Louisa felt the dampness under her arms. She looked down and saw the wet stain that showed so clearly on the blue chambray blouse. Quickly she got up and took off the blouse. He had said to wear blue but she would have to put on the white nylon. With that it wouldn't show. Her hands trembled as she buttoned up the blouse and then unzipped her skirt to stick the tail in. He was inside now; she could hear his voice.

Quietly Louisa eased her way down the steps and stood in the dining room just outside the living room door.

"No ma'am—Navy," Ellery was saying.

"Oh," her grandmother said. "Louisa's father was in

the Army. He got two medals. Her grandfather would have gone in the Army too. He always admired the Army but he had a hernia. Had it all his life. Wore a truss. It's still hanging there in the closet. Never could bring myself to throw it away. I suppose I should give it away to someone but it just seems—that—oh, Louisa, here you are. Your friend is waiting and he's brought me such a lovely little gift. Made it himself."

Louisa looked at the little hand-painted gourd sitting on the table next to her grandmother for minutes before she could bring herself to turn and say hello to Ellery. But when she did she saw he wasn't looking at her.

"Well," he said to her grandmother, "don't like to rush off like this but I thought we'd get the early show. Don't want to keep her out too late. Young myself once."

"Oh, you go right along," her grandmother said, laughing and clapping her hands. "Have a good time. Don't worry about a thing. Just enjoy yourselves."

Ellery helped Louisa on with her coat with such aggressiveness that for a minute Louisa was afraid that he might try to button it for her. "Good-bye, Mrs. Brown. It's been a pleasure," he said and taking Louisa's elbow firmly he steered her out of the house and down to the curb to a gray Chevrolet that had dents in the front and back fenders. When he had gone around and gotten into the driver's seat, he turned toward her.

"Let me look at you," he said. Louisa could think of no way of stopping him. "Ah, yes—Renoir. I was right. Definitely Renoir." Sighing, he started the car. "Your folks dead?" he asked.

"Oh, just my mother," Louisa said and found herself chattering away, holding on to the doors as they turned corners so she would be sure not to lean against him and telling him how her father worked out in Colorado and she stayed with him summers only she came back here for school because the nearest school there was miles away and how she and her father sometimes drove fifty miles just to see a movie and how she had her own horse and rode almost all the time and the horse's name was Blackbird and he always shied at barbed-wire fences not that there were many, what you had plenty of out there was space.

"Yes, I know," he said. "I've been out there. Visited a friend in a tuberculosis sanatorium."

"Oh," Louisa said and she was silent while he parked the car. Her father always said the one time he didn't want to hear a lot of jabbering was when he was parking the car. They walked the half block to Zaring's Egyptian Theater, which was lighted up on the outside by spotlights hidden in the hedge that surrounded it so that it looked like some kind of public monument. On the marquee was the title of a movie about Africa that Louisa had seen twice.

"You haven't seen it, have you?" Ellery asked as they stopped in front of the box office.

"Oh, no," Louisa said.

"Good," he said. He steered her right by the popcorn down the aisle to seats much farther forward than she ever sat. They had come in just at the beginning of the newsreel. Ellery helped her off with her coat and then stood up and took off his own and draped it on the empty seat in front of them. The feature started and it had just got to the part where the hunter agrees to take the girl to look for her long lost husband when Ellery reached over and took her hand. Louisa decided that the only thing to do was to pretend that it was someone else's hand, but this was hard to do because it kept sweating. Finally Ellery took out a handkerchief and wiped off his own hand and then hers and then held her hand again. Her elbow was resting on the arm of the seat and she felt her arm and hand grow numb but she did not move them. Perhaps if it fell asleep it would stop sweating. But half a dozen times during the movie Ellery went through the wiping operation. When the trailers came on Ellery said, "Who cares. Come on, let's go."

Her arm dangling at her side, Louisa followed him out of the movie house and started to turn right toward the car but he caught her by her good arm. "How about a snack?" he said. "I'm kind of hungry. How about you?"

"Oh, sure," Louisa said and when they sat down at the counter in the little luncheonette she started to flex her fingers frantically so that her arm would wake up.

"Hamburger and coffee for me," Ellery said to the girl behind the counter. "What about you?"

"Oh, I'll have a hamburger with onion and a Coke," Louisa said. She could lift her arm now and in a minute she'd be able to pick up her glass of water.

"Onion?" Ellery asked.

"Yes. They don't taste like anything without onion."

"Make that two with onion," Ellery said to the girl.

"Gotcha," she said.

Ellery had finished his hamburger almost before Louisa had finished putting salt and pepper and relish and catsup on hers and he drank his coffee thoughtfully, not looking at her once while she finished. He was quiet, too, in the car and Louisa felt that for some reason he did not want to talk. Her father got that way sometimes and she always knew that his stomach must be acting up. Louisa was silent until they pulled up at the curb a good half-block away from her grandmother's house.

"Oh," she said. "It's much farther down the block."

"I know it is," Ellery said. "But I want to talk to you. I must talk to you." He turned and put his arm up on the back of the seat. "Louisa." He hesitated and put his hand up over his eyes for a moment. "Louisa, there's something I must tell you, but first you must promise that you won't hold it against me." He reached over and took her hand in both of his. "Promise. Say you'll promise."

Louisa nodded her head.

"No, say it. Say 'I promise.' "

"I promise," Louisa said, thinking that she would promise almost anything if he would just stop holding her hand.

"Well, it's this," he said and he did stop holding her hand and began kneading his own together. "It's well—I'm not really a painter, Louisa. But I couldn't help it. When I saw you that day I—I had to talk to you. You looked so much like her." She had started to scratch her nose when he threw himself against her, his face in her shoulder and she got her elbow out of the way just in time. He was sobbing. Louisa folded her hands on her lap and waited for him to stop or do something else.

"I'm sorry," he said finally, lifting his head. There were no tear marks on his face. When men cried maybe they didn't have tears. She had never seen one cry before. But it wasn't the way she cried. When she cried, she cried quietly with lots of tears. "I couldn't help it," Ellery said. "I told you about my friend in the sanatorium. Well—that was her—Genevieve. When I saw you I couldn't believe it. It might have been her. She was beautiful, too."

He had her hand again and his face was in her neck and he seemed to be trying to nibble at her. I'll have to take out the part about his being a painter, Louisa thought. Then he shifted. "Ah, your sweet bosom," he said. "Many is the time I have rested thus on Genevieve's sweet breast." Louisa put the heel of her hand on his forehead and pushed.

"I have to go in now," she said.

"Oh, Louisa," he said and he kissed her hand. "Can't you see? Don't you understand? My darling," and he grabbed her chin and kissed her. Louisa held her mouth tightly together and took his hand from her knee and put it on his own knee and pushed him away. "I have to go in now," she said. Her mouth felt all wet and she wiped it with the back of her hand. "Thank you for the movie and I am sorry about Genevieve." She started to open the car door but he said, "Wait, let me drive you," and since he reached over to start the car, she stayed in. She kept her hand on the door but when they stopped in front of the house he got right out and came around and helped her out. But at the door he grabbed her again. "Genevieve, my darling," he said, breathing heavily, "You've come back to me. God has sent you back."

Louisa stood stiffly in his embrace for half a minute and then said, "Well, good night now," but he held her tighter and tried to pull her face around. Freeing one arm, Louisa reached over and rang the doorbell long and loud. He let her go immediately. "Okay. Okay," he said. "If that's the way you want it. See you around." As he walked away to the car, he looked so small and sad that Louisa wanted to call out to him, but she could think of nothing to say. He had slammed the door of his car and driven off before she had put the key in the lock. "Oh dear," Louisa said to the darkness of the living room, "I've made him angry." When he called she'd tell him she was sorry and he'd say he was sorry but he hadn't been able to help himself.

"Is that you, Louisa?" her grandmother called.

"Yes, Grandma. I'm sorry I thought I'd left my key and then I found it."

"You woke me up."

"I know," Louisa said, coming up the stairs. "I'm sorry."

"I'll never get back to sleep."

"I'm sorry," Louisa said, facing her grandmother now.

"That won't help me get back to sleep," her grandmother said and she closed the door of her room.

Louisa undressed quickly and took out her good pen and got into bed and reached under the mattress for the "Chap Record." It fell open at her page. Neatly she scratched out "Painter" and then after "Will go bald" she wrote, "Terribly sweet. Can't say yet but perhaps 'the not impossible He.' " She blew on the ink until she was sure it would be dry and then put the book and the pen under her pillow and reached up and snapped off the light.

About the Author

Rosanne Smith Soffer spent her early childhood in St. Petersburg, Florida. She attended high school in Indianapolis, Indiana, and graduated from Northwestern University. She worked on the staff of *The New Yorker* for several years, then became a free-lance writer of articles and short stories for magazines. Her short stories have appeared in such magazines as *Harper's Bazaar, Charm, Cosmopolitan, Epoch,* and *Quixote.*

Married to a professor of chemistry at Smith College, Rosanne Smith Soffer now teaches advanced high school English at Northampton High School in Massachusetts. "The Impossible He" was included in *The Best American Short Stories, 1957.*

REBELLION
Ruth Harnden

Last year, at fifteen, she had been a private person, and next year at seventeen, so far as she knew, she might expect to be so again. Only this year she seemed to have been thrust into the public domain, made to feel as conspicuous, and at the same time anonymous, as though she were ludicrously fat, or suffered from any condition that was the accepted butt of stale, universal humor brought out again and again with the zeal of discovery. *Sweet sixteen.*

"What a lovely thought, Dr. Mulcahey, or Mr. Byrne, or Colonel McGuire," she would have liked to say, looking stonily back into their archly smiling faces. "Did it just come to you? Or is it a quotation, perhaps?" Or she might simply say, "I feel sour, thank you. Quite sour!" and turn and walk out of the alien, enormous room filled with the aged or the aging who had no respect for her whatsoever, only a terrible, stripping curiosity.

She was either interested in people—deeply, passionately—or she barely saw them at all. But now she began to wonder whether she, too, was doomed to arrive one day at this peculiar, repulsive condition in which interest had given place to a dull, sly curiosity for something that had lost all reality.

An only child, too much of her life had been lived in an adult world. As a result she was mentally precocious, which she knew, and emotionally somewhat in arrears, which she was only beginning to know. The latter awareness manifested itself in a nameless impatience. She had become very critical, was frequently short-tempered, and was ridden by a continual unrest. It was partly on this account that her parents had chosen this season to ship her off to her uncle and his wife, who had no children of their own and an "interesting life" in the diplomatic service.

"You're a born rebel, Susie," her uncle had begun to say almost from the day she arrived, and it did seem as if her unrest was a kind of imminent rebellion that any minute, or any day, she would find the strength to express properly. In the meantime it came out in small intellectual attacks fairly well within the bounds of good manners.

"What's the matter with having *both* central heating and open fires?" she wanted to know when it was explained to her that many people could afford central heating, that some had even had it installed and then never connected it because they preferred the intimate comfort of fires in every room.

"Why don't they pasteurize their milk?" she demanded when she learned that it was customarily left raw, and that tuberculosis was rife in the country. But the chief object of her attack was the terrible inequality, the lack of democracy. At first it had seemed to her that people here must be wealthier than the same sort of people at home, but her aunt put her straight on that. "Heavens, no!" she said, "it's just the other way around. This is a poor country, and America's one of the richest." It was the servants, Susan explained. "Oh—that!" her aunt said. "But they're so cheap here. We can get four servants for the price of one in the States."

"You mean," Susan pointed out unsparingly, "that a great many people have nothing so that a very few can have everything?"

"Highty tighty," her uncle broke in at that. "A disciple of Marx?"

"No," she said coldly, "but if I lived here I'd probably become one."

"Of course it spoils us dreadfully," her aunt admitted with one of her gestures of delicate, side-stepping surrender that no one could mistake for defeat. She was a small, fastidious woman who managed to look fragile and feminine even in the most robust tweeds. At an age when she should have faded, the soft moist Irish weather had given her skin a renascent bloom. She kept her graying hair short and exquisitely groomed, and had never neglected the care of her hands. Beside her Susan felt a little gross—overgrown and underorganized. She was likely to do clumsy things, drop a teacup or a walking stick, stumble over a rug, although she was normally well-coordinated. But more devastating than her aunt's person was her bland, humorless sweet temper that could uncurdle the sourest wit, that blunted the edge of argument so effectively that even discussion died stillborn.

"We have to take things as we find them," her uncle had said in a terminating voice. He found them very comfortable indeed and this knowledge only increased Susan's critical impatience. They were old and they had given up. They would rather be comfortable than alive.

And being very uncomfortable, she told herself that she would rather be alive. But still she had this uncertainty of her own life; not that it had ended, but that it was unbegun. During that single, suspended week of freedom on the boat it had seemed likely at any moment to begin. She had played Ping-Pong and danced a few times with an older man, a Swiss who traveled for Du Pont. He was perhaps thirty and had given her a heady sense of imminent danger. But nothing at all had happened, and in recollection the whole thing gave her the feeling she got from developing a film that turned out to have been light-struck in the camera so that even her anticipation had been meaningless. She told herself in honest hindsight that he had treated her like a nice kid, as though she wore her obstructing innocence like a brand. And if she did—if that were the case—then how could anything happen? And if nothing happened, then how was it lost?

There were only two things in which she was uncritically content because in them she could be wholly involved as nothing else in life any longer seemed willing or able to involve her. She loved to drive a car and to ride a horse, particularly the latter. Occasionally she would ride badly, failing to quite manage the horse, and at these times she would need to take out the car, to drive it with a combination of abandon and precision that almost restored her self-esteem. But it wasn't the same thing, and she knew it with a glancing, secret contempt for the inert manageability of machines. You had no relationship with a machine, and along with the speed and the exhilarating presence of potential danger, which removed her restlessness, it was exactly the *relationship* she craved. The lonelier she felt in this alien place, in the embarrassment of her conspicuous youth, the more she needed it.

Dublin was a good place to have come to if you liked riding. Diplomatically it was not a brilliant post, but for that reason neither was it taxing. After some ten years her aunt and uncle had relaxed into a close resemblance, at least, of the amiable, indolent ways of the county born and bred. Their frequent receptions had preserved a formality—in the dress, in the food and liquor served, and in the conversational interchange or the musical intrusions. These gatherings usually showed, too, a considerable urban variety of guests. But their weekly At Homes had pretty well boiled down to the informal hard-riding set, who might occasionally talk of their gardens but never got any further away than that from the turf. Prosperous farmers or titled gentry, they had identical hard-planed, weather-burned faces and conducted their conversations in an identical manner, the voices booming, the diction blurred. Men and women dressed alike, in the tough, unregarded tweeds that never seemed to reach retirement, and it even appeared to Susan that there was little other difference between them, except that the women were apt to have deeper voices, and their faces were frequently harder.

Through this florid, shouting, unintelligible crowd she would move every Thursday afternoon at the same hours, passing buttered bread or refilling teacups and saying, "No, I don't hunt," for the hundredth time, or "No, I haven't been out yet." "Hunt?" or "Started to hunt yet?" was offered to her over and over, or perhaps simply "Been out yet?" which she learned quite soon could have, in their changeless context, only the one reference.

She had done a little jumping at home, but only over the simplest hurdles. After a trial hour in the field with her uncle it had been decided that she was not, or not yet, up to the banks. Evidently an Irish invention, the banks were towering, beveled mounds of earth. She had no notion of their actual height but would have guessed it at no less than twelve feet. Put at the bank, the horse would leap and then scramble up the angled sides, pause briefly on the leveled top, and then plunge headlong to the ground at the far side. It was the downward leap that appalled her, that sent her frightened, betraying hands to the saddle, and that formed the basis for her uncle's decision.

"You'll go out every morning," he told her, "with one of the grooms." In point of fact their horses were supplied by the nearby army post and the "grooms" were any of the enlisted men whose services were an added diplomatic courtesy on demand. The actual arrangements were made by her aunt on the telephone. Any course might be determined by her husband, but its execution, the applied diplomacy, usually fell to her lot. She had to a high degree that capacity for verbal indirection which results in the most unmistakable directness.

After the first few days the stolid, middle-aged sergeant her aunt had unerringly selected, sight unseen, was unexpectedly hospitalized with a ruptured appendix. On Saturday morning, at the customary hour, a young corporal came up with the horses. He was a thin, tallish boy who looked to be little older than Susan herself. While he adjusted her stirrups, standing at her horse's head, she examined his stark boy's face with the fine pink girlish complexion, the intent, impersonal gray eyes, and it came to her that he knew all about horses and that he knew nothing else. As far as people, as far as Life was concerned, he was way back there at the beginning with herself. Out of the simplicity of this bond and this freedom she began to talk to him as easily as she could talk to no one else in this place, not even thinking how to begin, as she had had to think with the sergeant so that she'd never begun at all.

"First I thought I'd never be able to handle a horse on a snaffle," she told him. "At home we use the curb, too, you know. Or if it's a single rein, then it's the curb. That's what they use in the West. That's what the cowboys use."

"For a fact?" he said, interested, his intent, unconcealing eyes coming up to hers without embarrassment or curiosity even, except for the words she was saying. "Anyone could hold a horse on a curb," he said then, swinging into his own saddle.

"I know it," she said just as naturally. "And I still don't know how I'd handle him on a snaffle if he wanted to run." He laughed at that. "Why would you be wantin' to hold him in that case?" he asked her. "Sure he'd have to stop when he got to the sea." That made her laugh, and presently they were cantering across the sere, stubbled grass of Phoenix Park as if they'd been doing it every morning of their lives.

There was no end to what they found to say without ever leaving the subject of horses and riding. He was teaching her a great deal but she was able to tell him a lot too. "This is the way the cowboys ride," she'd say, sitting to the trot, "taking the jolts on their stomachs. Of course they prefer a single-foot," she might add, "and anyone can sit to that."

"You can train 'em to that sometimes," he'd say, "sending 'em against the bit. But you've a better chance if they're inclined that way."

"But I like to post," she told him. "I *enjoy* it." She was even able to confess to him that she was scared of the banks. "I grabbed the saddle," she said, looking him straight in the eye, daring him to accept this and still go on knowing her.

"You've a good seat," he told her, looking straight back as if there were no disgrace standing between them. "Just leave it to the horse. Give him his head and leave it to him."

"I'd have to stop when I got to the ground?" she asked him, and they laughed together over this for a long time.

There was so much to say that by the end of the week she found herself talking to him when he wasn't there, asking him questions or explaining something to him, or going back over some point that had come up the day before, or that morning.

He never called her "Miss" the way the sergeant did, and still he'd never used her name either. It was just "you" or else he was simply talking as if she were anyone, or a number of people. But she knew that it wasn't like that. If it were he could have used her name. She knew this without knowing that she knew it until the day that he used her name.

They had gone up into the hills that morning for another try at the banks. "We'll take 'em together," he suggested. "Just give the horses the office and relax." But she decided that she'd rather, the first time, he waited for her on the far side, and finally he agreed to do that. It was on the far side, reaching the ground, that her horse stumbled and then fell. It seemed to her, reviewing it afterward, and even dimly at the time, that she'd barely felt the earth with her shoulder before he was off his horse and standing over her saying, "Susie, are your hurt? Are you hurt?" and it wasn't only her name but the sharp pain in his voice that she heard. "You're shakin'," he said, helping her up, holding her against the tension of his arm. "Are you all right?"

"Just dirty, I guess," she said, trying to laugh. He took out his handkerchief and dabbed at her forehead, her cheekbones, but when he got to her mouth he stopped and stuffed the handkerchief back in his pocket. "The thing to do," he said, speaking quickly in an oddly light voice, "is to get straight back on again. You've always got to do that at once or you'll maybe never do it again. Come along now," he said, busying himself with the two sets of reins he'd caught up through his arm, "up and at it again. You did fine—just fine! It was only for the beast stumblin' or you'd be in the saddle now easy as sittin' in the barn." It was like the time on the boat, and it was entirely different, because this time the nothing that had happened had happened to both of them.

It was more than a week before her aunt caught up with the fact that a substitution had been made in her plans. She happened to drive up from town just as Susan had got into the house, so of course she met the corporal coming down the driveway leading the second, riderless horse. "Hullo. Was that Sergeant Blair?" she asked casually, standing in the hall stripping the string gloves from her hands.

It was a minute before Susan could think who Sergeant Blair was. "Oh!" she said then, remembering. "Oh, he's in the hospital. His appendix broke. Two weeks ago, I guess it was. Or maybe it was ten days."

"Really?" her aunt said, examining herself in the hall mirror. "As long as that?"

"It seems much longer," Susan told her innocently, out of the moment's disarmed surprise. "It seems like a month at least that I've been riding with Jimmy."

"Really?" her aunt said again, having turned from the mirror now, and after a minute the irresolution in her face, studying Susan's, resolved itself in a smile. "How nice that you've made a friend," she said. "We must meet him. Would you like to ask him for dinner one night?"

"Oh, no!" Susan said out of the unexamined but certain instinct of an animal sensing an ambushed trap. "We just like to talk about horses," she said quickly, reaching for some protection of this thing that was hers alone in this alien place, this estranging time.

"In that case," her aunt said sweetly, "just have him in Thursday," and she put her gloves down on the table, the tough leather palms turned up, and went into the morning room.

She ought to have thought quicker, and further. She ought to have seen past the logic of Thursday when everyone who came talked about horses. But the moment was past and she was caught. She was caught beyond escape in her aunt's logic, and in her graciousness—switching at once to the thing that Susan might prefer.

She waited until the end of their ride on Thursday and then, getting off at the house, handing him her reins, she gave it to him the way it was: not a thing that needed accepting, or could possibly be refused. "Aunt Helen wants you to come for tea. About four they usually come. Any time between four and five. I'll see you then," she told him, and turned and went into the house without waiting to see what it might be that finally found its way to the surface of his intent, uncomplicated face.

It was perhaps four-thirty and everyone had gathered when she saw him at the threshold to the room, his young face looking exposed and raw hanging in uncertainty above the poise of her aunt's head. "I'm sure you know the army people already," her aunt was saying when she got to them, "though I'm afraid they're all aged career men."

"Hullo," Susan said, searching his face for any sign

that he, too, had heard how her aunt had taken away with the one word what she had given with the other. There was nothing to be read but a certain wariness when he said, "How do you do?" speaking as distinctly as if the words belonged to a foreign tongue. "Introduce Corporal Faley to the Colonel, darling," her aunt said, "and to Captain Sweeney and to Major Cunningham. And then get him a cup of tea," and she moved away.

"Come on," Susan said, not looking at him any longer, her face set in the stubborn, reckless hope that something might still be saved.

Colonel McGuire opened his mouth and barked something that might have been an acknowledgment of the introduction in this room where introductions were not made, and might as well have been the beginning of the story he launched into at once: some incident from the week before when he'd been out with the Killing Kildares. No one needed to ask the corporal which hunt he rode with, or even if he hunted at all. No one seemed to feel the need to ask him anything at all, and after a minute Susan said, "I'll get you some tea," and moved away from the identical faces which had assumed a further identity now. Without exception they were united at this moment in the bland, incurious conviction that anyone who was at all worth knowing they knew already.

She never did get him the tea although she made three tries going back after another cup when the first one was taken by Mr. Kavenaugh, stopping her in the middle of the room. Everyone all at once was determined to stop her, to engage her in conversation, to deflect her eyes searching the room for his face, from old Lady Closs, who wanted to know if she was going to any of the dances, to Mr. Byrne, who expressed a sudden interest in her political views. She knew she was being wooed, and she knew why. She knew exactly what was going on, and had known from her aunt's first words. But when she was stopped with the third cup, her stubborn frustration went down to helpless defeat. She felt it go as certainly as she might have watched a sentinel leaving his post. But it was no less gone for that.

She was one of them now. No longer anonymous, and briefly comical, she was addressed, consulted, attended. She might have been grown up; she might have been eighteen. And she began to hear her own voice rising on the competitive tide, her own words running together in expedient haste. It was a kind of intoxication, heady and numbing at once. She had really forgotten Jimmy's presence when her aunt's voice broke the spell at last. She thought Susan ought to know that Corporal Faley was leaving and surely she wanted to see him out.

He was standing alone in the hall, his back to the broad mirror that alone preserved the image of his integrity—the squared competent shoulders, the stark attention of the head. "I'm sorry——" she began, and then she stopped, and it was perhaps after all the only thing she had to say.

"That's all right," he said very quickly, possibly to spare her or perhaps to spare himself further. Into the unaware, youthful dignity of his face had come the beginning of adult confusion. His eyes shifted to some focus beyond her. "I'll . . ." his lean, assured boy's hand that was so certain on a horse's mouth lifted in a faltering gesture, as though it moved toward a cap he wasn't wearing. "I'll bring the horses 'round in the morning," he said in final definition of the status they had assigned him. Without looking at her again he crossed the hall, treading the carpet lightly, and let himself out the front door.

For a minute she stood alone in the hall. Behind her, across the wide house, the shouting unintelligible crowd sounded like one voice now, single as the voice of the pack. Her rebellion flared briefly, a last time. *Why did you let them?* she asked of the door that had closed behind him. If he hadn't fallen into their trap; if he hadn't accepted that identity they gave him; if he hadn't proved their point—her rebellion guttered and died because she had proved their point herself, as well. She belonged to the hunted no longer. She had become a member of the hunt.

About the Author

Ruth Harnden spent a school year studying in Ireland, the setting for her story, "Rebellion." She graduated from Radcliffe College, and worked in several bookstores and publishers' offices. The author of two adult novels and numerous short stories, she has recently turned to writing for children.

She is the author of *Golly and the Gulls, The High Pasture* (winner of the 1964 Child Study Association Award) and *Summer's Turning,* and is presently at work on a fourth children's book. A native of Boston, she now lives in Cambridge, Massachusetts.

A CHAIN OF LOVE

Reynolds Price

They had observed Papa's birthday with a freezer of cream even if it was the dead of winter, and they had given him a Morris chair that was not brand-new but was what he had always wanted. The next morning he was sick, and nobody could figure the connection between such nice hand-turned cream that Rato almost froze to death making and a tired heart which was what he had according to Dr. Sledge. Papa said "Tired of what?" and refused to go to any hospital. He said he would die at home if it was his time, but the family saw it different so they took him to Raleigh in Milo's car —pulled out the back seat that hadn't been out since Milo married the Abbott girl and spread a pallet and laid him there on pillows with his head resting on the hand-painted one off the settee, the gray felt pillow from Natural Bridge, Virginia that he brought Pauline his wife six years before she died, off that two-day excursion he took with the County Agent to the model peanut farms around Suffolk.

Much as she wanted to, Mama couldn't stay with Papa then. (Mama was his daughter-in-law.) She made him a half a gallon of boiled custard as he asked her to, to take along, and she rode down to Raleigh with them, but she had to come back with Milo in the evening. It worried her not being able to stay when staying was her duty, but they were having a Children's Day at the church that coming Sunday—mainly because the Christmas pageant had fallen through when John Arthur Bobbitt passed around German measles like a dish of cool figs at the first rehearsal—and since she had organized the Sunbeams single-handed, she couldn't leave them then right on the verge of public performance. So they took Rosacoke and Rato along to sit for the first days till Mama could come back herself. Dr. Sledge said there was no need to take on a full-time nurse with two strong grandchildren dying to sit with him anyhow.

And there wasn't. From the minute Papa had his attack, there was never a question of Rosacoke going if Papa had to go—no question of *wanting* to go—and in fact she almost liked the idea. There was just one thing made her think twice about it, which was missing one Saturday night with Wesley. Wesley Beavers was Rosacoke's boyfriend even if Mama didn't like the idea of her riding in to town with a boy two years older every Saturday night to the show and sitting with him afterwards in his car—Rato there on the porch in the pitch-dark looking—and telling him good-bye without a word. That was the best part of any week, telling Wesley good-bye the way she did when he pulled his Pontiac up in the yard under the pecan tree, and if it was fall, nuts would hit the car every now and then like enemy bullets to make them laugh or if it was spring, all those little rain frogs would be singing-out over behind the creek and then for a minute calming as if they had all died together or had just stopped to catch their breath. But Wesley would be there when she got back, and anyhow going to the hospital would give her a chance to lay out of school for a week, and it would give her extra time with Papa that she like to be with. Rosacoke's Papa was her grandfather. Her own father was dead, run over by a green pick-up truck one Saturday evening late a long time ago, almost before she could remember.

But Rato could remember. Rato had seen a lot of things die. He was named for their father—Horatio Junior Mustian—and he was the next-to-oldest boy, nearly eighteen. He didn't mind staying with Papa either. He didn't go to school, hadn't gone in four years, so he didn't have the pleasure of laying out the way Rosacoke did, but seeing all the people would be enough for Rato. Not that he liked people so much. You could hardly get him to speak to anybody, but if you left him alone he would take what pleasure he needed, just standing there taller than anybody else and thinner and watching them.

Dr. Sledge had called on ahead, and they didn't have any trouble getting Papa in the hospital. He even had the refusal of a big corner room with a private bath, but it cost twelve dollars a day. Papa said there was no use trying the good will of Blue Cross Hospital Insurance so he took a ten-dollar room standing empty across the hall, and they wheeled him in on a rolling table pushed by a Negro who said he was Snowball Mason and turned out to be from Warren County too, up around Sixpound, which made Papa feel at home right away and limber enough to flip easy onto the bed in all the clothes he insisted on riding in. But before he could get his breath good, in came a nurse who slid around the bed on her stumpy legs as smooth and speedy as if she was on roller skates with dyed black hair screwed up and bouncing around her ears. She called Papa "darling" as if she had known him all her life and struggled to get him in one of those little nightshirts the hospital furnished free without showing everything he had to the whole group. Everybody laughed except Rosacoke who had undressed Papa before and could do it in the dark. She gritted her teeth and finally the nurse got him fixed and stepped back to look as if she had just made him out of thin air. Milo said, "Papa, if you have somebody that peppy around you all the time, you won't be tired long." The nurse smiled and told Papa she would be seeing lots of him in the daytime and then left. Milo laughed at the "lots" and said, "That's what I'm afraid of, Papa–you getting out of hand down here," but Rosacoke said she could manage fine and wasn't exactly a moper herself and Papa agreed to that.

Soon as the nurse got out–after coming back once to get a hairpin she dropped on the bed–they began inspecting the room. There was a good big sink where Rosacoke could rinse out her underwear that she hadn't brought much of and Rato's socks. (Anywhere Rato went he just took the clothes on his back.) And Mama liked the view out the window right over the ambulance entrance where you could see every soul that came in sick. She called Rato's attention to it, and the two of them looked out awhile, but it was getting on towards four o'clock, and much as she wanted to stay and see what Snowball was serving for supper, she told Milo they would have to go. She couldn't stand to ride at night.

Practically before the others left the building, Rosacoke and Rato and Papa had made their sleeping arrangements and were settled. There was one easy chair Rosacoke could sleep in, and since Rato couldn't see stretching out on the floor with his bones, he shoved in another chair out of the parlor down the hall. That dyed-haired nurse saw him do it. She gave him a look that would have dropped anybody but Rato dead in his tracks and said, "You camping out or something, Big Boy?" Rato said, "No'm. Setting with my Papa." Then he went off roaming and the first thing Rosacoke did was open her grip and spread out her toilet articles all over the glass-top bureau. They were all she had brought except for two dresses and a copy of *Hit Parade Tunes and Lyrics* so she could get in some good singing if there was a radio and there was—over Papa's bed, two stations. And at the last minute Mama had stuck in what was left of the saltwater taffy Aunt Oma sent from Virginia Beach that summer. It seemed like a good idea—nurses hung around a patient who had his own candy like Grant around Richmond, Mama said—so she took a piece and gave one to Papa and began to paint her face, trying it out. Papa gummed his candy and watched in the mirror. Mama would have jerked a knot in her if she could have seen the sight Rosacoke was making of herself but Papa smiled. He had always said Rosacoke looked like an actor, and since the only picture show he ever saw was *Birth of a Nation*—and that was forty years ago in the old Warrenton Opera House with a four-piece band in accompaniment—then it must have been Lillian Gish he thought Rosacoke looked like. And she did a little that winter—not as small but thin all the same though beginning to grow, with a heart-shaped face and long yellow hair and blue eyes. That was what Rosacoke liked the best about her face, the eyes. They were big and it was hard to say where the blues left off and the whites began because everything there was more or less blue, and out the far corner of her left eye came this little vein close under the skin that always seemed to Rosacoke to be emptying off some of all that blue, carrying it down to her pale cheek.

But she couldn't stand there staring at herself all the time—she wasn't that good looking and she knew it already—so after the doctors began to ease up with the visits on the second day, Rosacoke got a little tired. That is, till the Volunteer Worker from the Ladies' Guild came in in a pink smock and asked if maybe they wouldn't want some magazines or a deck of cards maybe? She had a pushcart with her full of razor blades and magazines and things, and all Rosacoke had to do was look at Papa, and he—so happy with a lady visitor—pointed to his black leather purse on the table. The best thing she bought was a deck of Bicycle Playing Cards, and Mama would have jerked another knot if she could have seen Rosacoke right on Papa's bed, teaching him to play Honeymoon Bridge and Fish which she had learned awhile back from town girls on rainy days at little recess. But she never mentioned Slap Jack, her favorite game. She knew in advance Papa would get excited waiting for a Jack to turn up and maybe have a stroke or something so they stuck to quiet games which Papa took to easily, and you could have knocked Rosacoke off the bed with a feather when *he* started teaching her and Rato to play Setback, playing the extra hand himself.

They could count on the cards keeping them busy till Sunday, but they would have to do something with them then. Mama had said she would come down on Sunday to sit her turn with Papa. Milo would bring her after Children's Day. Milo was her oldest boy and he pretty well ran the farm alone with what help Rato could give him.

He would probably have to bring Sissie along for the ride even if Papa couldn't stand her. Sissie was Milo's new wife. Just try leaving Sissie anywhere.

The doctors didn't tell Papa what was wrong with him, and he didn't tell them but one thing either which was that he wanted to die at home. He told them they had been mighty nice to him and he appreciated it, but he couldn't think of anything worse than dying away from home. They said they would take care of that and for him to rest till they told him to stop and they would send Dr. Sledge a full report. And Papa didn't worry. He had left it in their hands, and if a doctor had walked in one morning and said he had come to saw his head off, Papa would have just laid his neck out on the pillow where the doctor could get at it. But the doctors didn't bother him for much of his time, and taking them at their word, he slept the best part of every day. That was when Rato would roam the halls, never saying "p-turkey" to anybody, just looking around. And when Rosacoke could see Papa was asleep good, she would tip over and listen to his chest to make sure his heart was beating regular before she would walk across the hall to the corner room, the one they had offered Papa. It was still empty. The door stayed open all the time, and she didn't see any reason for not going in. There was reason *for* going—the view out the window of that room, a white statue of Jesus standing beside the hospital, holding his head bowed down and spreading his hands by his side. His chest was bare and a cloth was hanging over his right shoulder. Rosacoke couldn't see his face too well, but she knew it, clear, from the day they brought Papa in. It was the kindest face she had ever seen. She was sure of that. And she went to that empty room more than once to look out at him and recollect his face the way she knew it was.

But that didn't go on long because on the third day Rato came in from sitting in the hall all morning and said they had just now put some fellow in that empty room. Rosacoke was sorry to hear it. It meant she wouldn't get to go over there in the afternoon anymore but she didn't say that. She would rather have died than tell Rato how much time she spent there, looking out a window. Papa wanted to know who it was that could take a twelve-dollar room, and Rato said it was a big man. Papa was disappointed too. He had got it figured there was something wrong with that room, lying empty three days or more. Rato said the man's wife and boy were with him—"I expect it was his boy. Looked like he was anyhow. The man hisself didn't look a bit sick. Walked in on his own steam, talking and laughing." Rosacoke wanted to know if they were rich, but Rato couldn't say, said he didn't know. You couldn't ever tell about Rato though, how much he knew. He wasn't anybody's fool. He just liked the idea of not telling all he knew. Keeping a few secrets was everything Rato had. So Rosacoke said, "Well, he's getting a beautiful room" and then walked over and buttoned Papa's nightshirt. She made him stay buttoned square up to the neck all the time because she couldn't stand to look at his old chest. Papa said he was hot as a mink in Africa and that his chest had been that hairy ever since he shaved it to be Maid of Honor in the womanless wedding Delight Church put on when he was seventeen years old.

The night before, when the lights were out but they were still awake, Papa asked Rato to name the best thing he had seen since arriving, and Rato said, "That old lady with all the cards in the big ward down the hall." Rosacoke said, "What sort of cards?" "Every sort there is—Mother's Day, Valentine, Birthday, Christmas . . ." Papa said, "Get-Well cards?" "She ain't going to get well. She's too old." Rosacoke said, "How old?" and Rato said, "What's the oldest thing you know?" She thought and said "God." "Well, she's something similar to that." Rosacoke and Papa laughed but Rato said, "I'm telling the truth. Go take a look if you get the chance. She sleeps all the time." Then they went to sleep but Rosacoke knew he was telling the truth, and anyhow he spoke of his doings so seldom she thought she would take his advice. So the afternoon the man took the twelve-dollar room, she went down while Papa was nodding, and at first it looked the way Rato promised. There was a lady older than God in the bed by the door (saving her a walk past nine other beds), covered to the chin and flat as a plank with no pillow under her head, just steel-colored hair laid wild on the sheets. Rosacoke stepped close enough to see her eyes were shut, and thinking the lady was asleep, she looked up towards a sunburst of greeting cards fanned on the wall over the bed, but she hadn't looked fifteen seconds when the lady shot bolt-upright and spoke in a voice like a fingernail scraping down a dry blackboard—"Praise my Jesus." Rosacoke said "Yes'm" and the lady smiled and said, "Step here, honey, and take a seat and I'll tell you how I got saved at age eighty-one in the midst of a meeting of two hundred people. Then I'll show you my cards—sent by my Sunday school class and my many friends"—and commenced scratching her hair. But Rosacoke said, "No thank you, ma'm" and walked out quicker than she came. She went a few feet outside the door and stopped and thought, "I ought to be ashamed, getting her hopes up. I ought to go back and let her talk." Then she heard the lady's voice scraping on to the empty air so she said to herself, "If I went for five minutes, I'd be there all afternoon, hearing about her cards. Papa is *my* duty." And anyhow she didn't like the lady. It was fine for your friends to send you cards, but that was no reason to organize a show as if you were the only person in the hospital with that many friends and all of them with nothing in the world to do but sit down and write you cards all day. She thought that out and then headed for Papa.

She was walking down the mile-long hall when she saw him—not right at first. At first she was too busy looking at people laid back with their doors open. She didn't know a one of them, not even their faces the way Rato did. The only thing she knew was Snowball Mason in one room, talking to some old man that looked so small in his little outing pajamas with his legs hanging off the bed no more than an inch from the floor like thin dry tan gourds swinging in a wind on somebody's back porch somewhere. Snowball saw her and remembered her as being from Warren County and bowed. She stopped to talk but she happened to look towards the left, and there he was—Wesley—sitting way down across from Papa's door, dressed to the ears and watching the floor the way he always did, not studying people. Still he had come sixty miles to see her so she whispered to Snowball she had to go and went to meet Wesley, holding back from running and trying not to look as if she had seen a ghost which was close to what she had seen, considering this was the last hope she had. He hadn't seen her yet and she could surprise him. She hadn't really missed him so much till now, but when she got nearer she knew how sorry she would be to miss this Saturday with him, and she speeded her steps but kept them quiet. She was almost on him and he put his hands across his eyes—it would be Wesley all over to go to sleep waiting for her—so she came up to him and smiled and said, "Good afternoon, Mr. Beavers, is there something I can do for you?"

But it wasn't Wesley at all. It was somebody she hadn't ever seen before, somebody who didn't really look very much like Wesley when she thought about it. It took whoever it was a little while to realize she was speaking to him, and when he looked up he looked sad and nearly as young as Rosacoke. He looked a little blank too, the way everybody does when you have called them by the wrong name and they don't want you to know it. In a minute he said, "Oh no, ma'm, thank you." "No, ma'm"—as if Rosacoke was some kind of nurse.

It just about killed her to have done that like some big hussy. The only thing left to say was "Excuse me," and she almost didn't get that out before shutting Papa's door behind her, the hot blood knocking in her ears. Papa was still asleep but Rato was standing by the window, having some Nabs and a Pepsi for dinner, and when she could speak she said would he please peep out and see who that was sitting in the hall. As if Rato had ever peeped in his life. He had done plenty of looking but no peeping so he just pulled open the door as if he was headed for dinner and gave the boy a look. Before he got the door closed good, he said, "Nobody but that man's boy from across the hall. That man they moved in today." Rosacoke said, "Thank you" and later on that afternoon she wondered if since he looked like Wesley, that boy could say good-bye like Wesley could.

If they didn't do anything else, those people across the hall at least gave Papa something to think about. They kept their door shut all the time except when somebody was going or coming, and even then they were usually too quick for Rato to get a good enough look to report anything. Something was bound to be wrong though because of all the nurses and doctors hanging around and the way that boy looked whenever he walked out in the hall for a few minutes. Rato reported he saw the man's wife once. He said she was real pretty and looked like she was toting the burden of the world on her shoulders. Even Rato could tell that. So Papa couldn't help asking Snowball the next time he got a chance what was wrong with that man. Snowball said he didn't know and if he did he wouldn't be allowed to say and that made Papa mad. He knew Snowball spent about two-thirds of his time in the man's room, taking bedpans in and out, and he told Snowball at the top of his voice, "That white coat you got on has gone to your head." Rosacoke could have crawled under the bed, but there was no stopping Papa once he got started. You just pretended hadn't a thing happened and he would quiet down. She could tell it got Snowball's goat though and she was sorry. He walked out of Papa's room with his ice-cream coat hanging off him as if somebody had unstarched it.

But that evening when it was time for him to go home, Snowball came back in. He didn't have his white coat on, and that meant he was off duty. He had on his sheepish grin, trying to show he had come on a little social call to see how Papa was making out, but Rosacoke knew right off he had come to apologize to Papa who was taking a nap so she shook Papa and said Snowball wanted to speak to him. Papa raised up blinking and said, "Good evening, Snow," and Rosacoke couldn't help smiling at how Snowball turned into a snake doctor, dipping up and down around Papa. He said he just wondered how Mr. Mustian was coming on this afternoon, and did they have any old newspapers he could take home to start fires with? Papa said he was tolerable and hadn't looked at a newspaper since the jimpson weeds took over the Government. What he meant was the Republicans, and he said, "The bad thing about jimpson weeds, Snow, is they reseeds theyselves."

Snowball hadn't come in on his own time to hear that, though, and it didn't take him long to work his way to Papa's bed and lean over a lot closer than Papa liked for anybody to get to him and say it the same way he would have told a secret. "Mr. Mustian, they fixing to take out that gentleman's lung."

"What you talking about?"

"That Mr. Ledwell yonder in the room across the hall. He got a eating-cancer. That's what I hear his nurse say. But don't tell nobody. I just thought you might want to know so soons I found out . . ."

"A eating-cancer? That's what it is?"

"They don't seem to be no doubt about it. I done already shaved his chest for surgery. He taking his operation in the morning at eight."

Papa wanted to know, "Is he going to live, Snowball?"

"Can't say, Mr. Mustian. He spit the first blood today, and alls I know is they ain't many lives past that. They ain't many. And if they lives you almost wish they hadn't. That's how bad they gets before it's over."

And Papa remembered that was the way it was with Mr. Jack Rooker who swelled up to twice his natural size and smelled a long time before he died. "I can recollect sitting on the porch in the evening and hearing Jack Rooker screaming clean across two tobacco fields, screaming for his oldest boys to just let him rest because there won't nothing nobody could do for him, not nothing. And I'd say to Pauline, 'Pauline, it don't look like

Jack Rooker is ever going to die, does it?' " But that was a long time ago when Papa was a lot younger and a lot farther away from dying himself. That was why he could feel so for Jack Rooker back then. It had just seemed as if Jack Rooker was going through something wouldn't anybody else ever have to go through again.

Snowball was nodding his head up and down, saying, "I know. Yes sir, I know," but Rosacoke could tell he had made his peace with Papa and was ready to leave so she stopped Papa from running on about Jack Rooker and told him it was time for Snowball to go home. Papa thanked Snowball for coming in, as if he had never been mad a minute, and said he would count on him keeping them posted on all that happened to that fellow across the hall.

Rosacoke followed Snowball out. "Snowball, what's that man's name again?"

"Mr. Ledwell."

"Is he really going to die, you think?"

"Yes'm, I believe he is. But Miss Rosacoke, you don't have to worry yourself none about that. You ain't going to see him."

"I know that. I just wondered though. I didn't even remember his name."

Snowball said he would be stepping along and would see her in the morning. But Rosacoke didn't hear from him till way in the next afternoon. Papa was taking his nap and she was almost asleep herself when Snowball peeped in and seeing Papa was asleep, whispered that the gentleman across the hall was back from his operation.

"How did it come out, Snow?"

"They tell me he doing right well, Miss Rosacoke."

"Has he waked up yet?"

"No'm, he lying in yonder under his oxygen tent,

running on about all sorts of foolishness like a baby. He be in some pain when he do come to though."

"Are his people doing all right?"

"They holding up right well. That's his two sisters with his wife and his boy. They setting there looking at him and waiting to see."

She thanked Snowball for letting them know and said she would tell Papa when he woke up. After Snowball left she stepped into the hall herself. The door over there was closed, and for the first time it said "No visitors." She wanted to wait until somebody opened it. Then she could at least hear the man breathing, if he was still breathing. But there wasn't a sound coming through that oak door thick as her fist, and she wasn't going to be caught snooping like Rato so she went back in to where Papa was awake, spreading a game of Solitaire which that dyed-haired nurse had taught him to play. That was *all* she had done for him.

Since they were away from home, they went to bed around ten o'clock. That is they cut out the lights, and Rosacoke would step in the closet and undress with the door half shut. The first evening she had shut it all the way, and Papa told her there was no use to be so worried about him seeing her as he had seen her stripstrod naked two or three hundred times before she was old enough to walk, but she kept up the practice, and when she was in her nightgown, she would step out and kiss Papa and tell Rato "Sleep tight" and settle in her easy chair under a blanket. Then they would talk a little about the day and home till the talk ran down of its own accord though Papa was liable to go on another hour in the dark about things he remembered. But it would all be quiet soon enough, and Rato would be the first to sleep. After

Rosacoke's eyes had opened full to the dark, she could look over and see her brother stretched sideways in his chair, still dressed, with his long hands caught between his drawn-up knees and his head rolled back on his great thin neck and his mouth fallen open. Most people seemed to be somebody else when they were asleep. But not Rato. Rato went to sleep the way you expected he would, like himself who had stopped looking for a while. Then Papa would fall off, sometimes right in the middle of what he was remembering, and Rosacoke could see him too, but he was different—sweeter and with white hair that seemed in the night to be growing into the white pillow his dark leather head rested on, holding him there forever.

After Papa slept Rosacoke was supposed to but she couldn't this night. She kept thinking about it, the man and his boy. Papa had forgotten all about Mr. Ledwell. She hadn't told him anything about the operation, and she had asked Snowball not to tell him either. She didn't want Papa to start back thinking and talking about that poor man and asking questions and sending Rato out to see what he could. She had it all to herself now. Snowball had told her Mr. Ledwell's boy was staying there with him through the nights. Mr. Ledwell had made the boy promise him that before he would go to the operating room, and the boy would be over there now, awake maybe with his father that was dying and she here on her chair trying to sleep with her Papa and Rato, her Papa turned into something else in the night.

Still she might have gone on to sleep if she hadn't thought of Wesley. If she was at home she could go to sleep knowing she would see Wesley at seven-thirty in the morning. He drove the school bus and went nearly four miles out of his way on the state's gas to pick her up first so they could talk alone a few minutes before they looked up and saw all those Gupton children in the road, knocking together in the cold and piling on the bus not saying a word with purple splotches like thick cobwebs down their legs that came from standing by an open fire, Mama said, and in winter afternoons Wesley would put her out last into the cold white yard that would be nearly dark by five, and she would walk on towards the light that was coming already from the kitchen windows, steamed on the inside like panes of ice stretched thin on frames. And huddled there she thought how Wesley had said they would go to Warrenton this coming Saturday for a traveling show sponsored by the Lions Club—an exact copy of the Florida State Electric Chair with some poor dummy strapped in it, waiting for the end. Wesley was interested in anything mechanical, and she would have gone with him (no charge for admission the paper said, just a chance to help the Club's Blind Fund) if that was how he wanted to pass time—striking up friends with the owner of the chair whoever it was and talking till time to head back home. But that would have been all right with Rosacoke. She would have waited and been glad if she had got the chance, but she wouldn't now and like as not Wesley would take Willie Duke Aycock which was what Willie Duke had waited for all her life. That was just Wesley. Let her miss school even two days at hog killing and he practically forgot her.

It was thinking all this that kept Rosacoke from going on to sleep. She tried once or twice to empty her head the way she could sometimes at home by closing her eyes and thinking way out in front of her, but she couldn't manage that tonight so she listened till she heard slow breathing from Rato and Papa. Then she got up in her bare feet and felt for the closet door and took down her robe from a hook and put it on. It was peach-colored chenille. She had made it herself and it had been honorable mention at the 4-H Fall Dress Revue in the Warren County Armory. She took her shoes in her hand and opened the door. The hall was empty and the only light was the one at the nurses' desk, and that was so white, shining into both ends of the long hall and against the white charts hanging in tiers. The two night nurses were gone or she could have talked to them. She hadn't ever talked to them, but they seemed nice enough not to mind if she did want to talk. She guessed they were out giving sleeping pills so she walked towards the big ward to pass time.

It was dark down there and all these sounds came out to meet her a long time before she got to the door like some kind of Hell she was hearing from a long way away —a little moan strained out through old dry lips and the grating of each private snore as it tore its way up the throats of the ones who were already asleep. Rosacoke stopped in the open door. The nurses were not there. Nobody seemed to be walking in the dark anyhow. All she could really see was, close to the door, an old woman set up in bed, bent all over on herself and scratching at her hair real slow. But she knew the others were there, and she knew there ought to be something you could do for such people, something you could say even in the dark that would make them know why you were standing there looking—not because you were well yourself and just trying to walk yourself to sleep but because you felt for them, because you hadn't ever been that sick or that old or that alone before in all your life and because you wished they hadn't been either. You couldn't stand there and say to the whole room out loud, "Could I bring you all some ice water or something?" because they probably wouldn't want that anyhow, and even if they did the first ones would be thirsty again and pitching in their hot sheets before you could make it around the room. You would be there all night, and it would be like trying to fill up No-Bottom Pond if it was ever to get empty. So she turned in the open door and saw one nurse back at the desk and walked in that direction, stopping to look at the flowers waiting outside the room of an old man who said they breathed up too much good air at night.

She was some way off when she saw the man's boy. There was no doubt about it being him this time and she was not surprised. The boy walked fast towards the desk, his shirt open down the front, the white tails sweeping behind him in the light of the one lamp and his chest deep brown almost as if he had worked in the field but you knew he hadn't. When he got to the nurse he shut his eyes and said, "My father's nurse says please call Dr. Davis and tell him to come now. It's serious." His voice was low and fast but Rosacoke heard him. The nurse took her time staring at a list of numbers under the glass on her desk before she called. She told whoever she talked to that Mr. Ledwell had taken a turn for the worse. Then she stood and walked to his room. The boy went close behind her so she stopped at the door and said, "Wait out here." When she shut the door it stirred enough breeze to lift his shirttail again. He was that close and without stepping back he stood awhile looking. Then he sat by the door where Rosacoke had seen him that first awful time.

She looked on at it from the dark end of the hall (she was not walking by him in her robe even if it had won honorable mention), but she saw him plain because a table was by his chair and he had switched on a small study lamp that lighted his tired face. His chin hung on his hand like dead weight on delicate scales and his eyes were shut. Rosacoke knew if he looked towards the dark he might see her—at least her face—and she pressed to the blackest wall and watched from there. For a long time he was still. No noise came through his father's door. Then clear as day a woman's voice spoke in the open ward, "I have asked and asked for salt on my dinner" —spoke it twice, not changing a word. Some other voice said "Hush" and the boy faced right and looked. Rosacoke didn't know if he saw her or not (maybe he was just seeing dark) but she saw him—his eyes, far off as she was, and they were the saddest eyes in the world to Rosacoke, that pulled hard at her and called on her or just on the dark to do something soon. But she didn't. She couldn't after the mistake of that first time. She shuddered in the hard waves that flushed over her whole body and locked her there in the shadow. Once she put out her hand and her foot and took one small step towards the boy whose head had dropped onto his folded arms, but the bleached light struck her robe, and she dropped back the way one of those rain snails does that is feeling its path, damp and tender, across the long grass till you touch its gentle horns, and it draws itself back, hurt and afraid, into a tight piece you would never guess could think or move or feel, even.

She couldn't have said how long she stood there, getting so tired she knew how it felt to be dead, before the doctor they called came in. He didn't have a tie on, and sleep was in his eyes. He saw the boy and touched him and said something, and they both walked into the room. Before they shut the door a sound like a mad child catching at his breath after crying ran out behind them to where Rosacoke was. She didn't know what was happening, but the boy's father might be dying. She knew that much. She felt almost sure that if the man died they would make some kind of public announcement. But he didn't die and she had waited so long she was nearly asleep. The hall she had to walk through back to Papa's was as quiet now as a winter night in an attic room when you could look out the window and see a sky, cold and hard as a worn plow point shining with the moon. All those people in the ward were asleep or maybe they had given up trying and waited. It seemed as if when you waited at night for something—maybe you didn't know what—the only thing happened was, time made noise in a clock somewhere way off.

It was the next morning that Rosacoke made up her mind. If Mr. Ledwell had lived through the night, she was going to call on him and his family. It was the only thing to do, the only Christian thing to do—to go over there and introduce yourself and ask if there was anything you could do to help such as setting up at night. The way she felt she might have gone over that morning if the room hadn't been so quiet. She hadn't seen a soul come or go since she woke up. She didn't know how Mr. Ledwell was getting along after everything that happened the night before. She didn't know if he had lived out the night. All she could do was wait for Snowball to tell her. She wasn't going to ask Rato to do any more looking for her after the last time.

Snowball was late coming by that morning, but he got there finally and called her out in the hall to talk. He said Mr. Ledwell had a relapse the night before, and they thought he was passing away, but he pulled through unexpectedly. "He not going to last though, Miss Rosacoke. The day nurse tell me he full of the cancer. It's a matter of days, they say, and he know that hisself so all of us try to keep his spirits up. He ain't a old man. I old enough to be his Daddy. He resting right easy this morning, but he was bad sick last night. In fact he was dead for a few minutes before the doctor come and brought him around. They does that right often now you know."

That made Rosacoke think of the day the Phelps boy fell off the dam at Fleming's Mill backwards into twenty feet of water, and three men who were fishing dived in in all their clothes and found his body face down on the bottom and dragged it out, the mouth hanging open in one corner as if a finger was pulling it down. He had stayed under water four or five minutes, and his chest and wrists were still. They said he was dead as a hammer for half an hour till one man pumped air in him and he belched black mud and began to moan through his teeth. But what Rosacoke always wondered was, where did they go if they died for a while—Mr. Ledwell and the drowned Phelps boy—and if you were to ask them, could they tell you where they had been and what it was like there or had they just been to sleep? She had heard that somebody asked the Phelps boy when he got well enough to go back to school what dying was like, and he said he couldn't tell because it was a secret between him and his Jesus. Mama had said that was all you could expect out of a Phelps anyhow—that she wouldn't ask him if you paid her cash money and that you couldn't just suppose he had gone to Heaven and if he hadn't, you could be sure he wouldn't admit going elsewhere. (She had smiled but she meant it. She had never had a kind word for that branch of Phelpses since they bootlegged their way to big money some years before.) But not everybody felt the way Mama did. A church of Foot-Washing Baptists up towards South Hill heard about it and invited the boy up to testify but he wouldn't go. And from then on Rosacoke had watched him as if he was something not quite natural that had maybe seen Hell with his own eyes and had lived to tell the tale—or not tell it—and she had followed after him at little recess, hiding where he couldn't notice her so she could watch his face close up and see if his wonderful experience had made him any different. As it turned out it had. He was the quietest thing you could imagine, and his eyes danced all the time as if he was remembering and you couldn't ever know what, not ever.

By the time Rosacoke thought that, Snowball had to leave, but before he went she asked what he thought about her going over to see Mr. Ledwell and his family.

"It couldn't do no harm I can think of, Miss Rosacoke, if you don't stay but a little while. He can't talk much with his one lung, but he be happy to have a visitor. You wait though till he get a little of his strength back from last night."

She nodded Yes but she hadn't planned to pay her visit that morning anyhow. She had made up her mind not to go over there till she could take something with her. She might be from Afton, N.C., but she knew better than to go butting into some man's sickroom, to a man on his deathbed, without an expression of her sympathy. And it had to be flowers. There was that much she could do for Mr. Ledwell because he didn't have friends. He and his family had moved to Raleigh less than six months ago. Snowball had found out the Ledwells were from Baltimore. But of course there wasn't a flower for sale anywhere in the hospital, and anyhow it wasn't cut flowers Rosacoke had in mind. She got a dime from Papa by saying it was time she sent Mama word as to how they were getting along. Then she hunted down one of the Volunteers and bought two cards with the Capitol on them. She wrote one to Mama.

Dear Mama,
We like it here alot. I hope you and Baby Sister, Milo and Sissie are all O.K. Papa and I are getting plenty rest. Rato is the one taking exercise. When you come down here would you bring some of your altheas if they have bloomed yet?
Yours truly,
Rosacoke Mustian

She wrote the other one to Wesley Beavers.

Dear Wesley,
How are you getting along? I am fine but miss you alot. Do you miss me? When you go to see the Florida Electric Chair think of how much I would like to be there. If you see Willie Duke Aycock tell her I said hello. I hope to see you Monday early.
Your friend,
Rosacoke

Then she mailed them and waited and hoped the altheas had bloomed. Mama had got an idea out of *Life* magazine that you could force things to flower in winter, and she had dug up an althea bush and set it in a tub and put it in the kitchen by the stove and dared it not to bloom. If it had she would gladly pick a handful of oily purple flowers that bruised if you touched them and hold them in her big lap the whole way to Raleigh on Sunday.

And Sunday came before Rosacoke was ready. She woke up early enough (Rato saw to that—he could wake the dead just tying his shoes), but she took her time getting washed and dressed, straightening the room and hiding things away. She didn't expect the family till after dinner so it was nearly noon before she set Papa up and lathered his face and started to shave him. She had finished one side without a nick, singing as she worked—the radio was on to the final hymn at Tabernacle Baptist Church—when the door burst open, and there was Baby Sister and Mama close behind her with flowers. Baby Sister said, "Here I am." Rosacoke got her breath and said, "Blow me down. We sure didn't look for you early as this. Mama, I thought you had Children's Day to get behind you before you could leave."

Mama kissed her and touched Papa's wrist. "I did. I did. But once I pulled the Sunbeams through 'Come and Sing Some Happy Happy Song,' I felt like I could leave so we didn't stay to hear Bracey Overby end it with Taps. I know he did all right though. I hope he did—he practiced till he was pale anyhow. Then after leaving church like Indians in the middle of everything to get here early of course some Negroes drove up at the house just as we was starting—some of those curious Marmaduke Negroes with red hair. Well, they had heard about Baby Sister, and they had this skinny baby and wanted her to blow down his throat." (Negroes were always doing that. A child who had never seen its father could cure sore throat by breathing on it.) "It's a awful thing but Baby Sister enjoys it—don't you?— and I can't deny her any powers she may have, especially on Sunday."

(Nobody had denied Baby Sister—six years old and big for the name—anything she wanted since she was born six months to the day after her father died. Even the nurses didn't try. Mama marched her in past a dozen signs that plainly said *No Children Under 12* and Baby Sister in Sweetheart Pink and nobody uttered a sound.) All through her story Mama looked around, and when she was done she said, "Where is Rato?"

Rosacoke said, "Patrolling, I guess. He'll show up for dinner," and before she could wonder where were Milo and Sissie, they strolled in from parking the car. Milo kissed Rosacoke and said, "Wesley sent you that." Mama said, "No he didn't. We haven't seen Wesley." Then he laughed and kissed Papa—"Miss Betty Upchurch sent you that, but I don't tickle as good as her." (Miss Betty was a crazy old widow with whiskers that he teased Papa about.) Everybody laughed except Sissie. When they quieted down Sissie said, "Good morning" and showed her teeth and settled back to looking as if a Mack truck had hit her head-on so Milo explained it to Papa. "Sissie will be off the air today. She's mad—woke up mad but didn't find reasons till we were leaving home. Then she found two good ones. One was she had to shell butter beans all the way up here because Mama didn't read the directions and froze her damn beans in the shell. The other thing was she had to sit on the back seat to do it because Mama and Baby Sister had spoke to sit up front with me and the heater. Well, she sat back there shelling, and when she finished—it took her a hour and we were on the outskirts of Raleigh—she lowered the glass on her side, intending to empty out the hulls, but Baby Sister said, 'Shut that pneumonia hole,' and Sissie got flustered and threw out the beans instead. Mama capped the climax by laughing, and Sissie ain't spoke a word since except just now." He turned to Sissie who was already staring out the window—"Say something, Doll Baby. Turn over a new leaf." She wouldn't even look so Milo laughed and that did seal her. It was a good thing. Nobody could make Papa madder than Sissie when she started running her mouth.

Mama frowned at Milo and said, "Everybody calm down. We got half a day to get through in this matchbox." She meant Papa's room that was ten by twelve. Then she went to the bureau and while Rosacoke scraped chairs around, she took off her hat and her white ear bobs and combed her hair and put on a hair net and slipped off her shoes. She went to the chair where Rato slept—in her stocking feet—and said, "Rosacoke, get me my bed shoes out of my grip." Rosacoke got them. Then Mama settled back and blew one time with relief. She had come to stay and she had brought three things with her—dinner for seven in a cardboard suit box, her grip, and enough altheas to fill a zinc tub. She made it plain right away that Rosacoke would go on home with Milo and Sissie and Baby Sister but Rato would stay on to help her with Papa. Milo said he planned on leaving between eight and nine o'clock. (What he had in mind was to pacify Sissie by taking her to supper at the Chinese café she liked so much and then going on to a Sunday picture. But he didn't tell Mama that.) And Rosacoke couldn't object to leaving. In some ways she would be glad to get home, and Milo's plans would give her time to pay her visit to Mr. Ledwell, time to do all she wanted to do, all she thought she could do—to step over when she had seen her family and pay her respects and give them the flowers that would say better than she could how much she felt for Mr. Ledwell, dying in this strange place away from his friends and his home, and for his people who were waiting.

So she had that day with her family (Rato appeared long enough for dinner), and the day went fine except for three things. One thing was Sissie but nobody ever looked for Sissie to act decent. Another thing was, after they had eaten the dinner Mama packed, Papa reached over to his bedside table and pulled out the playing cards. Rosacoke had taken pains to hide them way back in the drawer, but Papa pulled them out in full view and set up a game of Solitaire and looked at Mama and grinned. She made a short remark about it appeared to her Papa was learning fancy tricks in his old age. Papa said couldn't he teach her a few games, and she drew up her chair and said she had gone nearly fifty years—seven of them as a deaconess in Delight Baptist Church—without knowing one playing card from the other, and she guessed she could live on in ignorance the rest of the time. But she didn't stop Papa. He just stopped offering to teach her and lay there the rest of the afternoon, dealing out hands of Solitaire till he was blue in the face. He played right on through the nap everybody took after dinner. You couldn't have stopped him with dynamite. The third thing was after their naps. When they all woke up it was nearly three-thirty and the natural light was dim. Rosacoke stood up to switch on the bulb, but Milo said, "No don't," and even closed the blinds. Then he went to Papa and pointed at his necktie and said, "Watch this. Pretty soon it'll start lighting up." It was something he had got that week by mail, and he claimed it would say "Kiss Me In The Dark!" when the room got dim enough, but they waited and the only thing the tie did was shine pale green all over. Rosacoke was glad he didn't get it working but Papa was disappointed. He asked Milo to leave the tie with him so he could test it in total darkness and show it around to the nurses, but Milo said he was intending to wear it to some crop-dusting movies at the high school that coming Thursday.

In a few more minutes it was five o'clock, and Milo started his plans by saying he and Sissie were going for a little ride and for Rosacoke to be packed for home by nine. Then he got Sissie up and into her coat and they left. Whenever Milo left a place things always quieted down. Papa went back to his Solitaire, and Mama crocheted on a tablecloth that she said would be Rosacoke's wedding present if the thread didn't rot beforehand. Even Baby Sister, who had pestered all afternoon to make up for Sissie being on strike, was worn out and sat still, sucking her thumb, so in the quiet room Rosacoke took down her grip and packed in almost everything. But she kept out her only clean dress and took it down to the nurses' utility closet and pressed it and put it on. She had washed it in the hall bathtub the night before. When she came back to the room, nobody paid her any mind. They thought she was just getting ready to go home. She washed her hands and face and stood in front of the mirror, combing her hair and working up her nerve. She turned her back to Mama and put on a little lipstick and rouge to keep from looking so pale. Then she took the altheas up out of the water Mama set them in and dried the stems with a clean towel and wrapped tissue paper around them. Mama said, "You are dressing too soon," and Rosacoke said, "I reckon I am," but before anybody had seen her good, she slipped out the door in her yellow dress, holding the flowers. She had tied a white card to them. Snowball had got it for her the day before. It said "From a Friend Across the Hall."

She took three steps and stopped and stood in front of the oak door, taller than she would ever be, that said "Ledwell." Behind it was where Mr. Ledwell was and his people that she didn't know, where he had laid down that first day Rato saw him talking and laughing, where he had gone out from to take his operation, and where it was not his home. Rosacoke was nervous but she told herself she looked as good as she could, and she had the altheas in her hands to hide the shaking. She knocked on the door and she must have knocked too soft because nobody came. She knocked again and put her ear to the wood. There were dim sounds coming from the other side so she pushed the door open a little, but the room was dark and quiet as an open field at night with only the sky, and she was drawing back to leave when the moving light of candles caught her, streaming from a part of the room she couldn't see into, drawing her on. So she went inside and pressed the door silent behind her and stood up against it, waiting till her eyes had opened enough to halfway see. There were five or six people in the room. Mr. Ledwell was a ridge on the bed that the sheets rose and fell over in gullies like after a rain, and his boy was by his head, holding one of the candles. In the yellow light the boy looked a way Wesley Beavers might never look, and the same light fell through a clear tent that covered his father's head and chest. A little of it fell on three ladies off in a corner, kneeling on the hard floor, and on a man standing near the bed by a table with two candles on it. He was all in black and falling from his neck was a narrow band of purple cloth with fine gold crosses at the ends. He was talking in words Rosacoke didn't know, almost singing in a voice that was low and far away because he was old with white hair and was looking down, but finally he looked up at Mr. Ledwell's boy, and the two of them pulled the tent back off him. Rosacoke knew he was alive. She could hear the air sucking into his throat, and his eyes were open on the boy and on the yellow candle.

The old man in black moved his hands in the air three times carefully, wide and long over Mr. Ledwell. Then he took a piece of cotton and waited for Mr. Ledwell to shut his eyes. He wiped the cotton over the lids, and they were shining for a second, wet and slick under the light before Mr. Ledwell opened them again and turned them back to the boy. The boy rolled his father's head to one side and then to the other while the old man touched the cotton to the ears that looked cold, and all the time Mr. Ledwell was trying not to take his eyes off the boy as if that sad face in the soft light that came and went was what kept him from dying. And except for that same soft light, the walls of the room would have disappeared and the ceiling, and Rosacoke could have walked out through where the window had been that she used to stand by. It seemed to be time for her to leave anyhow. She didn't know how long this would go on. She didn't know what it was. She only knew they were getting Mr. Ledwell ready to die in their own way, and she had taken the first step to leave when the boy's face turned and saw her through all that dark. His face changed for a minute, and you might have thought he smiled if you hadn't known that couldn't have happened now, not on his face. That was why Rosacoke didn't leave. He had looked at her as if he knew why she was there, almost as if he would have needed her if there had been time. But the old man touched Mr. Ledwell's lips, and Mr. Ledwell strained his head off the pillow and sucked at the cotton before the old man could pull it back. He thought they were giving him something to drink. And it went on that way over his hands that had to be pulled out from under the cover and his feet that seemed to be tallow you could gouge a line in with your fingernail. When they finished with his head, they put the tent back over him, and Rosacoke couldn't hear his breathing quite so loud. From his feet the old man walked back to his head. He put a black wood cross that had Jesus, white and small, nailed on it into Mr. Ledwell's hand. Then he shook a fine mist of water over him and made the sign again, and Rosacoke heard words she could understand. The old man told Mr. Ledwell to say, "Thy will be done." Mr. Ledwell nodded his head and his eyes opened. He took his hand and tapped on the inside of the clear tent. When his boy looked at him, his voice came up in pieces—but Rosacoke heard him plain—"Don't forget to give Jack Rowan one of those puppies." The boy said he wouldn't forget. Mr. Ledwell looked easier and when the old man reached under the tent to take the cross and Jesus away from him, he nodded his head over and over as he turned the cross loose.

The old man went over to speak to the lady who must have been Mr. Ledwell's wife. She was still on her knees, and she never took her face out of her hands. That was when Rosacoke left. They might switch on the light, and there she would be looking on at this dying which was the most private thing in the world. She had stayed that long because the boy had looked at her, but he might have forgotten by now. He had never looked again. A chair was by the door. She laid her flowers there. In the light somebody might see them and be glad that whoever it was stepped over to bring them, stepped over without saying a word.

She waited in the hall for the sound of his dying because he had seemed so ready, but it didn't come—nobody came or went but a colored girl, pushing a cart load of supper towards the ward—so she had to walk back into Papa's room, dreading questions. The room was dim though and still with only the light over Papa's bed that shined on his hair and the cards spread out on his knees. But he was just turning them over now, not really playing, and when Rosacoke shut the door, he looked and put one finger to his mouth and pointed towards Baby Sister, asleep at last in Mama's lap, and Mama nodding. Rosacoke thought she was safe and halfway smiled and leaned on the door, waiting for breath. But Papa stared at her and then tried to whisper—"You are leaving me, ain't you?"—and Mama jerked awake. It took her a while to get her bearings, but finally she said, "Where in the world have you been with Papa's flowers?" Rosacoke said, "To see a friend." Papa said, "I didn't want no flowers. Who is your friend?" She said, "Mr. Ledwell" but Papa didn't show recollection. Mr. Ledwell hadn't crossed his mind since the operation, but just to say something he asked was the man coming on all right? Rosacoke said, "He ain't doing so good, Papa" and to Mama who had never had a secret, never wanted one, "Mama, please don't ask me who that is because I don't know."

Then she went to her grip and turned her back on the room and began packing in the things she had left till last. She was almost done when Rato walked in. Nobody had seen Rato since dinner. He walked in and said it the way he might walk in the kitchen and drop a load of wood in the box—"That man over yonder is dead. Ain't been five minutes." Mama said she was always sorry to hear of any death, and Rato said if they left the door cracked open they could see the man because a nurse had already called the undertaker to come after the body. But Rosacoke faced him and said, "No" and said it so Rato wouldn't dare to crack the door one inch. He just left fast and slammed it behind him. But Baby Sister slept through it all, and Mama didn't speak for fear of disturbing her so the room was still again. To keep her hands busy Rosacoke rearranged the few little things in her grip, but she stood sideways to look at Papa and have him to fill her mind. Papa had his cards that he went back to, but he dealt them slow because he was thinking. He was so old himself you couldn't expect him to be too sad. Lately he always said he knew so many more dead men than live ones that there wasn't a soul left who could call him by his first name. And that was the truth. That was what took the edge off death for Papa—grieving over so many people, so many of his friends, burying so much love with each one of them till he had buried them all (everybody he had nearly) and pretty nearly all his love, and death didn't hold fear for him any more. It wasn't as if he didn't know where he was going or what it would be like when he got there. He just trusted and he hoped for one thing, he tried to see to one last thing—for a minute he stopped his card playing and asked Mama could he die at home, and Mama told him he could.

That was what made Rosacoke think so long about Mr. Ledwell who had died in that dark room. She wouldn't be able to go to his funeral, wouldn't even be asked. But that wasn't so bad. She had done what she could, being away from home, hadn't she, and didn't she know his name at least and hadn't he died not cut up or shot or run over but almost in his sleep with his wife and his boy there, and with all that beautiful dying song, hadn't he surely died sanctified? If he had to die wasn't that as good a way as any, leaving his living picture back here in that boy? But she hadn't ever seen him alive really. She hadn't ever told him or any of his kin—out loud—that she felt for them. She hadn't ever said it so loud she could hear her own voice—that Rosacoke Mustian was sorry to see it happen. That was why she spoke at last. She had been quiet so long, and now her slow lean voice cut through all the dark in the room. "It don't seem right," she said. "It just don't seem right. It seems like I had got to know him real well." And her words hung in the room for a long time—longer than it took Papa to pick the cards up off the bed and lay them without a sound in the drawer, longer even that it would have taken Rosacoke to say good-bye to Wesley if it had been Saturday night and she had been at home.

About the Author

Reynolds Price grew up in the North Carolina country he re-creates so well in "A Circle of Love." It was during the Depression years and his father moved the family to several Carolina towns as he sold, first, insurance and then electrical appliances. What he remembers of those years, he says, are "our family, the terror of financial ruin, hundreds of solitary days in the woods up trees in vines (suspecting I was miserable) and a lot of laughter."

He attended Duke University and then Oxford University in England, where his first short stories appeared in *Encounter* magazine. He returned to teach English literature at Duke, where he still teaches half the year. His first novel, *A Long and Happy Life,* was published in 1962, and a collection of short stories, *The Names and Faces of Heroes,* in 1963. His latest novel is *A Generous Man.*

THE LOVELY NIGHT

Shirley Jackson

Natalie Waite leaned her chin on both her hands and looked at the soda clerk thoughtfully: What would happen if she went over very casually, smiling, and asked him to marry her? Or run off with her to Italy? Would he stare at her blankly, or would he, possibly, conceivably, smile and say, "Sure"? Suppose, worst of all, she went over very casually, smiling and hardly looking at him at all, very casually indeed, and asked him to take her to the informal dance at the high school? She shivered, and closed her eyes suddenly; it was horrible. ("How would you like to take me to the informal dance tonight? No one else seems to ask me, and it's getting pretty late.") Horrible.

"What on earth *you* thinking about?"

Natalie opened her eyes. "Nothing," she said. She tried very hard not to look impartially on her companions; almost constant companions they were, by now, and any clear look at them gave Natalie such a look at herself that she was helplessly depressed, and almost frightened. Doris, on her right, was the sort of girl who invariably finds her own level in any group of people so loosely interrelated as the student body of a small high school; Doris was fat, and badly dressed, and stupid. She was the center of a little group of girls who did things by themselves, went to movies and had excruciating parties which they referred to as "hen" parties, went swimming in the summer, in a gay chattering body whose animation never quite concealed the fact that they were unattractive and unpopular.

Ginny, on Natalie's other side, was pale, without distinguishable color in eyes or skin or hair; she played sentimental tunes very poorly on the piano, and was given to giggling flirtation with her teachers; she seemed incapable of admiring the pleasanter side of anything or anybody; incapable, indeed, of believing that anything or anybody *had* a pleasanter side.

When Natalie sat in the drugstore with Doris and Ginny she knew that she was marked, just as irremediably as though they had all worn distinctive uniforms, as one of the little group around Doris, the aggressively sociable outsiders.

"What *are* you moping about?" Doris said again, insistently. "You thinking or something?" She and Ginny began to laugh the more uproariously because there were other people in the drugstore: women at the next table drinking coffee after an afternoon's shopping; two girls at the counter drinking Cokes and talking to each other in quick, low voices; the clerk.

"*Honestly,*" Doris said, and their laughter rose.

Why am I here, Natalie thought miserably, what made me be here, marked out by these girls as their friend, instead of off somewhere by myself, or sitting somewhere with people I like? Why am I here? She smiled defensively at Doris and Ginny. "I don't know," she said ineffectually, and they laughed harder.

"Listen," Doris said to Ginny, suddenly serious, "listen, you've got to be ready at eight, remember. None of this waiting around."

"I'm always ready," Ginny said, loudly for the benefit of anyone who might be listening. "Never-late Ginny, that's what they call me."

"You be ready, too," Doris said, turning her heavy eyes on Natalie. "We'll come and get you, Ginny and me, about five after."

"What for?" said Natalie blankly. She looked at Doris and then at Ginny; they were grinning at her.

"Doesn't hear a word," Doris told Ginny.

"Deaf as a post," Ginny told Doris.

Doris pushed Natalie's hand on the table. "The dance, stupid. Didn't you know we were all going to the dance?"

Natalie frowned, uncomprehending, and Doris said easily, "I guess in the high school you come from they don't have dances like this. This is a kind of a dance they have a lot here. You don't need a date to go."

"It's not as though they had a real *band,"* Ginny put in quickly. "We go all the time."

"Sure," Doris said. "We all go and we have fun."

"Fun" was one of the things that Doris and her friends kept having. Natalie smiled, to seem polite, and said, "I couldn't possibly go. Really, I can't."

"Don't be silly," Doris said, and Ginny said, "We're all going. Don't be scared."

"You mean just anybody goes?" Natalie said.

"I guess in your old high school—" Doris began, and Natalie said hastily, "I went to a girls' high school. A sort of private school. We only had a couple of special dances each year."

"Well, that's why, then," Doris said, greatly relieved. "This is a different kind."

"I was hoping—" Natalie began; she was about to say that she had been hoping that someone—anyone—would ask her to the dance, but she stopped herself suddenly. Doris and Ginny would only answer that they had just asked her; perhaps, after all, if it really was an occasion to meet people, and people did do it all the time, and it certainly wasn't possible to ask the soda clerk if he . . .

She smiled to herself, and Doris said loudly, "Well, that's settled, then. You coming?" She referred, this time, to their leaving the drugstore, which was done with so much noise and laughter and dropping of pennies and exclamations over the counter display of compacts and lipsticks that Natalie held back, reluctant, until Doris' bold shout across the store brought her hurrying. "Hey, Nat, you coming?" Doris shouted, and Ginny added piercingly, "Got to rush home and get ready for the dance."

They don't care about anything, Natalie thought, feeling the contemptuous eyes of the shopping women, the two girls at the counter, and the clerk; they don't care what they sound like, and they think I don't care either. . . .

She wanted to leave them quickly, outside on the sidewalk, but there it would be worse; the three of them standing in a hesitating little group in the middle of the people moving past, talking loudly, laughing, pushing one another. Doris always talked back to people who pushed against her in a crowd and Ginny seconded her. Better, Natalie told herself grimly, as she had fifty times before, better to walk along with them and say good-bye on some neutral street corner, better to have the neighbors see me with them than try to get away in public.

"Honestly," Doris said loudly as they pushed their way through the crowds of people on the streets; it was just after five, and everyone was hurrying. "Honestly, I can't *wait*." She nudged Natalie significantly. "Wait till you get there," she said. "Honestly."

"Who do you dance with?" Natalie asked timidly, low-voiced, for fear someone passing might hear her talking to Ginny and Doris about a dance, as though they, of all people, could tell her.

"Well, really," Doris said. She laughed loudly. "Listen," she said to Ginny, and people passing them glanced up quickly and then away, "she wants to know who we dance with."

Ginny laughed too, and Natalie, between them and helpless, walked as rapidly as she could.

Ten minutes' walking with their frequent pauses before shop windows, Ginny's turning to look after men, and her audible comments, brought them to the corner where Natalie left them; they lived next door to each other not more than two blocks away from Natalie. When Natalie saw her own front door from the corner, she grew more restless and nervous.

"Don't dress up much," Ginny assured Natalie before they parted. "It's not *that* much of a dance, see?"

"But we'll have fun," Doris promised.

"Just don't get all dressed up as though you expected something special," Ginny said.

"Really," Natalie said, encouraged by being so close to her own home, "I don't think I'd better go."

"Honestly," Doris said. She turned and regarded Natalie coldly.

"If you never want to have any *fun*," Ginny said.

"Listen," Doris said to Ginny, "she's just scared. She

wants to go, but she's scared. In that high school she came from—"

"It's nothing terribly fancy, this dance," Ginny said.

In order to escape from them at all Natalie had to promise that she would go with them; to herself, she modified her promise into going with them as far as the door. I'll see what it's like, she thought, and then if it looks like—I can always say I've got a headache, or I've got something to do at home. Maybe if I don't dress up at all, don't even change my clothes, no one will think I intended to go to the dance at all. . . .

Doris and Ginny progressed slowly up the street toward their own homes, stopping to turn back and call, "Be ready, now," with much laughter, and, in case someone might be listening, in loud voices, "Honestly, Nat, we can't wait!"

When they were far enough away for her to ignore, safely, their waves and shouts, Natalie turned and hurried down her own street; she was almost late for dinner. Being late would be bad enough if her mother and father minded it; it would be worse if they were gratified, supposing that she was late because she had been having such a gay time with her new friends, the pleasant young people she had met, become close to, so readily in this new high school.

Natalie went into the house. In the dining room, the dinner table was set, her own napkin ring where it had always been, the coffee pot ready to plug in by her mother's place, the carving knife readied for her father. The one quick look she gave her own dinner table effectively dislocated Natalie from Doris and Ginny; it was completely impossible that any girl coming home to dinner at a table like that should have spent the afternoon being frightened, bullied, shamed, by Doris and Ginny.

In the living room Natalie could hear the low voices of her mother and father, waiting for her, waiting for the pleasant dinner that found them nightly around the table together, the three of them beautifully close to one another in love and understanding. Natalie hesitated in the doorway to the living room, waiting for the last echo of Doris' voice to clear out of her head before she spoke to her parents.

"Natalie," her mother said with pleasure, and her father looked up and smiled.

Natalie smiled back. "I'm so *glad* to see you," she said, as though she had not parted from them only that morning.

At dinner, with some hesitation, Natalie told them about the dance. "You see," she said, trying to explain and yet not wanting to identify Doris and Ginny too clearly, not wanting to confess to her mother and father that she was hopelessly entangled with the wrong people. "You see, it's just that I don't know very many people yet, and girls going to a dance alone sounds wrong, somehow."

"Take you myself if I could still dance," her father said.

"He can waltz," her mother confided to Natalie. "He never learned anything else, so far as I know."

"I'd even only waltz," Natalie said earnestly.

"I know exactly what you mean," her mother said. "My mother used to make the boy next door take me. She'd call his mother." Natalie's mother made a rueful face, remembering. "Sometimes he'd try to get out of it," she added, "and we'd hear him arguing with his mother, all the way over at our house."

"Lucky you got me finally," Natalie's father observed.

They can't really see it seriously, Natalie thought without criticism; it's so far back, and so mixed up with everything that's happened to them since, that they've really forgotten. They're trying hard to cheer me up. "But shall I go?" she asked her mother. "What shall I do?"

"Natalie dear," her mother said gently, "if it frightens you, don't go. Don't let these girls, whoever they are, talk you into doing anything you don't really want to do. But just remember this." Natalie's mother put down her coffee cup and leaned toward Natalie. "The only way to be friendly with people is to want to know them. And probably the best way to get to know people is to go where they are. Isn't that true?"

"I suppose," Natalie said, confused; somehow her mother's words had nothing to do with Doris and Ginny.

"And listen to this, too," her mother said. "Perhaps there is some boy, some specially nice boy, who's never noticed you particularly in school, perhaps because he sees you every day in the same old surroundings, or perhaps because you've never done anything to stand out in his mind—oh, any one of a dozen reasons for not noticing a girl particularly. But then, if that same boy sees you—tonight, for instance—in a different setting, a gayer atmosphere—well." Her mother sat back and spread her hands eloquently.

Natalie's father nodded. "You're a pretty girl," he said to Natalie.

Natalie felt herself blushing. Anyone's mother and father can think she's pretty, she told herself, it doesn't mean anything; but she continued to blush. Her mother laughed.

"The way you describe it," she said, "it can't be much of a dress-up affair. You might wear your new blue sweater. You look very nice in that."

Just as her mother and father were a refuge from Doris and Ginny, and from all the troubles outside, so Natalie's own room was a refuge from her mother and father and their wealth of affection. When Natalie came into her own room after dinner, she sat down at the chair before the desk and told herself over and over, "If it *could* be possible to keep your children from hating growing up, *surely* my mother and father would do it for me."

When she lifted her head, quieted somewhat, and perhaps a little braver, it was twenty to eight; there was only just time to dress and get outside if she hoped to head off Doris and Ginny before they rang her front doorbell. They were, she knew from horrible experience, dismayingly, brutally punctual, not liking to miss a minute of their fun.

She put on the blue sweater her mother had recommended, and combed her hair carefully. Although she did not admit it to herself, her mother's suggestion that someone—some nice boy—might notice her under new circumstances stayed in her mind, and she combed her hair to make it slightly different, almost blushing to herself in the mirror when she remembered her father's odd notion that she was pretty.

As she hurried, at last, down the stairs, her mother was standing at the bottom, waiting for her. Natalie checked herself, embarrassed, and her mother smiled at her. "Chin up," her mother said, and touched Natalie's shoulder lightly.

"Good night, Dad," Natalie said at the door of the living room.

Her father winked at her and blew her a kiss. "Have a fine time," he said.

Outside she was barely in time to catch Doris and Ginny before they started up the front walk. *"Honestly,"*

Doris said. "We really thought you'd back out, didn't we, Ginny?"

"We were all set for an argument," Ginny said. "We were going to keep at you till you came. You didn't dress up much, did you?"

Ginny had chosen to array herself in a sleazy silk dress; Doris was wearing a particularly unfortunate blouse and skirt combination and gaudy costume jewelry. They eyed Natalie and her blue sweater dubiously.

"Listen," Ginny said, "aren't you going to wear anything better than *that*?"

Natalie stopped herself before she spoke; if she wore anything but a school sweater, went all dressed up to the dance, it would look as though—would look, at any rate, very strange if she carried through her now decided plan of leaving them at the door.

"I thought I'd wear this," she said inadequately.

Ginny snickered, but she and Doris were too pleased with themselves to trouble more about Natalie. On the way up to the high school Ginny hummed and did small dance steps on the sidewalk; Doris nudged Natalie and giggled excitedly.

"Place is all lighted up like a Christmas tree," Ginny observed as they came in sight of the high school.

Natalie was staring at the high school; it was so familiar to her in its everyday aspect that seeing it by night was a shock. Instead of being dark and forsaken, the way it should be when classes were over and all the students gone, it was lighted and noisy. The lights from the windows of the gym shone onto the lawns and the sidewalks; the only dark windows she could see were on the second floor, in rooms she knew so well, where she read Shakespeare and fumbled her algebra, and pounded doggedly away at French.

It was like her first day at the high school, Natalie thought, when she had come timidly up the walk, longing to be back in the safe small class at Miss Lang's, desperately afraid of these knowledgeable boys and girls who walked so assuredly along the halls. I won't go in, she told herself tonight, as she had told herself the month before when she'd come for the first time; I'll tell them I don't feel well and have to go home, or I'll wait till no one's looking and just run.

As she had done a month before, however, so she did tonight. She walked with fear up to the doors and inside. This time, with Doris on one side and Ginny on the other, she had no choice. Her first impression was that all the lights for basketball games, for gym classes, for special performances, were on and that everyone, the whole roomful of people, was laughing at her.

"See?" Doris said, so loudly that Natalie cringed. "See, it's just a regular dance. You'll love it, honestly."

"It's fun." Ginny squeezed Natalie's arm on the other side. "Let's look around first and see who's here," she said to Doris.

Arm in arm, the three of them made their uneasy way around the outside of the gym floor. Natalie, hardly looking to right or left, was sure by what she saw from the corners of her eyes that she was being stared at with smiles and snickers. It's your imagination, she told herself fiercely, you always think people are staring at you when you feel uncomfortable. No one's even noticed you.

Doris and Ginny, giggling, pushing their way, sometimes pinching Natalie in their excitement, were carrying on their usual loud conversation.

"It's a swell dance," Doris announced, apparently for the benefit of the entire assembly.

"There's Helen Rockwood," Ginny announced.

"Dancing with John Grover. She's in our English class, Nat. See her?"

Still out of the corner of her eye, Natalie saw a laughing face turned to her, a blue sweater much like her own. Helen was certainly laughing at her, and Helen's partner was laughing, too.

They came closer and Helen said, still laughing, "Hi, Natalie."

Miserably, without lifting her head, Natalie said, "Hello."

"Come on," Doris said jubilantly to Natalie. "You want to dance?"

If anything could have increased Natalie's misery, it was the realization that in Doris and Ginny's group, the girls danced with one another. It was something that Natalie had dimly known from the moment they had suggested the dance, but the thought of moving out onto the dance floor with Doris, under the eyes of Helen Rockwood and the others, made Natalie shiver.

"Not now," she said confusedly. "I don't think I want to dance, not right away."

Doris shrugged and laughed, and she and Ginny went out onto the floor together. Natalie stood alone by the wall, wishing she did not now have to go halfway around the gym to get to the door and the welcome darkness outside. After a few minutes, when no one came near her or spoke to her, she gathered courage to look up at the dancers, and saw with surprise that no one was staring at her, or laughing; they were all completely and satisfactorily intent on their own business.

She could follow the course of Doris and Ginny around the dance floor, partly by watching for Doris' showy blouse, partly by the little wake of confusion they left behind them. Wherever they had passed through the crowd of people dancing, there were stares and laughter, occasionally an expression of annoyance from a couple Doris and Ginny had blundered into, a general murmur of comment. None of it seemed to have any perceptible effect on Doris and Ginny: they moved on, apparently oblivious of the quality of attention they drew, talking loudly and swinging each other around in wild gaiety.

But don't they *know*? Natalie thought, watching them across the room. She was so far separated from them now, she could see them for a minute divorced from herself and they seemed to her infinitely pathetic: a large clumsy girl and a small noisy girl who were attracting unpleasant attention to themselves because they so terribly, desperately wanted attention of any kind, secured in any manner—anything at all, if it could save them from being forgotten or overlooked. Why? Natalie thought, not aware that she saw them clearly, apart from her own fear, for the first time; they're not unkind or mean or anything—all they want is for someone to *notice* them.

She was suddenly overwhelmed with the weight of Doris and Ginny as they swung into her and against the wall.

"Come on, Nat," Doris said, breathlessly.

Natalie shook her head. "Maybe later."

Then, as they moved away again, she was acutely aware of standing alone. She glanced quickly around the gym and could not see any other girl standing by herself, although across the hall there was a group of boys, laughing and talking with great gestures, their backs to the dancers.

If only one of *them* would come and ask me to dance, Natalie thought, and then the idea of being spoken to by a stranger filled her with fear again, and she looked pointedly away from the group of boys, praying that none of them had noticed her glancing toward them, and hoping that no one at all, ever, under *any* circumstances, would think that *she* wanted to dance. She felt herself putting on a look of disdain, of indifference toward the dance and the dancers—the look of someone who would never dream of dancing at a dance—and would have laughed at herself if she had not been so miserable.

A boy passed her, a boy she remembered slightly, although in her panic she could not remember in which class she had seen him; he was coming directly toward her, with a determined look on his face, and for a dreadful moment it seemed that he might speak to her. When at the last minute he turned and stopped a couple dancing near her, Natalie was first filled with relief and then with anger. He *could* have asked me, she thought; after all, it's only common politeness to ask a girl who's not dancing. Doesn't he think I came here to dance? She dropped her look of disdain and put on a smile of interest, as of a girl who was a really good dancer and was only resting between partners. Then she realized that her smile was directed at the boy who had come near her, and she canceled the smile, and frowned fiercely instead.

Doris and Ginny came close to her again, and Doris waved and Ginny pointed significantly at the floor, asking if Natalie wanted to dance. Natalie, relieved that they did not shout at her, shook her head violently, and she could see Ginny shrug, and hear her voice beginning, "Some people—"

When she glanced, as though in meditation, at the big clock at the end of the gym, Natalie was shocked to find that it was nine-thirty. She had been at the dance for over an hour. What does everyone think of me, she wondered, seeing me stand here all by myself all this time.

It was too much, and she fled; behind her she heard

Ginny's voice calling out, "Nat, where you going?" and she ducked into the first place she could find, which was the girls' room. There, in this room to which the girls flocked after gym class, she found a refuge; it was, somehow, a link with the world she had partly conquered the first day she took a deep breath and walked into the school, and where (studying Shakespeare, worrying away at algebra) she could at least hold her own.

Wretchedly she sat on the window sill, and wondered what to do. Doris and Ginny were not going to let her step out quietly. It was impossible to get across the gym and outside without their seeing her, and Natalie knew that she didn't have the courage necessary to resist them, with everyone in the gym watching their antics.

She turned her head quickly to the window when the door opened, and saw in the glass the reflection of Helen Rockwood, who, after a brief glance at Natalie, turned to the mirror with her comb. "Hi," Natalie said into the window.

Helen glanced around. "Having a good time?"

"Wonderful," Natalie said.

Helen turned to face Natalie, as though she had come to a sudden decision. Her voice was curious, but not unkind, when she said, "How come you're here with those"—she hesitated—"those girls?" she finished finally.

Natalie wanted to say, "Because no one else asked me," but what she actually said was, "I don't know."

"It's not my affair, of course," Helen said. "I know you're new around here, and maybe—" She finished, this time, with a helpless gesture.

"It's hard to make friends in a new place," Natalie said. She wanted to say more, but did not dare to.

"I know," Helen said. She turned again to the mirror

and began to apply her lipstick. "I was new here last year," she added.

She smiled at Natalie in the mirror, slipped her lipstick and comb into her pocket and said, "Have a nice time, anyway," before she went to the door and out again, leaving Natalie alone.

For a minute Natalie sat perfectly still, wondering what Helen had perhaps wanted to say and, like Natalie, had not dared. And, suddenly, it all fell into place—what her mother had meant, telling her about the boy next door, what her father had tried to say, actually, when he could only manage to tell her she was pretty, what Helen meant by saying it wasn't *her* affair, she had been new herself last year.

I've got to do it by myself, Natalie thought, surprised when she heard herself speak aloud; it's no good waiting for other people to take care of me—I've got to do it myself. Everyone else is too busy taking care of himself.

She did not know yet what she was going to do, but she stood up with determination, and went over to the mirror and combed her hair and put on lipstick just as Helen Rockwood had done. Then, boldly, her hair newly combed, she opened the door of the girls' room and stepped out. She was no longer part of the dance, neither desiring nor fearing partners, and she looked around unafraid. Everyone seemed to be having a good time, she noticed, and those two unfortunate girls were still creating a stir wherever they went.

Mr. Brandt, the chemistry teacher, was dancing with a pretty young woman who was probably his new wife; the chemistry class had greeted him with a cheer when he came back to school after his honeymoon. Helen Rockwood went by, in the blue sweater so much like

Natalie's own, and she smiled and Natalie smiled back. There was a boy standing with his back to her, leaning against the wall not ten feet away. He was watching the dancers as though he had stopped momentarily and was resting for a minute before dancing again.

Resolutely Natalie walked over to him and touched his arm. He turned and Natalie said, without looking to see if he were surprised or not, "I want to ask a favor of you, please. Will you walk with me as far as the door? I want to go home."

He did not speak, and Natalie realized that she had undoubtedly surprised him. "I know it sounds silly," she said, her voice weakening, "but it's important to me. If you wouldn't mind."

"Of course not," he said. Natalie saw with relief that he had been recollecting his manners, that even if he would never think of asking her to dance, his mother had certainly taught him not to be rude. For some reason Natalie felt a swift thankful joy for her own mother, and then she said, "Please, can we go right now?"

"Of course," he said, and with solemn formality offered her his arm.

Just as solemnly, Natalie put her hand through his arm, and they walked sedately toward the door at the farther end. Natalie felt that if she tried to speak, she would spoil her enormous dignity with a giggle, and perhaps the strange boy felt the same way, because they walked in strict, careful silence along the aisle between the dancers and the wall; once a dancing couple blundered into them, and Natalie's escort moved her out of the way, nodding at the excuse offered by the dancers.

Again someone waved at him and called, and he waved back, and for a minute Natalie was afraid that he might abandon her, but he walked on beside her.

They had nearly reached the door when Natalie found Doris and Ginny standing in front of them. Doris looked sullen and angry; Ginny had her hands on her hips, and she looked Natalie and her escort up and down and said, "Pretty quick to snub her old friends, isn't she?"

"*Some* people," Doris agreed. "*Of* all the nerve!"

It's the dragon on the road, Natalie thought hysterically—can my knight get me past? He had stopped, and looked from Natalie to Doris and Ginny in confusion.

"Listen here," Ginny began shrewishly, "if you think—"

She was cut off, suddenly, by Helen Rockwood and her partner, who swept quickly between Natalie and Doris and Ginny, and Helen took Natalie by the arm. "You two leaving so early?" Helen said; her glance included the knight as well as Natalie. "Do you really have to go, Natalie?"

"Yes, I have to go home," Natalie said; she was incapable of saying more.

Helen turned and made an elaborate display of looking at the clock.

"You're probably right," she said. "I have to go pretty soon myself." Doris' "Well, of *all* things," and Ginny's "Some people think they're pretty smart," were lost before Helen's voice.

At the door, Helen's smile touched Natalie quickly and Natalie smiled back.

"Good night, Natalie," Helen said politely.

"Good night, Helen," Natalie said politely. She walked out through the door, accompanied by the strange boy. Once outside, she released the arm she had been clinging to, and said weakly, "Thank you very much."

He glanced back at the lighted doorway and then at Natalie, hesitated, and then said, "I better come a little farther with you. It's pretty late."

Bless his mother, Natalie thought, and almost laughed. "No, thanks," she said. "I only needed to get across the gym. I don't want to keep you from the dance."

"That's all right," he said. "I think I ought to take you home. It's pretty late."

He's going to go on saying that, Natalie thought, until he manages to think of something else to say. It made her feel more assured to know that he was conversationally helpless, so she said, "Thank you," and they turned and began to walk down the path. Natalie debated briefly whether to tell him about Doris and Ginny, decided it was not really important, after all, and finally said pleasantly, "Are you in my French class?"

"I think so," the boy said. "You're Natalie Waite, aren't you?"

"Yes." She was absurdly pleased to recall that the French class—formerly one of her greater terrors—met three times a week.

"I'm Bob Lennox," he said.

Natalie placed him immediately; he sat in the middle row, usually, and his French was almost as weak as hers.

"Irregular verbs," she said, and shuddered.

"Golly," he said, and they both laughed.

They turned the corner and Natalie could see the lights in the living room of her own house. Her mother and father were still up waiting for her, to see what kind of time she had had. When they came to her house, she was going to invite Bob in, and she knew already that he would accept, politely and awkwardly. Her mother and father would like him, Natalie thought.

Walking along in the pleasant darkness, with the sound of his footsteps echoing hers, Natalie rehearsed happily their entrance into the house.

"Mother, Dad," she was going to say, "I want you to meet Bob Lennox. A friend of mine."

About the Author

Shirley Jackson was born in San Francisco in 1919, and spent her early life in California. She attended Syracuse University, where she founded, edited, and was the main contributor to the college literary magazine. Shortly after graduation, she married Stanley Edgar Hyman, the well-known writer and critic.

She lived in North Bennington, Vermont, where she painted, wrote, studied black magic, and took care of her four children. She is best known for her stories of eerie fantasy and witchcraft, but she is also the author of two humorous books about bringing up children, *Life Among the Savages* and *Raising Demons.*

Her books include *The Haunting Of Hill House, Hangsaman,* and *We Have Always Lived In the Castle.* Her short story "The Lottery," which was first published in *The New Yorker* in 1948, is now considered a classic of its kind. Shirley Jackson died in Vermont on August 9, 1965.

THE STRANGE THING

Emily Hahn

The sun on her body was painful, but she lay quiet on the pier with her arm over her eyes, and thought. She would have a headache by dinner time, but it didn't matter. Under the sun she was getting sleepier and sleepier: the slightest movement made her dried bathing suit pull uncomfortably, so she didn't move. There was not even a watery slap against the poles as the water swayed about them. Down the shore on the public pier they were screaming and splashing but it sounded much farther away than the music in her head. Violins in her head were playing while words went on, voiceless words. The violins were the voice.

Gaze into the tea leaves, just a moment, love, with me.
Read the ancient legend written there in leaves of tea.

Ancient legend; that was beautiful. But there was no sense in saying leaves of tea again except that it made it easier to dance to, if you were a tall slim slippery girl with high-heeled slippers, dancing with a man. The music made the sense, really; and then the way the drum helped it along and the violins played louder to meet the drum:

Telling of the million prayers that wait at the gate of the gods.
Just a skein of tangled threads, countless ends and odds. . . .

She jerked a little as she reached that part: it was the same place that something had happened to her last night. The orchestra was playing "Tea Leaves" and people were dancing by her where she sat against the wall next to Mother. She was just sitting there watching them: the bronze girl in peacock blue and the man with yellow hair and a brown face and the little shiny man with white trousers and the old lady with gray hair and pink cheeks, holding up her train while she danced.

"—that wait at the gate of the gods."

The drum grew loud. In her head something opened up and there she was, looking at herself. It was exactly like waking up, except that as soon as you wake up you forget what was happening in your dream, and this time she could remember both sides of that second equally clearly. Before, she wasn't there in that room, not the way the bronze girl and the old lady and Mother were: then afterwards suddenly she was. First she was something like God, looking on at everyone, and then she was both God and Catherine, looking at herself. Perhaps she couldn't be God any more, but just Catherine. Catherine in pink organdy, crumpled in the back where she had sat on it at dinner, and flat-heeled white kid shoes.

It had been that way ever since. She had been cross and snappy all morning, at Jennie for trying to make her stop reading and come to lunch, and at Mother for everything she said. She had a sort of grudge against Mother for being stupid and letting her go to a party in crumpled organdy when she herself was too young to know any better. Now, though, it would be different. If they didn't let her wear high heels and clothes like Harriet's she would not go to any more parties. She would spend all her time reading and swimming. When summer was over it would be all right because at school it doesn't matter what you wear: the only thing to worry about at school is gymnasium and "lights out."

The wind was probably rising: she couldn't open her eyes, but she heard a creaking sound out on the lake that was a passing sailboat. It was getting late. She would open her eyes and dive in, just to wake up; then into the house. There would be time to read awhile and to eat an apple, if Mother didn't scold her for spoiling her dinner.

She had paced out to the end of the board and was poised for a dive when she saw that the boat was too near for safety. She stopped and waited for it to pass. Pinky Sinclair was sailing it and there was another man smoking a pipe, wearing a white shirt and a bathing suit. Pinky waved at her and she raised her hand, waiting for them to go on. The man with the pipe said something to Pinky and the boat shifted and he called out, "Come on out for a ride."

Surprised, she shook her head. It was late. Then she changed her mind and dived in. The boat was so near that she was almost there at the side when she came up. They helped her in, pulling her up by the arms, and their fingers hurt a little. She laughed at her clumsiness and gasped at the shock of the water.

"This is Bud Milford," said Pinky, and went on with the business of sailing, which was all he ever cared about.

Bud smiled slowly at her and she looked away. She felt a little shocked: there was something to think about. He smiled at her as if he knew all about the secret. He knew that she was Catherine. They were the only ones in the world who had found out: Pinky didn't know, any more than Mother did, or Harriet. Perhaps this man knew because it was the first time he had seen her: it was his first impression. She looked at him again and he was still looking at her: his eyes were blue but you could hardly see them, they were so narrow.

All the rest of the afternoon they sailed slowly back and forth on the lake, saying hardly anything at all. Pinky sailed and Bud smoked and sometimes smiled at her, and she looked at the shore. Whenever the boat turned, Pinky called out and they ducked to avoid the swinging sail, and sat on the other side of the cockpit. When Bud didn't smile but just went on looking at her she felt uneasy; knowing he was in on the secret. Now and then she thought that it was all crazy, and then remembered that she always felt crazy after lying in the sun for a long time.

It was when they came in to Pinky's pier that the thing happened. They stopped there because it was deep; Pinky said he would take her home in his canoe. He jumped out first to tie up. The boom hung in the middle of the boat, swinging back and forth, and she crouched down to avoid bumping her head. So did Bud. They were out of sight: even the pier had disappeared. He took hold of her shoulder: his hand was so big that it covered her shoulder entirely; he held her casually but strongly, and he kissed her on the mouth. She was surprised and yet she didn't say anything. She lay quietly against him, against his chest in the white shirt, and he kissed her for a long time. She felt his heart beating calmly and strongly.

There didn't seem to be anything to say. Perhaps people always acted like this.

Then they stood up as if nothing had happened, and he helped her out to the pier and told Pinky not to bother, that he would take her home in the canoe. He paddled with deep long strokes, and looked at her. There was nothing to say.

As they glided up next to the dock, he held to the boards while she climbed out and said:

"Can I see you tonight?"

She could hardly talk: something funny had happened to her breath. She said that her mother didn't let her go out; that . . .

"Pinky's going sailing," he interrupted. "You can go out with Pinky, can't you? All right, we'll come by for you at eight. Meet you down here."

"All right," she said, and he paddled away. She ran so hard up the steps to the house that she was almost sick when she got there, and there was no time to rest before dinner.

Harriet was there, wearing the new yellow dress with the full skirt. There was a party, but Mother was not going at all. That left the evening free for Catherine. Harriet was excited about the new dress, and she didn't look at Catherine at all. It was a good thing. She would have noticed something.

Mother said gently, "You're late, Catherine. I don't like your swimming in the evening."

"I wasn't swimming. I was sailing with Pinky."

"Pinky?" asked Harriet. "He took you sailing? Why?"

"Why, Harriet!" said Mother, mechanically.

"I didn't mean it just that way," Harriet said. "I mean he doesn't usually let anybody ride on that precious boat. Especially kids. He's getting ready for the races with Bud

Milford. That's a sweet boy, Bud Milford."

"Milford? Robert Milford's son? I didn't know he was here."

"Just for the races. He was perfectly pie-eyed the other night: I think he's too old for that sort of thing. He must be twenty-five."

Mother laughed. "Is there any standard? Well, darling, please come home early. You're so nervous when you need sleep. Remember what a busy day we're going to have."

"Oh, bother," Harriet said. "I'm not Catherine. There isn't so much to worry about: you know Jennie'll take charge anyway."

It was a quarter to eight, and the sun was sitting on the trees across the lake. Catherine stood up, crumpling her napkin.

"Do you mind if I don't wait for dessert?" She kept her eyes on the chair so that Harriet would not look at her. "I'm going out on the lake for awhile."

"Alone? I wouldn't, darling. I don't like you to go paddling alone." Mother always said no at first, to everything.

"I thought maybe Pinky would let me take a ride. It's a nice boat."

"Oh, Mother!" cried Harriet. "Don't let her go tagging after that poor boy!"

Mother turned toward her with offended dignity. "Please remember that you cannot manage the entire family. If Pinky doesn't seem to mind, why—"

Catherine slipped out, picking up a sweater on the way. It was still too early, but she was afraid to sit in the room with Harriet, who would surely notice. She went down the stairs as slowly as she could, stopping on each step to put both feet squarely in the middle. This took up a certain amount of time. It was getting dark when she reached the bench on the pier and sat down. Someone was passing in a canoe, but it was too early to be Bud. She sat without thinking until the canoe had gone by, trembling.

She had been trembling ever since Harriet had made that crack about his being twenty-five. It was amazing. He was old, he knew all about things, and yet he had recognized her. He had said to himself: Here is a girl, Catherine. You are Catherine; I am Bud and in the same world with you . . .

He swung the canoe toward the pier, said "Hello," in a sleepy voice, and waited for her to step in. They paddled out to the sailboat tied up at the buoy: Pinky was there already. He nodded at Catherine and went on untying ropes. They left the canoe at the buoy and sailed off across the lake toward the point on the other side. It was quite dark now, and yet there was a lightness about the air as if it were waiting to shine up again.

The boat made a little swishing sound, cutting the water. Catherine sat in the dark with Bud so close to her that down her side there was a warmth that came from him, although they were not touching. After awhile they came close to the other shore and Pinky called out and they ducked. Instead of coming up and sitting on the other side, she stayed down in the corner of the cockpit. He made her do it: his hand held her shoulder and pushed her into the corner against the pile of cushions. He sat on the edge of the cockpit with his hand down by his knee, on her shoulder, and she watched him looking out across the lake, smoking his pipe. What was he thinking about? He looked sad and far off. What memories were in his head? So many things must have happened in twenty-five years.

The boat creaked and rushed along under the rushing stars. It sounded much faster down where she couldn't see the lights crawling by over on the shore. She closed her eyes, feeling the warm place on her shoulder where his hand held it. All her other thoughts had gone away. She couldn't think about anything at all: she didn't try. The faint fishy smell of the lake, the varnish smell of the cockpit, the white sail in the black air and a warm feeling on her shoulder: it was like sleeping.

They had stopped. Pinky was tying ropes again. She sat up and rubbed her eyes: they were tied up somewhere down the shore. Pinky called Bud to help him lower the sail a little so that they wouldn't drift. She wrapped a blanket around her shoulders and waited for him to come back; it was cold without him. No one said anything. He came back and sat down in the cockpit and took part of the blanket for himself, smiling at her; Pinky was tuning his banjo.

They all sang: fraternity songs and ballads and new numbers, and after awhile Bud asked Pinky to sing "The Hermit of Shark Tooth Shoal," which was quite long. Under the blanket he put his arm around her. It felt tense and controlled, and she could not keep her eyes open. She had to close them and lean against his arm. What was he thinking about? Perhaps he felt just the way she did: empty.

Pinky said that they must go home because the breeze was dying. All the way back, Bud's arms were around her. He turned her until she was facing him and he kissed her once, for a long time, just as they glided up to the buoy. She fought not to close her eyes. She opened them and looked at him after he had kissed her: his eyes were shut and his face had a curious peaceful waiting look, as if something were sure to happen.

They left the boat and went back in the canoe. Pinky got out at his pier; then instead of turning toward hers, they headed out into the lake again.

"Oh, I must go home," she said. "Mother will be worried. She'll be mad. Look!" She pointed up to the house. Against the lighted window of Mother's room, some one was looking out at the lake.

"She can't see. It's too dark."

"But I've got to go to bed. We're leaving tomorrow. We're going back to New York on the noon train."

"Are you?" He straightened the paddle and looked at her quickly. He laughed. "I never saw it fail. It happens every time. Every time."

"What?"

"This." He went on paddling out into the lake and didn't say any more. When they reached the sailboat at the buoy again he sat down by her and took her into his arms. She closed her eyes promptly and he ran his finger over her eyelashes.

She stirred, uneasy. "I'm sure Mother can see us."

"Well, then—" he stood up and held out his hand. "Get into the boat. It's more comfortable."

There was a tarpaulin over the pit and now no one could see them. They crouched down in the shadows, on the cushions.

"Just like a little house," he said, and looked at her, and then he kissed her terribly hard, as if he wanted them to grow together, and she let go of herself and forgot that she had become Catherine or anybody special at all, until he let her go.

He pushed her away and leaned back with his hands behind his head, looking at the sky. He lit a cigarette.

He looked very sad. She felt sad too: there was no reason, but she did. Why should everything be so sad? She loved him sitting there, smoking a cigarette. She couldn't stand it. She leaned over and kissed his cheek.

"Don't," he said, and turned his head away.

It was incredible. It was horrible. Very slowly, she woke up.

"Why?" He did not answer.

After a minute she shivered, and rose to her knees, struggling not to step on the hem of her skirt.

"I've got to go home."

"Yes," he answered immediately. "We shouldn't have come at all."

But why? She started to clamber out, and he took hold of her arms and looked hard at her.

"You ought to be careful, Catherine," he said. "You're too forward."

It was very strange. Wondering about it, she said nothing until they reached the pier: he kissed her and watched her as she went up the stairs, then he paddled away without waving good-bye to the top of the staircase.

Mother was too busy, looking over Harriet's clothes in front of the big trunk, to say anything about the time. Catherine went to her room and sat by the window. She was languid but not exactly sleepy: it would be hard to go to sleep. For a long time she sat there trying to figure everything out, but her mind would not stay with the subject. She began to think about poetry, little stray bits of big poems that she couldn't remember perfectly . . .

She vanished. In the sounding town
Will she remember, too?
Will she recall the eyes of brown
As I recall the blue?

And there was another that was lovely:

And the star I laugh on tilts through Heaven
And the heavens are dark and steep . . .
I will forget these things once more
In the silence of sleep.

But she couldn't. The stars were getting dark, as if night were just now really falling. . . .

And England over
Advanced the lofty shade . . .

No use; she couldn't go on with it. There were only the few bits that made her shiver when she said them to herself: they didn't really mean anything without the rest.

Too forward. What did he mean? He must mean something; real people always mean something; it's not like poetry. All of this that happened had something to do with love. She had been in love ever since the afternoon, and he wanted to do something about it, and she had been too forward. . . . Oh. She understood all of a sudden, and it was awful. She put her hands up to her face, but she couldn't stop knowing. The greatest crime in the world, everyone said, and she had committed it. Too forward. She had let him get all worked up: that was the phrase, and it was the worst thing a girl could do. Everyone said so and it was in all the books.

After a long time while she kept her eyes covered, she went to bed and tried to sleep. But first she burst into tears and sobbed until the pillow was clammy under her face and her head ached. When it was over and there was nothing left but a stupid heavy feeling, she went to sleep.

Coming in from hockey, hoarse from screaming and laughing, she almost forgot what a nuisance it was to change clothes twice in the middle of the day. Afterwards in the study hour when the air was bad and she was afraid that she would doze off at her desk, she thought again of how tiresome it had been. The Latin text blurred again and again no matter how often she blinked her eyes; all the words were indecipherable and only the ink spots stood out on the page. She sighed, for the tenth time in three minutes, and shifted her feet. Miss Cochran was reading at the head of the room: the light from the window just touched her hair and left the rest of her in deep shadow. Catherine rested her cheeks on her hands and stared at the book, beginning to think it all out again. She always came round to it in study hour.

There had been (a long time ago) a sailboat and a man, twenty-five years old, and a girl. The girl was too forward. She made the man want something that he couldn't possibly have. She didn't mean to, but that's what happened. He wanted to do something that he couldn't, and he suffered. It was dreadful and irrevocable. It had started so naturally, and then. . . .

Catherine moved spasmodically and knocked a pencil off the desk. Miss Cochran looked up and frowned, then went on reading.

It was irrevocable. She would never be able to forget it. She could forget everything else in reading, but whenever she finished a book she remembered *that* again. Everything would remind her of it, forever.

There was a folded piece of theme paper in the Latin book. Slowly, stopping to think of words, she wrote on it:

"I suppose you have never forgiven me. I couldn't

expect you to. You'll never get this letter and I'll never see you to explain, but it is the only way I can think of to say how sorry I am. I didn't mean to be so forward. It is too late to do anything about it, but I've got to say I'm sorry. I'm terribly sorry. I didn't understand. I was young. I understand now."

As she was signing her full name the bell rang, loud and peremptory. She jerked violently and hid the letter in Caesar until she could put it with the others in the candy box back in her room. There were a lot of letters there.

Sitting up in a private box was very thrilling, even though she was only with Harriet and Mother and Uncle John. If no one looked too hard at her they might almost think that she was wearing a regular evening dress: the color and the length were right. It was only the sleeves that made it all wrong: Mother had been very stubborn about sleeves. But she stopped worrying about herself when the music stopped and the curtain went up.

Halfway through it seemed to lag, and she looked down at the people beneath. It would be fun to take a huge fan and brush all their heads off into the lobby like so many marbles. Then she saw him.

He was sitting in the fifth row with a girl. He was in a dinner coat and looked older. Of course he looked older: it had been a long time. She must be looking older too. There he was, and she could tell him all about it. She began to tremble: she trembled so hard that surely Harriet would notice. What could she do? Could she wait until afterwards and see him in the crowd, going out? But perhaps he would get out before they met. Could she wait for intermission?

Harriet turned around and looked at her.

"Are you having a chill?" she asked. Then Catherine went crazy.

She said, "Look down there. There's Bud Milford. I've got to see him."

"Why?" Harriet was looking at her very hard. "You don't have to see him. Don't be crazy. What's the matter?"

"Sh-h-h-h," said Mother.

Catherine gripped the edge of the box and tried to make her teeth stop chattering.

"I've got to. I've got to. Let go of me."

She ran out of the box, down the stairs, to the white lobby. There was an usher there who looked at her. She caught his arm.

"Listen—I haven't any money to tip you with but there is a man in there I've got to see. Will you get him or let me in to see him?"

"Why," said the usher, "I guess I better get him. Where is he sitting?"

"In the fifth row next to the aisle. With a girl. He has yellow hair."

He went in and she stood perfectly still, a statue in the mirror. Bud came out, arguing with the usher. Then he saw her.

"Why, Catherine!"

She stood there, trying to talk.

"Why, Catherine! It's fine to see you."

She started to say something but couldn't.

"What's the matter? How are you? It's been a long time since I've seen you."

What could she say? What was there to say?

"Is there a mistake? It is Catherine, isn't it?"

There was nothing to say. She stood there looking at him, trying to think what it was, what it was all about. But there was nothing to say.

She turned and ran away.

About the Author

Emily Hahn began her career as a mining engineer for an oil company in St. Louis. She then became a geology instructor at Hunter College, and later served with the Red Cross in the Belgian Congo. While she was there, "because I was too broke to buy a ticket home, I wrote this little story. I was probably homesick for northern lakes and sailboats and the tight, safe little life I had left behind me in the Midwest." It was "The Strange Thing," her first published story.

Since then, Emily Hahn has written many books, fiction and non-fiction, for adults and children, and she is a regular contributor to *The New Yorker*. She is particularly noted for her books on China, where she lived for seven years.

She now lives in England with her husband, Major Charles Boxer, and her two children.

LITTLE BASEBALL WORLD

Robert Lowry

Helen turned it on very low so that nobody else in the house would know she was listening (she'd sworn before them all never to listen again, because they'd kidded her about it) ; and then as soon as she heard the score she turned it off and sat staring at the backyard.

The score was five to two in favor of the Cubs and it was only the last half of the third inning with the Reds at bat—who was batting? Lombardi? Lombardi was a good hitter, you couldn't tell what they were going to do now. Of course the Reds would lose eventually, they always lost, they were so dumb, they did so many dumb things just when they got you all excited about how good they were, then somebody did something so dumb you wanted to throw the radio out of the window. Who was batting anyhow? She turned on the radio again, very softly, and listened, leaning forward in her rocker.

"Lombardi on second, Harry Craft at bat with one ball and two strikes—" Lombardi on second! She leaned forward to listen.

They were so dumb though, they'd never do anything right, they'd lose this one too. "All right," said the announcer. "Bill Lee is ready—" And the black-eyed buxom girl rocked back and forth in the rocker before the radio; she was ready too, it was evident; she was waiting for whatever was sure to come. She just had no faith at all in the Reds any more, they lost yesterday and they'd lose today, they weren't going to be leading the league for much longer. . . . Like what happened yesterday, they were winning until the first of the ninth, then that dumb Johnny Vander Meer let the bases get full by walking so many, and Hartnett came in to pinch-hit and made a home run, and that was the end of your old ball game. That was the way they always did—got you all worked up then betrayed you.

". . . hits a long fly ball into right field—and he's *out!*"

"Oh my God," Helen said, and snapped the radio off. She went to the kitchen, got herself a glass of water, and came back into the dining room. She sat stiffly in her rocker, staring out at the backyard. She wouldn't turn it on for ten minutes, then she'd see what happened. Not that she expected anything good to happen.

But all the radios up and down Gorker Street were blaring forth the game, and before three minutes were up she couldn't resist, she turned it on very low.

"—and the Reds are out in front again! Now let me turn you over to Dick Bray who has a few words to say about the Breakfast of Champions . . ."

She'd missed the best part—the score and everything. That silly Dick Bray was talking away in his tenor voice about Wheaties, the Breakfast of Champions—he wouldn't tell it.

"Shut up about your Wheaties and tell us the score,"

she said out loud. "We know all about your Wheaties, just shut up and tell us something we want to know."

But no, he never would. Finally Red Barber came on to announce the first half of the fourth, and she found out the Reds were leading six to five.

Well, that was better than nothing—she rocked away in her rocker. They'd lose it anyhow, though. They always did something good, then went ahead and lost it anyhow. They didn't care how hard you rooted.

She'd certainly done her part—been here by her radio since the opening game in spring, shouting at the announcer, getting angry when the Reds fumbled, furious when the Giants or Cards or Phillies made a run. Anyhow the Reds were leading the league, even if they wouldn't win the pennant. It was the last of July, everybody else on that street was sure they were going to be champions and play in the World Series, but she laughed at that, you never could depend on them just when you thought they were so good. That was when they always lost.

"Well, the Reds are out in front now with that one-run margin," Red Barber said, "but don't forget we still have six-long-innings to go and—"

"Six long innings is true," Helen said right back. "And don't kid yourself that plenty can't happen between now and then."

She knew enough about it, this was her second year listening and they'd made plenty of mistakes in that time. Of course she *wanted* them to win—stayed tuned in even on Sundays when the club officials wouldn't let the game be broadcast because it hurt attendance. She read the *Ladies' Home Journal* or *Liberty* in front of the radio then and waited for the pause in the recorded music when Red Barber gave the runs, hits, and errors at the end of each half-inning.

Seven days out of the week she was here, but she didn't care. People could just leave her alone to sit here, they could mind their own business. Her mother never told her to go out and get a job or anything, but she knew that was what they were all thinking she should do, and she didn't care. Her brother Tom would make some remark to her, and she'd tell him off. Just let me alone, just go away and never speak to me.

She didn't care if she *never* went out of the house again. She almost never did either, except to go downtown to the library. She hated clothes, she hated getting all dressed up. She felt so conspicuous on the streetcar. Wearing those silly gloves.

They didn't understand, nobody else had anything wrong with them. They didn't have to wear silly gloves when they went out. Tom thought he was smart and could do anything he wanted, go anywhere he wanted. He was a boy seventeen, two years younger than she was —she'd wanted a sister anyhow.

Well, yesterday she'd told her mother off, all right. Her mother had said, "Why don't you ever go out any more? Why don't you and some of your girl friends go to the movies?" She'd told her mother then. "Because of my hand, that's why. Because I'm crippled," she'd said right out. Her mother had begun crying and Helen hadn't even felt sorry. "Now you know, so just stop crying. I'm not ever going anywhere again, so just don't bother me. I'm not ever going to go out and get all dressed up and wear those silly gloves again."

They could all just leave her alone, she was perfectly happy. She was glad she was all through with high school

—glad she had no friends—glad she didn't have anything to do but listen to the baseball game—glad she was crippled. If anybody didn't like it they could just not look at her, that was all. She knew she was ugly and they could just all stay away.

Baseball was more interesting anyhow. She'd never seen a game but that didn't matter, she didn't want to. She knew all the players, she read the papers and listened to all the sports broadcasts and she liked the players better than any people she knew. Paul Derringer was the best of them—he was tall and slender and always going out to the night clubs so sometimes he couldn't play the next day. She liked little Eddie Joost too—he was like a grade-school boy, always doing something crazy like fumbling the ball when it was an easy play. Ernie Lombardi supported a lot of his relatives out in California and she felt he played awfully seriously—not like Frank McCormick who was good-looking and so sure of himself.

Her mother asked once how could she know what a ball game looked like if she'd never seen one, and she'd got mad and told her mother she didn't *want* to know. But she knew all right—she could picture Harry Craft "shifting his chaw of tobacco from the left side of his mouth to the right and stepping up to the plate" or Whitey Moore "pounding his fist in the palm of his glove and glancing over at first." Red Barber was a really good announcer, he could say funny things about the players and make it all humorous. Of course he made a lot of mistakes too, sometimes got so excited he forgot what he was saying and you had to wait till he calmed down to find out if it was a hit or an out.

Well, here we go into the first of the ninth, she thought. Cubs at bat. The Reds better watch out with their old one-run lead—they usually were leading up to the last inning and then threw the game away by making errors. Who was batting anyhow?

"Quit talking about last inning and tell us who's batting," she said to Red Barber, and he answered by saying: "Whambo! It's a *hard* bouncing ball down to Joost at third—and Joost *fumbles!* He picks up the ball and makes the throw to first—but too late!—and Wilson is tucked away there safely with—"

"Did you do those dishes?"

She turned scarlet and whirled around on her mother standing in the doorway. "Let me alone!" Helen shouted. "Can't you see I'm listening?"

"If you're not going to do them *I* will," her mother said. "They've been around here all afternoon and I'm sick of seeing them."

Her face was toward her mother but her plump body was bent eagerly toward the radio.

"Just tell me," her mother began again, but Helen really turned on her then: "Now you made me miss who was next at bat! Don't bother me! I'll do them! Just let me alone now!"

It was a long fly ball—that dumb Craft would never catch it—going back, back, the sun in his eyes—oh, he caught it! She looked around then, and her mother was gone.

The rest of the inning was nothing, a ground ball and a strike-out, so the Reds won and they were lucky they did. She turned the radio off and rocked away. She had to admit that she *wanted* them to win even if she didn't really believe in them—days they won she felt so good.

Her brother came into the room from outside. "What'd they do today, lose?"

She felt her hand clench. "Well, they almost did but

they didn't," she said. "It was a crazy game—the Cubs got five runs in the third inning, then the Reds got three more runs and it was six to five. So the Cubs couldn't do anything till the first of the ninth and Wilson got on first—that crazy Eddie Joost had a ground ball and he fumbled it. The next batter up hit a long fly and I thought Craft would never catch it; he had to go all the way back to the stands. So they won all right—but I bet they're still shaking in their boots!"

"That's all right," Tom said, "just so they won. It won't be long till they have the pennant clinched, if they just keep winning."

"Well, they better do better than they're doing if they're going to beat out St. Louis," Helen said. "All the fumbles they've been making. Wait'll the series next week when they meet the Cards. Johnny Mize made two home runs yesterday."

"That don't mean anything," Tom said. "How about Lombardi yesterday? He made a home run and a double."

"Yes, he has to hit a home run or not get anything, he's so slow! Red Barber said that double yesterday would have been a triple if Bill Werber or Craft had hit it. The other team makes fumbles and everything and they still get old Lombardi out."

"How about Goodman?" Tom asked. "He made a triple yesterday."

"Goodman!" she shouted. "Don't talk to me about Goodman! Today when he came up to the plate in the first inning the crowd was clapping and everything because of that triple, and all he did was just stand there while Bill Lee whizzed three of them over, and he went back to sit down. The crowd was so stunned it didn't know what to say. All Red Barber said was, 'Well, that's the way it goes'—Red Barber says such dumb things sometimes."

She was feeling all warmed up, the way she always did whenever she talked about baseball. Her brother was the only one in the family who really knew anything about it. He'd played on the Turkey Bottoms Blues when he'd been in grade school, so she always liked to hear what he had to say. Sometimes she would even flatter him by asking his opinion on something.

"I feel like going sometime," Tom said. "I haven't seen them play all this season."

"It costs too much," Helen said. "It costs a dollar and ten cents just for regular seats."

She felt him looking at her intently, but she wouldn't look back at him—she never did know what he was thinking. "Let's get tickets and go to the World Series if the Reds win," he said.

Helen's hand clenched up tight against her breast and the color all drained out of her face. She couldn't answer: maybe he was making fun of her because she just sat here all day. She looked at one of the Aimsley fox terriers smelling at something in the backyard.

"I think Cokie Myers's father can get me tickets, he works at the park," Tom said. "Should we go if I can get them?"

"You can't get them," she said loudly. "So just don't bother me!"

"I can get them."

"Just don't bother me!" she said. "You can't get them so just don't even talk to me about it!"

"I tell you I *can* get them!" he said, getting mad too. "Will you go if I get them?"

She jumped up from the chair, her face white, her hair all mussed. "Just leave me alone!" she shouted at him. "Just quit bothering me and leave me alone!" And she went out into the kitchen and turned on the hot water for the dishes.

At supper table that night she got so mad, her mother and her brother were so optimistic about the Reds' chances and they didn't know anything about it. When they said some of the things they did, she just couldn't help shouting at them. They *always* thought the Reds were going to win.

"They're not going to win tomorrow," she shouted. "They always lose on Friday. Joe Aston in the sports page yesterday analyzed how many times they lost on Friday and it turned out to be eight out of ten times."

"That doesn't mean anything," Tom said, breaking a piece of white bread and mopping up gravy with it. "They're in a winning streak now and they're going to keep on going. I bet you they win tomorrow."

She just got furious, she waved her hand and could hardly speak, he made her so mad. "Why? Why?" she demanded, leaning forward, her black eyes jumping out of her head, her hair falling around her face. "How can you say they're going to win tomorrow?"

"Because of Derringer, that's why."

"Yeah, yeah, Derringer!" Helen stopped eating altogether and sat back in her chair. "Look what he did in his last game—got knocked out of the box in the second inning by the Boston Bees! Derringer! Don't talk to me about Derringer!"

"Well, Derringer *is* good," her mother put in innocently. "He's a good pitcher," she added.

Helen turned on her mother with a fixed expression of horror, her right hand clenched in close to her and her left thrown out as if to defend herself. "Good pitcher!

Yes! Good pitcher! He pitches good when he wants to, but that's only about twice a month! I know him!"

For five minutes there was silence while her mother and brother ate, but she could hardly eat anything, they made her so mad. Then she turned on Tom suddenly when he was just about to put a forkful of peas into his mouth and said: "You should have heard the booing the crowd gave Joost today when he dropped that bunt! Boy!"

She liked to sit in the dark like this: the kitchen light was on but it didn't shine on her rocker by the radio at all. The Sports Round-Up program had been a disappointment; Dick Bray and Red Barber hadn't had time to do anything but give their opinions on the Reds' pennant chances, and she already knew what *their* opinions were, they were so optimistic.

There was just dance music now and she didn't feel like dialing around. She was tired, she'd been so keyed up all day. She was glad her mother was taking a nap upstairs and her brother was out to Ray's Place. Sometimes she just didn't want to be with anybody at all, she just wanted to be alone. She only felt natural when she was alone, and they didn't like her anyhow. She didn't care, they could just leave her alone if they didn't like her.

Well, her father would be down soon—she heard her mother stirring around now, waking him. "Come on, William, get up. It's ten o'clock."

She went out to the kitchen and poured herself a glass of milk. She began to feel better, thinking about the day's game—wait till her father heard what almost happened in the ninth inning!

"Hello, Helen," he said—still a little sleep-dazed so that

she felt he hardly saw her out of his eyes. It was funny, he always seemed about a foot smaller in the evening, when he got up, than when he came home from work in the morning. A small man with a pot belly and arms too thin and long for his body, he was dressed in a blue work-shirt buttoned at the collar and brown whipcord pants. She always felt strange with him, maybe because he didn't really look like her father. His face was altogether different from hers: he had a strong nose with a little bend in it and small gray eyes under gray eyebrows. A kind of bony face. She looked like her mother—round like her mother, with large brown eyes and full lips.

"Old Bucky Walters thought he was so good today!" she said as he went to the icebox and brought out a large plate of sliced tomatoes and cucumbers and a bottle of beer. "He had to go and let the Cubs get three hits in the first inning and everybody thought the Reds were sunk."

He sprinkled huge amounts of salt and pepper over the salad and opened the beer. "Yeah?" he said, sitting at the table.

"Then they got two more runs in the second, and we got two runs. That made it five to two. You should have heard the crowd booing the umpire when he called Frey out at third in the fourth inning! That was when Werber singled and it looked like we were going to get some runs. The umpire was the only guy who believed old Frey was out. Red Barber said it was the worst booing he'd heard in years."

He drank the beer and wiped the foam off his mouth. He was always so quiet when he was sleepy—he only really talked a lot when he came home from Ray's Place in the afternoon.

"Well, who won?" he asked finally.

"Oh, we won," Helen said, hating to tell him the end of the game first. "But it's a wonder. Red Barber almost threw a fit when Joost fumbled in the ninth inning and the Cubs had Wilson on first. We were only leading by one run—six to five. But then Craft did something good for a change: he made a one-handed catch all the way back to the stands with the sun in his eyes and, boy, the crowd really cheered then, I thought the radio was coming apart. Then there was a ground ball and a strike-out and that was all. Oh, I forgot to tell you, they put in Gene Thompson to pitch in the eighth inning."

"Gene Thompson?" he said. "I didn't know he was playing with the Reds any more."

"Sure he is. They always talk about trading him but they never do. He did pretty good too, except for that last inning. If Craft hadn't been awake for a change, Thompson would just have another loss on his record."

She followed him out in the hall, where he put on his blue work coat. "Tomorrow the Giants come to town, then we'll see! Carl Hubbell is supposed to pitch—and after what he did to the Reds last time, they better be lying awake tonight thinking about it."

She followed him back into the kitchen, where he stuffed a handful of kitchen matches into his pockets for his stogies. She watched him, trying to think of something else to say, as he took out his gold pocket-watch and noted the time. She always felt desperate when he was leaving in the evening—she never got to tell him half of what had happened.

"Ten-forty," he said. "Got to get down there."

Following him to the front door, she said, "Everybody's so sure they're going to win the pennant, but *I'm* not so sure. If they can take two games out of three from the Giants, they'll be all right."

"Oh, they'll win," he said. "Good night."

She watched him through the window as he stopped to light a stogie on the front porch, and then she turned and went upstairs. She didn't feel tired now, she felt all excited again. But she thought she might as well go to bed anyhow—there was nothing else to do.

She went right on through August with them, never missing a game, and she never gave them the benefit of the doubt but they kept winning anyhow, doing plenty of things wrong but somehow pulling through. She still wouldn't believe they were going to be champions even when they were within two games of clinching it. They'll do something dumb, she kept thinking, they always do. And besides, Johnny Vander Meer has a sore arm and can't pitch.

But then they took a game from Philadelphia and they were only one game away from the pennant and she was so nervous the next day because they didn't play, they were on their way back to Cincinnati to meet St. Louis, and that was the hardest team of them all—St. Louis had all the batters, Johnny Mize, Enos Slaughter, all of them. She didn't talk back to Red Barber very much during that St. Louis game, she just sat there with her heart high in her chest and both her hands clenched, listening hard to every play. The radio wasn't turned off once during the game, and she got wildly irritated between innings when Dick Bray talked about Wheaties.

It was the last half of the ninth and Frey was on second, the score was still nothing to nothing and she wasn't making a sound. Jimmy Ripple was coming up to the plate and Red Barber gave a minute description of everything he did—dusted his hands with dirt, picked up the bat, stepped over to the plate, dug in his right toe. She was leaning forward, her head almost touching the radio, her teeth clenched together, when suddenly the scream of the crowd hit her full in the face—

"It's a smashing line drive into left field and Frey is rounding third—"

He was scoring, he was scoring! She couldn't sit down, she jumped up and walked around the room, her mouth open, her eyes blazing, her hand clutched in tight against her breast.

"—and the Cincinnati Reds are now—"

All of Gorker Street was screaming. Mrs. Must next door was screaming to her husband Allen who was out in the backyard: "Allen, Allen, they did it—"

She stood very still in the middle of the room, no longer hearing the radio, her body full and free, all her doubts gone. Should I go up and wake him? she thought, but instead she ran out on the front porch where her mother and Tom had been sitting in the swing.

"They—" she said, but they already knew, they were both standing up shouting something at Mrs. Tellmacher across the street and here came Mrs. Aimsley up the walk.

"What's the matter?" Mrs. Aimsley asked.

"The Reds just won the pennant," Tom said.

"My God, I thought war was declared or something."

Helen's mother was beaming, "Tom's going to get tickets and take you," she said.

"What?" Helen asked, looking from Tom to her mother.

"Tom's getting tickets from Mr. Myers to one of the World Series games and he's going to take you."

She felt like crying—she hated them, they were always making fun of her. "You leave me alone," she said, the tears popping into her eyes. She began to scream: "All of you just leave me alone, I'm happy the way I am, so just leave me alone!" She ran off the porch around to the backyard.

"I don't care!" she said. "I'm not going!"

Tom had the tickets in his hand. "You want me to tear them up?" he asked. "Just say tear them up and I'll do it right now."

She didn't know what to say. But she knew why he'd gone and got them: just because she didn't want him to. He was always making fun of her, she listened to the game all the time and he thought she was silly. That's why he'd got the tickets, just to show her up.

"You can go by yourself!" she shouted and ran out on the front porch. She just wanted to get away from all of them, she hated them.

But they were at her day and night, they acted as if they couldn't understand why she wouldn't go. As if she wanted to get all dressed up and wear those silly gloves!

Her mother kept pounding away at her till she thought she'd go crazy. "It would be so nice for the two of you to go out together once in a while," her mother said, and that almost made her burst a blood vessel.

"Nice!" she said. "Nice! Do you think I want to go out with *him?* He doesn't like me and I know it. He can just go out by himself whenever he wants to."

"Why don't you go with Tom?" her father said one evening while he was eating his snack. "He got those tickets and now you won't go with him."

Somehow she never really got angry with her father, he didn't talk at her like her mother did. But now she felt so emotional she couldn't answer him, and she left the room. They were all the same—none of them understood. None of them would leave her be, they all had to keep picking on her.

The day before the game she came into the kitchen where her mother was pressing her blue dress.

"You can do all that you want," Helen said, "but I'm not going!"

Her mother didn't answer her—just went on pressing. And Helen sat down and watched her mother working, wishing she'd argue. "Tom doesn't want to take me anyhow—he just did it because you made him." But still her mother didn't answer and finally Helen got up and left the room.

The sun wasn't even up! She looked at the alarm clock beside her bed: five-twenty. And then she remembered, this was the day! Today we'll see, she thought. Today we'll know whether they're any good or not. Derringer was going to pitch—she wished it were Bucky Walters. Derringer was more brilliant sometimes, but Bucky could really be depended on more.

She wondered if Tom would try to make her go. Well, she wasn't going, that was all; he could put that in his pipe and smoke it. All of them could try to make her go, but she wouldn't.

She couldn't stay in bed, she was too excited. She'd never been so excited about anything in her life before. She got up and dressed and went downstairs. There were some sliced peaches in the icebox so she ate them and drank a glass of milk. Then she went out on the front porch and Gorker Street looked so strange, the air smelled good and the street was quiet, deserted. Just Mr. Timpkins's car parked down the street, but none of the kids who were always around. Wait a minute—here came Mr. Daugherty up the street. She ducked back into the house, she didn't want him to see her.

At eleven she was sitting on the front porch reading

the *Ladies' Home Journal* but not really getting anything out of the story because she was so excited, when Tom came out. She wouldn't look up at him but he came over to her anyhow.

"You better get dressed," he said.

She still didn't look at him, there was a strange feeling in her chest. She surprised herself when she jumped up. "All right then, I will." And she went into the house and up the stairs.

When she was all dressed, she stared at herself in the mirror. I don't look so fat when I'm dressed up, she thought. She wore her blue dress with the little white collar, and on her head was the hat she'd got last spring —a white, off-the-face hat with a black bow on it. She hadn't been out for three months, she'd almost forgotten how it felt to be all dressed up. . . .

"You can wear your new gloves," her mother said when she arrived down in the kitchen. And she didn't get mad, she just took the gloves from her mother and started working the right one on. She had a hard time, the hand always persisted in clenching up hard whenever she wanted to do anything with it, but finally she succeeded and then worked the left one on by using the edge of the table. Tom and her mother did not watch her: Tom was looking out the back door and her mother was washing a skillet at the sink.

She wished her mother wouldn't come out on the porch with them, but she didn't say anything. She felt so strange all dressed up, she just knew that people were looking out of their windows at her as she came down off the porch steps behind Tom. For a moment she almost decided to dash back into the house, but then they were on their way, going past Mrs. Must's. Tom turned once at the top of the street and waved to his mother, but she didn't. She didn't even want to look at that house, besides it was silly to wave.

They climbed the footbridge over the railroad tracks and then they were standing side by side at the car stop on Eastern Avenue. She couldn't resist looking at Tom as they stood there—he did look handsome in his brown suit and his tie. She got car tickets out of her purse. "Here, drop these," she said, as the trolley came swaying toward them from the end of the line. And then they were on the car, bumping against each other as they sat on the straw seat.

Part of a swarm, she moved forward toward the high wall that was the ball park, Tom somewhere behind her, but she didn't look around. She felt that life had caught her and was dragging her along toward something she must know . . . something so inevitable she could not escape now even if she struggled. She was carried in through a doorway cut in the green wall, Tom was handing over the tickets, then they were free again, going up the ramp into the grandstand. And suddenly she thought: Is this the day I've been waiting two years for? The battle she had put up against coming certainly did seem ridiculous now that she was here. Nobody even noticed her, they all just rushed along, nobody stopped and laughed at her and stared at her gloved hands.

They were following an usher down to their seats and she was so busy watching her step she didn't get a good look at the field till she sat down—and then she looked, and she couldn't believe it. It was so little! It was a dozen times smaller than she'd expected! She looked at the centerfield wall over which Lombardi had hit so many home runs, and it hardly seemed any distance at all. She looked at the diamond itself—the distance between the bases was so short! And she hadn't known about the signs out there surrounding the outfield—signs advertising insurance, loans, suits of clothes, ham. They made it all seem so commercial.

Tom bought two bottles of Coke and gave her one. "Did they really charge you fifteen cents each for these?" she asked. Everywhere were men in white suits selling things to the crowd—popcorn, Crackerjacks, score cards, souvenir pins. Red Barber had never mentioned the way they hit you over the head to buy things.

But the *players* don't have anything to do with it, she thought. These are just a lot of people trying to make money out of the game, they don't really care about baseball. . . . Well, it wouldn't be long now, the groundkeepers were smoothing out the infield. She watched them, trying to feel the same excitement she'd always had at home just before the game, but she couldn't: two men on her left were discussing Florida and in front of her a Spanish-looking fellow was pressing kisses on the cheek of a little blonde. Wasn't anybody interested in the game?

"Where's the broadcasting booth?" she asked Tom.

"It's up above us, you can't see it," he said. "But look down there, there's Dick Bray interviewing people."

"Fans in the Stands," she said—but Dick Bray was lost in a knot of people, she couldn't see him.

Then the band was playing—*The Star-Spangled Banner*—and everyone was standing. Why did she always feel so silly standing—feeling everyone would turn and look at her? "There's the Reds!" Tom said, nudging her.

She started, she strained toward them, even bending forward a little. They came stringing out on the field from their dugout, tiny loping men, each one like the other way down there—and she didn't know them!

She didn't know a single one of them. Had she been foolish enough to think they would be bigger than life, that she would actually recognize each one? They were all alike in their white suits with the big numbers on the back, just miniature men who seemed to have nothing to do with her or the rest of the crowd. And here came Derringer out to the mound—but it wasn't really Derringer at all, Derringer was taller than Gary Cooper, Derringer was nonchalant, masterful, and this was just a tiny man in a white suit, far away.

The game was starting—Derringer threw to Wilson. But she couldn't see the ball. She realized, as the first inning progressed and Detroit had men on base, that the game itself was just like the park: it was all in miniature, it wasn't like the game she'd imagined at all. They were just a lot of little men down there standing around, and she didn't know any of them. Even when the ball was hit, nobody seemed to do very much—one man out in the field ran around a little and then there was someone on first; Derringer had the ball again and was throwing to the plate.

The Tigers were making runs, but she didn't care. She didn't know any of those people down there, she didn't care what they did. The crowd was screaming because Detroit was scoring again but she felt disgusted, she felt unclean. It isn't mine at all, she thought. It belongs to everybody. It isn't anything.

The second inning had come along, but she wasn't even watching any longer, she wasn't even *trying* to identify the players. Instead of looking at them, she studied the ads on her score card, reading all about Pepsi-Cola and then about Chesterfields, They Satisfy. Her stomach was swimming in her, she felt she would drown if she had to stay the whole game, her head was bursting.

Just to get out of here, to run away from here she didn't care where. . . . "Tom," she said, but he didn't hear her, he was shouting something down at the players.

She stood up and someone behind her pushed her shoulder and said, "Sit down!" but she kept on going, stumbling over people as she headed for the aisle.

Just as she got to the exit, Tom appeared at her side. "Where you going?" he asked. She didn't answer, she walked on. "You can't leave now—"

She saw the sign, "Ladies Rest Room," and she rushed toward it, not even looking around at him. Nobody inside at all, that was good. She slumped down in an armchair: it was over. The crowd was screaming out there but she didn't care. She didn't care whether the Reds won or lost.

And suddenly she saw herself as she had been—wearing that sloppy house dress and sitting by the radio for two years. It was a dream, she thought, it wasn't real. I made it all up myself. There is no such person as Paul Derringer. Bucky Walters and Lonnie Frey and Bill Werber —they are all just people I made up. No one has ever seen them but me.

I have just told lies, that's all, she thought. I lied to myself every day of the week. It's really a silly game, with nothing important happening in it, but I made it the most important thing in the world. I acted as if they were playing for me alone, and here they weren't really playing for anybody. They wouldn't know me if they saw me, and I didn't know them. Really it was just something I dreamed. Just a silly dream.

Thinking this she began to feel better. She'd been sick, that was it. And after you'd been sick for two years you wanted to wash yourself clean and never be sick again.

These silly gloves, she said to herself, working off the

right one. These silly gloves that I've been wearing all my life. . . . She had to use her mouth to pull off the left one. Then she pushed up her sleeves and began. She washed her crippled hand last and most thoroughly.

Finished, she dried with a paper towel. So it's all over, she thought. It wasn't real and I don't want it. Now I will just have to change, that's all. I will have to be someone different.

She picked up her handbag and started to reach for the gloves, then turned quickly and hurried to the door.

About the Author

Born in Cincinnati, Ohio, in 1919, Robert Lowry began to write in his early childhood. In his teens, he established a printing and publishing company, The Little Man Press, which published some of his early short stories.

He wrote the first draft of "Little Baseball World" when he was in his late teens. Later, after his discharge from the Air Force in 1945, he rewrote it, and it was published in *Mademoiselle*. The story appeared in *The Best American Short Stories, 1947* and was later expanded by the author as part of a novel, *The Big Cage*.

Robert Lowry is the author of several novels and collections of short stories, including *Casualty; The Violent Wedding; Happy New Year, Kamerades!* and *Party of Dreamers*.

THE FIRST PROM'S THE HARDEST

Hildegarde Dolson

There seems to be a popular theory that little girls who have brothers learn very early to adopt an easy, bantering manner toward members of the opposite sex. In my own case, this theory held water like a sieve. It's true that in a rough game of croquet I could banter as well as the next one, or even bawl the daylights out of one of Bobby's friends. But when it came to social presence, I had none.

Every Saturday afternoon for several years, twenty-nine other little girls and I had sat on one side of the room at Miss Steele's dancing school and heard Miss Steele say, "Now choose your partners." At this, most of the boys would charge across the room as one man—but not at me. When the mists cleared away, and the belles of the place had more partners than they knew what to do with, Miss Steele stepped in. After spotting those of us who were leftovers, she'd rush up reinforcements by the napes of their necks, before they could escape to the hall. On the days when there weren't enough boys to go around, somehow I was always one of the girls who danced with a girl. As a wallflower, I was rapidly going to seed. My one respite came during the Paul Jones, when, as Miss Steele blew her whistle, every boy was honor bound to dance with the lady on his right. I must say that the whistle blew some really good dancers my way. They may have acted sullen, but at least they kept time.

Until I was fifteen, my social activities were confined largely to these gay Saturday afternoon dancing school whirls. I was now a sophomore in high school, and much more concerned over the fact that Mother wouldn't let me wear high heels than that I was undoubtedly about to flunk geometry. Even more acute than the high heels was the throbbing fear that I wouldn't be asked to the Junior Prom. I had a grim conviction that now was the test of whether I was to face the future as a withered old maid or a prom trotter.

Unfortunately, a freshman in short pants named Freddie Perkins settled the matter five days before the prom, by edging up to me at the end of Study Hall and requesting my company on May 29th. I think his actual words were, "My mother was talking to your mother and she said you hadn't been asked to the prom, so do you want to go?"

Somehow it had never occurred to me that it was possible to be asked to a prom by the wrong man—especially a man in short pants—and the stark horror in my face must have frightened even Freddie, because he backed away several paces and stood waiting for my answer. He had nondescript hair parted in the middle above goggle-rim glasses, and the whole effect was profoundly depressing. "I have to stay home and study geometry that night," I finally said sullenly. Freddie pointed out in a dogged manner that I could study all day Saturday.

I began concocting an elaborate excuse about going to Meadville to visit an aunt, when a nasty thought struck me. "Does your mother know for sure you were going to ask me?"

"Of course," Freddie said, obviously surprised that I could think him capable of such folly on his own hook. "She told me to."

The thought of what would happen when Mrs. Perkins cross-questioned Freddie and phoned my mother stopped me short. Frantically I tried to decide whether to take my chances on the prom-in-short-pants, or go home and face Mother's wrath. Quailing at the thought of her stern conviction that "Freddie is a nice little boy and his mother belongs to our church," I muttered something which the waiting Freddie took to mean consent. He trotted off without another word, and I went glumly down to gym class, brooding over the way Fate had gummed up my first big chance at Society.

While we were struggling into our middies in the locker room, Ellie May Matthews, a sharp-nosed girl I disliked with abandon, said maybe I could get my kid brother to take me to the prom. With that, I yanked up my bloomers and prepared to defend my honor. "I'm going with somebody else," I said haughtily. Looking her straight in the eye, I unblushingly added that as a matter of fact I'd had two invitations, but Mother had made me turn down the best one.

"Then who are you going with?" she persisted.

It was one of those moments when I'd gladly have traded my present setup for a desert island and a geometry teacher. "Freddie Perkins," I said.

The ensuing silence was hideous, with the thought of Freddie's pants hanging unmentionably in the air. Even Ellie May was too taken aback to speak. "The family made me," I added hopelessly. My friend Betty Evans did her loyal best for a lost cause by saying that Freddie was awfully bright. "He's on the Honor Roll every month." As we filed onto the gym floor, she said delicately that maybe the Perkinses would buy Freddie a new suit.

For five days I silently implored Heaven to get Freddie out of short pants, and argued with Mother about my own costume for the prom. She was lengthening my pink organdy dress by adding a ruffle around the knees, and she listened unmoved to my wild-eyed descriptions of what the other girls were wearing. "I don't know what their mothers can be thinking of," she'd say firmly, making it clear that my chances of getting a pleated red crepe and high-heeled satin slippers dyed to match were as remote as Judgment Day. She was equally adamant about dangly earrings from Woolworth's, but she finally promised that if it were a nice warm night, I could wear her Spanish shawl, at present decorating the piano.

Cheered by a mental image of myself tossing a shawl about with Castilian grace and a rose in my hair, I concentrated on coaxing for a boyish bob. Alway before I'd had my hair neatly cut and clippered up the back of the neck by the same barber who did my brothers'. The one Ladies' Hairdresser in town was a man who charged seventy-five cents and often vanished for a week at a time, on what I now realize must have been binges of the first magnitude. Mother disapproved of him sharply, but worn down by my bulldog tenacity, she finally consented, on the afternoon of the prom, to my getting a stylish boyish bob by Mister Leo.

I think I must have caught Mister Leo in an off moment just before or just after a binge, because he whacked off my hair in what struck even me as a somewhat impetuous manner. Mother let out an involuntary shriek when I trotted home proudly to display my coiffure, and at dinner Bobby referred to me somewhat crudely as "Ratface," until Father threatened to send him from the table.

After dinner Mother got to work on me with a curling iron, and the Spanish shawl was dragged from the piano for my further adornment. Sally, whose bedtime had been postponed to allow her to watch this gilding process, was big-eyed with envy. What made her envious was not the fact that I was going to a prom, but that I was going to stay up late. If I'd been going out with a hoot owl, the effect, in my sister's mind, would have been equally impressive. "Will you stay up past ten o'clock?" she kept asking. I said Pooh, ten o'clock was early, and intimated that if there were a creak on the stairs toward morning, it would be Hildegarde Coming Home.

Mother, who was now brandishing the iron on my shortest back wisps, said amiably that twelve o'clock was late enough for a little girl of fifteen. However, she agreed that as long as I was with Freddie she wouldn't worry. In a way, I could see what she meant.

By 8:15 I was dressed to the teeth, and Sally had gone storming off to bed with the taunt of "Just wait till I'm as old as Hildegarde. You'll see." As I stood before the downstairs hall mirror, trying the Spanish shawl at every possible angle, the sound of the doorbell froze me in my tracks. Would Freddie have new pants or wouldn't he?

I opened the door, took one look at Freddie's legs, and experienced a primitive urge to push him off the porch. The fact that he was not only in short pants but carrying an umbrella filled me with sullen rage.

"It's going to rain," he said. "You'd better wear your rubbers."

Rather impulsively I shut the door in his face, knowing

that if Mother saw Freddie's rain outfit I'd never get out of the house without my rubbers. Grabbing up the shawl, I dashed into the living room to say good-bye. "Can't Freddie come in, dear?" Mother asked.

"No, he says we're late. Some other kids are waiting at the corner." Then I turned and bolted, with her "Have a good time" following me as I went out the door to my doom.

Freddie got up off the railing and stood patiently while I hitched the Spanish shawl up over one shoulder and anchored it at the left hip with my elbow. "What's that?" he asked.

"It's an evening wrap," I said fiercely.

In silence we started out for the high school. About halfway down the first block, Freddie asked me what I got in Latin last month. He also checked up on my marks in English, history and geometry, and then mentioned smugly that he'd had all A's. About that time it began to rain, and he hoisted the umbrella with the righteous air of a man who's always right. "It's a good thing I brought this," he said. I believe it was at this point that I remarked pleasantly I'd rather die of pneumonia than be seen carrying an umbrella.

We walked the rest of the way in damp silence, while I wished passionately that one of us would fall and break a leg—preferably Freddie. In those days, my vocabulary didn't contain the word "Dope," but we had other standards to judge by. A boy who wore a yellow slicker with everybody's nickname written on the back was *smooth*. A boy who got all A's and carried an umbrella was *dumb*. The fact that Freddie also wore short pants put him in some horrible category beyond description.

I felt this even more despairingly as we walked into the high school gym, past laughing groups of couples, all of whom I suspected darkly of laughing at Freddie's pants and my Spanish shawl. The gym was a brilliant glare, with Japanese lanterns strung along the walls for exotic atmosphere, and the five-piece orchestra a dazzling spectacle on a platform at one end of the room. Somebody handed Freddie a dance program with a dangling little pencil attached, and my heart went down into my damp white shoes as I looked at it. Ten dances to fill out. All around me were boys in white flannels and dark-blue serge coats, but I was doomed to dance all evening with a pair of short pants. In panic, I fled to the girls' dressing room. It was crowded with the same girls I sat with in classes, but now that they were all dressed up and laughing shrilly together, I felt stiff with loneliness. While I stood miserably in one corner, trying to decide where to put my shawl, Betty Evans came in. She admired my new boyish bob with heartening coos, and then turned all around so that I could get the full effect of her lavender crepe with lace panels. When we went back to the gym, I hung on her arm trustingly, because she'd been to three dances in the last year, and it reassured me to be seen with such a sophisticate.

Our escorts were nowhere in sight, but that didn't abash Betty in the least. She hailed one of the boys, a senior I viewed with awe because he played halfback on the football team. "Ooooooh, Stevie," she called gaily. "What I don't know about you."

Stevie promptly came over. "Yeah, what?"

"Oh, I couldn't tell for anything. You'd die if you knew."

This went on for several minutes, until Stevie insisted he'd get the second dance with Betty and make her tell. "Don't you dare," she squealed after him. I'd been listening in alarmed fascination, wondering what dark secret Betty had discovered, and as soon as Stevie had gone off to look for Betty's escort, I asked, "What *did* you hear about him?"

"Nothing," she said. "It's just a line. Boys always like you better if you hand them a line." I stared at her in shocked admiration, as her partner came to claim the first dance. Suddenly I felt nakedly young, with no line to guide me.

The next two hours still come back to me in nightmares. Freddie had exchanged dances with five members of the Freshman Debating Team and with Mr. Higgins, the Latin teacher, who was there with his wife as chaperon. To say that neither Freddie, his fellow debaters, nor Mr. Higgins were good dancers is to wallow in understatement. Freddie went on the principle that a dogged walk from one end of the dance floor to the other was good enough for any girl. Plowing back and forth with him until my legs ached, I tried desperately to look as if I'd never seen him before and was coolly amused at the mistake which had brought us together. Then I was passed on to the other dancing debaters, including one called Roscoe who jerked, and a youth who embarrassed me hideously by shouting above the music to give me his views on States' Rights. After him came Mr. Higgins, who did a sort of leaping quadrille and regained his lost youth by running around me in a spirited Highland Fling. As far as I was concerned, being made conspicuous by Mr. Higgins was a fate infinitely worse than death. After that dance, even plodding up and down the floor with Freddie had a certain restful monotony.

It was while we were plodding through the next-to-last dance that I heard somebody say, "Hi, Fred, mind if I cut in?" To my utter astonishment, ten seconds later I was gliding down the floor with a tall, handsome boy in a gray suit, while Freddie gaped after us like a surprised goldfish. "I'm Fred's cousin," the boy said. He mentioned something about stopping overnight on his way home from Allegheny College, but if he'd told me he'd just slain fifty dragons, I'd have accepted his story just as unquestioningly. "Aunt Helen sent me over here to see Fred," he added. We smiled at each other, and in a daze of emotions, I stumbled all over his feet. I apologized frenziedly, seized with the awful fear that he'd give me back to Freddie. "That was my fault," he said. "I was trying a new step they do down at school called the Charleston. See, it's kick to the side and then forward."

From then on I drifted along in a rosy haze, kicking to the side and forward. I think he had brown eyes and brown hair, but the important thing was that he was *smooth,* and he actually went to college. We exchanged names—his was Donald—and he told me he was coming back later in the summer to visit. "Now that I have a good reason," he said, tenderly squeezing my hand. At this, I was so overcome that I kicked in the wrong direction and landed a mean one on his shin. Even that didn't seem to discourage my dream prince. "Do you date Freddie very often?" he asked.

I shook my head violently and proceeded to make it very clear that Freddie had little part in my gay, prom-trotting existence. "The family made me come with him tonight and I was furious." Then, remembering that Freddie was his cousin, I added hastily that he was a very nice boy. "But I'd really rather date older men," I concluded brightly. My conscience gave a startled lurch as I said it, but it seemed to have a devastating effect on Donald, because he immediately invited me up for a football game the next fall. Somehow I managed to accept without swooning. We both forgot Freddie completely after that, until he turned up at the tag end of "Home Sweet Home." "Hel-*lo,* where've you been?" I said roguishly. Donald apologized like a gentleman for taking the last dance—a gesture which Freddie dismissed by saying his shoes hurt. They exchanged a few cousinly remarks, and then Donald asked where we were going to eat.

Freddie just stared, while I said glibly that everybody always went to Chacona's Ice Cream Parlor. It was not for nothing that I'd listened to Betty Evans. "We're off to Chacona's," Donald announced, taking my arm. Freddie pointed out that it was after twelve o'clock. He also said baldly that his mother had only given him enough money for the prom tickets. "She didn't say anything about eating."

Donald assured him masterfully that he'd take care of everything, and I went off to collect my shawl. In the dressing room I was surprised and gratified when at least ten girls greeted me fondly and told me I looked awfully cute. I was even more overcome when the most popular girl in the senior class came up to say that she simply adored my dress. She herself wore a short red taffeta evening wrap, and I was almost blinded by her glory.

"Who were you dancing the last two dances with?" she asked. All the girls crowded around to listen, and suddenly I knew, with belated feminine instinct, why they'd admired my dress. Instead of resenting it, my lungs nearly burst with pride. "Oh, that's a college man

I know," I said. "He's invited me up for a football game next fall."

In the midst of a rustling, respectful silence, I flung the piano shawl grandly over my last year's organdy. "He has a marvelous line," I said. Then I swept out the door to meet Donald.

The tide had turned and I had found my sea-legs.

In the next two years, our living room began to fill up with a modest number of men, or what Mother, in an unguarded moment, once referred to as "callow youths."

"Dear, do we know his family?" she often asked doubtfully.

To me, this was entirely beside the point. If they wore long pants and liked Guy Lombardo, then what was she fussing about? Jimmy and Sally had other standards to judge by. Any boy who brought me candy was their idea of a good, substantial Romeo, and even a stick of gum was better than nothing. When I received my first corsage, my younger brother and sister were honestly puzzled by my pleasure. After all, who wants to eat rosebuds?

About the Author

Hildegarde Dolson grew up in Franklin, Pennsylvania, and started writing at the age of nine. After attending Allegheny College, she went to New York City to become a writer. For five years she wrote advertising copy for Sak's Fifth Avenue, Macy's and other New York stores, and then became a free-lance writer, contributing to such magazines as *The New Yorker, Mademoiselle, Good Housekeeping* and *Reader's Digest.*

She is the author of *We Shook the Family Tree,* a humorous account of growing up in a small town, and several other lighthearted books. She has also written non-fiction for young people. Married to writer Richard Lockridge, she lives in Greenwich Village in New York City.

PARTY AT THE WILLIAMSONS'

Astrid Peters

It turned out to be quite a party, but no matter how many people came up the stairway, Kate, pushing the button and looking over the railing to see who it was, found she knew them all. She knew them by their first names, although they were people she never thought of at all. They were friends of her mother and father, and they had all been around while she had been growing up. She couldn't remember not knowing them. They were the people who had houses next to her family's on the Cape; people who were the parents of the children she had gone to school with or of the children who went to school with her seven-year-old brother, Joe; people with whom her mother and father would reminisce about gay times that had happened before she was born or when she had been too little to know anything about them.

"Hi, Kate!"

Bert and Paul Devries came up the stairs, and instantly Joe appeared in the doorway of his room. The apartment was a duplex in a brownstone house; the bedrooms were on the lower floor, and every time Joe heard the doorbell ring, he would get out of bed and stand half in the hallway, his eyes black and shining in the sudden light, twisting his bare feet, waiting to be noticed.

Bert was hatless, her gray hair fastened in a casual knot. Even for a party, she wore a heavy tweed suit, careful not to seem in competition with women who worried about looking pretty.

"How do you like the new school?" Bert asked Kate. Paul disappeared into the back room to leave their coats.

"Oh, I'm crazy about it," Kate said.

"Barbara's on her vacation, too." Bert leaned over and rubbed the top of Joe's head. "Hello, honey, you ought to be in bed. Come over tomorrow," she added to Kate as she started up the stairs to the living room.

"I'd love to," Kate said, watching Bert's broad, heavy body going up the stairs. She felt that Bert had disposed of her as though she were ten years old again. For a moment, she wished she hadn't come home for Christmas vacation. She was sixteen and she had known ever since she had been back that she was grown up. Until this fall, she had never been away from home, and from the moment she had waked up in her old room again, seeing the familiar pink curtains and the snapshot of Bandy sitting up begging on the beach, and underneath the snapshot, carefully arranged on the bureau, the little Indian dolls she had brought back from the summer in the West, she had felt alone, as though she were no longer a part of her family.

Her getting older had been going on for years, she thought curiously, but she would never have known it if she hadn't gone away. When she had been a child, grownups had just seemed like a different race. Now she knew the real difference was a difference of time, and it was like knowing a terrible secret. Their time was passing; soon it was going to be her time.

Kate turned suddenly and glared at her brother. There was something degrading about his willingness to accept the crumbs of the party. "Will you get back into bed, Joe!" she said. Then she went down the hall into the linen closet, almost pulling the door shut on herself, and dug toward the back, where the case of Scotch was stored. "All these people!" she whispered fiercely. "These old people!" She took out the two bottles her father had asked her to get, and stood in the dark for a second before she stepped out, a bottle held in each hand, her face remote and gentle. At the landing, she pressed back against the wall to let Max and Elsie Ganes pass.

"Hello, Kate!"

They greeted her loudly, as though amazed to see her there. Then, suddenly unable to think of anything else to say, they continued up the stairs. Max hesitated and looked over his shoulder with a little wave. "My, what a sight," he said. Kate didn't know whether he was referring to her or to the bottles she was carrying. They were both a little high already, she thought.

Upstairs, the sound of people was everywhere. Someone was playing records in the dining room. "Jada, jada, jada jada jing jing jing" rang through her head, and then, as she went by the living room, she heard her mother say clearly, "But that's been discredited."

Politics, Kate thought. "Don't ask any Trotskyites," her father had said. "They get so intense." And Kate had meant to ask him what the word really stood for. Trotskyite. It didn't sound political. It had a gay sound, like the kind of dance people would do in black leather boots.

In the kitchen, her father, his high, bald forehead

shining with perspiration, was making drinks. Helen McLean stood beside him. She was hitting herself on her behind with one hand and with the other she was holding out a tray of ice cubes. "It's like iron," she was protesting. "I've been playing so much tennis that I haven't an ounce of fat on me!"

Kate could tell by her father's face that he had been kidding Helen. She knew the look so well, even when it was just beginning: the funny stiffness around his nose, as though only by looking haughty, only by trying to look like someone else, could he keep from laughing.

"Honestly, Hank. Feel it. It's like iron!" Helen said, and Kate's father, still with one hand gripping the neck of a bottle, reached around and patted her gently. "Like iron," he said gravely, and poured another drink.

"Oh, you're just a stinker," Helen said, and when she laughed her brown face and big white teeth made such a merry pattern that Kate started to laugh without volition, the way one is won to laugh at something in a movie. Helen, suddenly aware of her, turned around. "Isn't he a stinker, Kate? Am I fat or flabby?"

"You're not fat at all," Kate said warmly. "Why, you're thin. Here's the Scotch, Hank." She leaned against the coolness of the refrigerator and watched him fill the glasses, so many with soda, and then, turning to the sink, so many with water. She wished he would never get through, so they could just stay in the kitchen forever.

He straightened up. "Do you feel like trying a highball, Kate?" he said casually. "I'll make you one if you want it."

"No!" she said, and then, trying to soften her vehemence, "not now, thanks, Hank. I ate too much dinner. I may take a Coke later."

Suddenly she looked right at him and they smiled at

each other. She never took a drink, but he had asked her this time because she had been away. For a moment, her love for him welled up inside her as though there was no hope for it.

She turned to Helen. "You do look really wonderful, and you're so brown. May I have one?" She took a cigarette from the pack Helen offered and for a second leaned close to her, getting a light. Then Kate's father picked up the tray of glasses and they followed him out to the hall. "See who needs a drink in the dining room for me, will you, Kate?" he said.

The dining room looked bigger than usual, with the long white table pushed against the wall, and the vase of Christmas greens and magnolia leaves made shadows that stretched out the wall as they went up to the ceiling. "Dearly beloved," someone sang sweetly, and then hummed with the record. The Poores and the Lavines were talking earnestly in a corner, but everyone else was around the phonograph. Sarah Kellogg was sitting cross-legged on the floor and Paul Devries was on one knee beside her. They were going through a pile of old dance records. " 'Hindustan'—remember that one?" she asked. "And here's 'The Sheik of Araby.' In school, we used to add, 'Without a shirt.' "

Kate took little nervous puffs at her cigarette and then put it out. There were glasses scattered on the table, some half full but deserted among the ashtrays. She picked up as many as she could carry and took them to the kitchen. When she came back, she brought a cloth and wiped the table. Then she emptied the ashtrays and wiped them clean.

In the corner, Ann Poore was talking very fast. She had a long, thin face, with a nose that reached down too far and a chin that came out to a point. Kate thought she was very ugly in a sad, frightened way, but from her neck down she was willowy and always very elegant in the latest fashion. As she talked, the soft tip of her nose quivered and shook like the nose of a mouse. She took little, quick gulps of her drink and talked like a person running for safety. Kate turned away, so as not to feel too sorry for her. She picked up the rest of the glasses, and when she came back from the kitchen, the Poores and the Lavines were gone.

Jack Crawford and some girl were trying to do a Lindy Hop, except that Jack wouldn't really try. He just improvised, twirling the girl around and waving his hands in the air, but the girl danced seriously, with a steady, even beat, accommodating herself to his fooling without ever breaking the rhythm.

"Remember the long, swooping steps and how close one used to dance?" Sarah Kellogg said. She was still sitting on the floor, and when Paul Devries leaned down to help her to her feet, she took his hand. But instead of her jumping up, they both stayed quite still, as though frozen in that position, looking at each other so expressionlessly that Kate wanted to cry out, "Be careful, you'll step on the records." Then suddenly the moment was past and they were up dancing. Looking at Paul's face, Kate was reminded of the way her brother Joe sometimes looked when she helped him get dressed. He would sit very quietly on the edge of his bed watching her, his lips parted, intensely concentrated on the little, mothlike sensations of having his shoes tied. Paul's face had the same look of willful helplessness. When the record came to an end, he and Sarah stayed for a second in the middle of the floor, and again they looked at each other with a strange lack of expression before they dropped their arms to their sides and walked back to the phonograph. Sarah went ahead of him primly, holding herself stiff and straight, as though to make up for all the movement before.

As Kate watched, Phil Burry came up in back of her and put his hand on her arm. "How about a twirl, Miss Katydid?" he asked archly. She shook her head, startled. "Oh, no, thank you," she said clearly, and his hand slid off her arm. She stood uncomfortably beside him without looking at him. She didn't know whether he had meant it as a joke or not. When her father came in the room, she turned to him gratefully.

"Anybody need a drink?" he called out. "How are you fixed, Phil? I think you could do with a little something there." He dropped his arm casually on Kate's shoulders. "Come on in the kitchen and help me, Baby," he said.

Then Jack Crawford came up with a little hopping step, waving an empty glass in one hand and shaking the forefinger of the other. "I'm a jitterbug, I'm a hepcat, I'm a crocodile," he announced, his sparse gray hair standing up in a wispy halo, and he hopped and bounced up the hall after them. Kate looked back. Over his head, Sarah and Paul looked stately as they passed in front of the darkness of the big window. They were dancing again.

The kitchen was full of people all talking at the same time, and Kate stayed out in the hall. One place was the same as any other now. While she had been in the dining room, the party seemed to have grown bigger. The people she saw were all the same, but now they seemed to take up more space. A boyish-looking man talking to Helen McLean kept sliding off the corner of the kitchen table. Every time he had edged himself up on it, he would slowly start sliding until he was standing again. When he threw his head back, Kate could see his face, looking tired and wizened. It was Allen Franklinker, and under the bright light he didn't look boyish at all. "He was a great man," she could hear him say. "I used to tell him that. 'You're a great man, Scott,' I'd say, but of course he wouldn't pay any attention to me." His voice sounded as though he were going to cry.

"It was a swell piece," Helen said soothingly. "It was time somebody wrote a piece about him."

"You think so?" he asked. "You really think so?" He looked at Helen intently and slid off the table again, and this time he caught her arm to steady himself.

Why, he's really drunk, Kate thought. It seemed odd for a poet to be drunk. She looked at her father, but if he thought anything of Allen Franklinker's drunkenness, he gave no sign.

"Kate, dear," her mother called to her, coming up the stairs. "Will you run down and stay with Joe a few minutes? He won't go back to sleep." She waved both hands in the air. "There's just too much noise, I suppose."

"Wait a minute, Libby," Kate said. She reached up, and her mother bowed her head docilely as Kate tucked in a lock of hair that was straying down. Marian Holbrook came up beside them, and Kate's mother, looking a little like a bird, with her head on her chest, said, "Did you get her all right?"

"Yes," Marian said. "They're both sound asleep and Johnny hasn't coughed once." She opened her eyes wide in a look of speculation. "I think—I'm going to have another drink!" The two women smiled at each other almost conspiratorially and her mother called out to the kitchen door, "Two Scotch-and-water!" "Coming up!" Kate heard her father answer as she started down the stairs.

In the hall, she passed the Morrisons with their hats and coats on. "Good night!" they called. "Good night,

Kate!" A second after they had disappeared, Mike Levy came up the stairs from the front door. "Hello," he said. He gave a half salute and, dumping his coat over the banister, kept on up the second flight to the party. He must have come in when the Morrisons went out, Kate thought.

The big bed in her parents' room was piled high with coats and hats, a soft mountain of fur and cloth, with an occasional glove looking creamy against the darkness. The bathroom door was open and she could see Sarah Kellogg standing in front of the mirror, putting on lipstick. As Kate passed, Sarah turned and suddenly smiled blindly—as though she didn't really see her at all, Kate thought. She went through the passageway to Joe's room and opened the door, but before she could say his name in the dark, she heard his breathing and tiptoed across the floor, feeling her way through the toys. He was lying with his arms flung over his head, and she took the two trucks that were on top of him and put them on the chair beside his bed. Before she went out, she stood still and listened once more to the sound of his breath, like a little pulse in the room; then she shut the door gently behind her.

The sounds of the party upstairs were all mingling together, and hearing them now, when she was alone in the passageway, made her feel that there was something sad in people talking and laughing, making so much noise, unaware that all the time she could hear them. She went down the passageway to her room, opening the door without putting on the light. Bandy looked like a dark shadow on the blanket she had put on the floor for him. He was getting old and he hated parties; whenever they had one, he was always shut up in her room, because the door to the terrace could be left open without freezing the house.

The room was cold and the air felt wonderful, as though she must have been gasping before. After a moment, it didn't seem dark—not as dark as she would have liked it to be. The light from the night outside was almost like moonlight. When she passed Bandy to go onto the terrace, he didn't raise his head, but he thumped his tail softly on the floor and she could see the water in his bowl gleam.

She was just about to step out on the lumpy crust of snow when she heard someone speak and she moved back from the door. "Oh, darling, oh, darling!" someone mortally wounded said.

At first, it looked like a big, thick person with blurred edges; then Kate saw it was two people with their arms around each other. They looked as if they were in some kind of combat, pressing and burrowing fiercely at each other. Kate felt a physical shock, like being hit in the stomach from inside. She knew at once who it was and she stood there watching, her heart pounding so she could feel it shake her with each beat.

Paul lifted his head for a second. "I love you," he said clearly to the night, and leaned down again. "My dear, my love!" Sarah said quickly, and they broke apart, so there was space between them, and stood looking at each other. Then, with a little groan, they kissed again, but finally this time, and hard, like a blow. Then they turned to go in the door to Kate's parents' room. She heard Sarah say, "Lipstick!" and saw a flutter of white. "No, use mine," Sarah whispered imperatively, and they leaned against the door a moment. Then they were gone.

Kate put her head out the door cautiously. Then she went back and sat on the edge of her bed. Why, they had been in love when they had been upstairs dancing. She tried to remember just exactly the way they had looked, and she thought it was as though she had known it before without knowing she knew. All the time she had watched them dance they had known they loved each other—and they were dancing in front of everybody!

What would they do, she wondered. Would they go upstairs and tell Bert and Mr. Kellogg? Were they telling them now? She looked up at the ceiling. No, she thought, not now, at the party. But for a second she could see the living room filled with people moving in violent confusion. It couldn't be true. She had known Paul and Sarah all her life, and it hadn't been at all like watching people make love in the movies. Paul and Sarah had looked so clumsy, and as though it hurt them, standing out in the cold on the grimy snow, surrounded by the bleak back yards and all the lighted windows.

Suddenly, she remembered looking at Sarah a long time ago. She had wanted to touch Sarah's stomach. Sarah had been very big, and even Kate had known that she was waiting to have twins born. It was queer to think that somebody who had had twins could be in love. And Paul had gray hair.

She sat slumped in the bed, shivering from the cold. She knew her mother must be wondering why she was so long and if Joe was still awake, but she felt, all at once, so stricken with tiredness that it was difficult to make herself move. Before she left the room, she glanced out the door at the terrace again. It looked empty and mysterious, and somehow larger, at night. She thought she could never look at it again without seeing Sarah and Paul holding onto each other as though they would fall if they let go.

Going up the stairs, Kate wondered that the sounds of the party were the same as they had been when she came down. She heard the brittle crash of a glass breaking, and as though it might be some kind of sign, her foot hesitated on the top step and her breath quickened. But the laughter and talk went right on. When she came to the door of the living room she heard another crash and someone said, "My God, that's the second."

Allen Franklinker stood by the fireplace, gazing down at the broken glass at his feet. As she watched, he leaned back against the mantel disdainfully; then his foot reached out searchingly and pawed the pieces into the ashes in back of him. He was going to scorch his clothes if he stood so close to the fire, Kate thought.

She looked around for her mother and saw her on the sofa, and, beside her, sitting on the arm of the sofa, resting one hand lightly on her mother's shoulder, was Sarah Kellogg. The two women were talking and Sarah was swinging one leg idly back and forth, her foot just clearing the floor. Kate could see only her back, but she could see her mother's face smiling, and as she started down the hallway, she heard her mother's soft laugh.

She didn't want to face anyone right now, and she walked past the kitchen, which was full of people, and went down the hall to the dining room. No one was playing the phonograph. Her father was talking to Helen McLean. They were both standing, and Helen had her hat on and her coat dangling from her shoulders. When Kate came up, she kissed her.

"I've had such a lovely time, darling. I just stand here and don't go home," she said. She was just being obstinate, Kate's father told her. The evening was young, and as for going home, she hadn't even finished her drink. Helen looked at the drink in her hand speculatively, then tossed it down with such a flourish that it spilled on her chin, and Kate's father lent her his handkerchief. "See?" Helen said. "I'm drunk. I've got to go home."

But she wasn't at all drunk, Kate thought. She was just joking. The three of them walked down the hall together, Kate on one side and her father on the other, pretending to hold Helen up, and they walked straight into Paul Devries.

"There you are, Hank," he said. "I've been looking for you. We've got to go home. Bert's down getting her coat on." He had come up so suddenly that Kate found she was looking right at him and it was too late to look away. He had no trace of lipstick on his mouth, she noticed. He said good night, touching them all on the hand or the shoulder—little, reassuring gestures of friendliness to take away from the bare good night—and then Kate's mother, seeing them from the living room, came out.

"Good night, Libby," Paul said. He leaned over and kissed her. "You give awfully nice parties." Sarah stood in back of her mother and she, too, said good night. "Good night, Paul," she said, and while she was saying something formal, about getting together soon, Paul suddenly stuck his hand out. They had been looking politely at each other, but now Sarah stared down at his hand as though she were going to cry, and Paul started to pump both their hands up and down violently.

Kate turned quickly to her parents. "Libby—" she began, without knowing what she was going to say.

"Darling," her mother interrupted, "did Joe go to sleep all right?" She was leaning dreamily against her husband. "I forgot. Oh, poor, poor Joe!" she exclaimed, as though, because she had forgotten, Joe was cold and naked out in the snow.

"He was sound asleep before I even got there," Kate

said. No one knew, no one saw anything—no one except herself, she thought despairingly. Then Sarah asked the time. "Oh, it *is* late!" she said, and gave an artificial laugh, which stopped abruptly, as though she had heard herself. "It is *not* late," Kate's mother said firmly, and as the rest of them went down the stairs, Kate looked over her shoulder and saw her mother herding Sarah back into the living room.

When Kate and her father had given the last wave over the banister and called good night to Paul and Bert, her father turned to her and grinned. "Around this time," he said softly, "I always wish to hell everybody would go home."

Kate leaned against the wall. "How old is Paul, Daddy?" she asked.

"About my age," he said.

"Your age!" she said, startled.

"Sure, why?"

"Oh, nothing," she said.

Her father looked at her alertly. "Why don't you go to bed, Baby? You must be tired."

"No!" she said crossly, but suddenly she knew she couldn't go upstairs again. The thought of the party horrified her, as though it were a scene of wild disorder. "I'm not tired, Daddy." Her head drooped and she felt she couldn't move.

"What's the matter, Kit?" It was the pet name he used to call her when she was little, and she lifted her head and smiled. "You go to bed," he said. "This minute!"

"Yes, Daddy," she said gratefully, and put her face up to be kissed.

"Good night, dear," he said. He rubbed her cheek with the back of his hand and she leaned against it. "Good night, Daddy," she said, and waited till he started her with a little pat down the hall.

Kate got undressed quickly and dropped into bed without washing her face or brushing her teeth, but after the light was out, she sat up in the dark. "Bandy!" she called.

When she was little, she had always refused to go to sleep unless Bandy slept on her bed, but as she had grown older, the habit had somehow been forgotten. It had been years since she had thought of it. Now, without knowing why, she wanted him to be there. "Bandy," she called again, and after a moment she heard his laborious movements as he got to his feet.

"Here, boy."

She patted the bed. Obediently, he heaved himself up beside her. "Lie down, boy," she whispered, and he turned around and then flopped down heavily. She slid lower under the covers, so she could get her arm around his neck. His fur was deep and silky. After a second she could feel the warmth of his body and she put her head against him.

From upstairs she heard the detached sounds of the party. Why, they're still going on, she thought sleepily.

About the Author

Astrid Peters intended to be a painter, and studied at the Pennsylvania Academy of Fine Arts, and the Art Students League in New York City. She worked briefly as a fashion illustrator, and began writing solely as a hobby. Her first story was sold to *The New Yorker,* and she has been writing ever since. Presently, she is at work on a novel.

Married to Robert M. Coates, former art critic for *The New Yorker,* she has two grown-up children and two grandchildren. She now lives in Old Chatham, New York.

SUNDAY AFTERNOON

Lucile Vaughan Payne

Outside the house, Vernay Street trembled in midafternoon sunlight. Elizabeth, pausing on her way from the kitchen to the porch, shifted her gaze from the scene framed by the screen and glanced at her watery image in the glass pane of the front door. For a moment she stared at herself stonily. Then her lips curled in an expression of utter distaste. The mouth that was reflected back at her grimaced vaguely in instant response.

Thinking of all the food she had just eaten, Elizabeth shuddered. I'm disgusting, she thought; I have no soul. How can you have a soul and still eat like a horse? Did Heloïse eat like a horse? Did Juliet sit and stuff her face with roast pork and green beans and candied yams? Revolted, Elizabeth opened the screen and walked out. Her mother was sitting in the pillowed swing, her hands folded comfortably in her lap as she watched with bright, unflagging interest her own particular stretch of Vernay Street. How can she stand it? Elizabeth wondered. How can she look so comfortable and so *interested*—yes, actually interested! What is there to see? Mrs. Rossiter bending over her flower bed. Simmons' cat washing its face. Nosy old Mrs. Sprunt squeaking away in her chintz-covered rocker and fanning herself.

Sunday afternoon. How I hate Sunday afternoons.

With lowering brows she watched Rose Marie Rossiter run out of the house and climb into Willie Kline's dusty roadster. She thinks she's so popular.

"Well, young lady," said Mrs. Kane. "What are you up to this afternoon?"

"Up to?" said Elizabeth. *"Up* to?" She spread her hands hopelessly. "What is there to be up to?"

Aware of her too-full stomach, she was smitten with sudden terror as she watched her mother relax placidly on the cushions. I am growing old and fat; soon I, too, will be sitting in the porch swing to watch the march of Sunday afternoons. Her hands curled at her sides. Life is passing me by. Maybe it's just around the corner. Maybe it lurks on Vine Street, or Logan, or Mackay. It is not here.

"I think I'll go for a walk," she said broodingly.

"My, in this hot sun? Why don't you sit down and enjoy the breeze?"

Because, Mother, this house, this street, this very atmosphere is driving me crazy. Very simply, it's driving me crazy. "No. . . ."

She went down the steps, sauntered slowly down the walk. Beneath her feet the blossoms of the catalpa tree disintegrated, leaving a faint impalpable odor on the summer air. A fat russet worm made his leisurely way across the sidewalk, and the patterned shade of the trees moved lightly. Dappled with sunlight, the lovely young creature . . . yes, Mrs. Sprunt, I know you are sitting there on your porch watching me. Don't expect me to look up. I will not. I will not.

She looked up and waved vaguely at the old woman. I know what you're thinking. There goes Elizabeth Kane, you're saying; just look at that, getting so grown up. Getting a figure, isn't she? Yes, I'm getting a figure, so what about it? Be sixteen pretty soon, won't she? *All right!* Say it, say it, Almost-Sweet-Sixteen-and-Never-Been-Kissed. It's none of your business, none of your business, none of your . . . she passed out of the range of Mrs. Sprunt's vision and felt the tension leaving her muscles. When I think somebody is watching me, my legs begin to jerk and my neck gets stiff. That's a funny thing. I don't like it. I don't like to have people watching me. It's none of their business.

Do you suppose I'm the only girl in this town who is almost sixteen years old and hasn't a date? At the next corner, three houses down, that's where Robert Mayo lives. What do you care where he lives? You must not, under any circumstances, Elizabeth, turn your head to look in that direction. He's probably at the ball game or something, anyway. Or maybe he's out with a girl. Jealousy spread through her chest like heat. Some of the girls say he's too shy to ask anybody for a date, but I bet he does; he's just the secret type and doesn't let anybody know.

She raised her head high and crossed the street at Robert's corner, sternly keeping her eyes straight ahead.

What's so wonderful about Robert Mayo? Just another dumb boy. All boys are dumb. Maybe if I walk just as slow as I can he'll see me, and maybe if he sees me, he'll . . .

She breathed more easily as distance grew between herself and the corner. She looked furtively at the houses along the street. They were set farther back on their lawns than those in her section, and she saw nobody near enough to hear. She muttered to herself, tentatively, "I love you, Robert." The words had a foreign, choppy sound. It embarrassed her to say them. How did you learn to say it naturally? Like Elizabeth Taylor, or Sophia Loren, or Ingrid Bergman. Especially Bergman. She tried it the Bergman way. More "lov" than "love," she decided; sort of between them. "I lov you, Robert." She closed her eyes, floating along the sidewalk. "Oh, dawling, I lov you so much. . . ."

She was swept with sudden laughter and ducked her head, biting her lip to keep the laughter inside herself. They'll think I'm a crazy woman, she thought, darting a glance at the houses lining the street. But saying the words had released something in her. She felt extraordinarily gay and daring and she began to walk more swiftly.

I shouldn't make fun, she told herself severely. For you know, Elizabeth, down deep in your heart, that it's true. She was touched with gravity. I love you, Robert. As long as she did not say the words aloud it was all right; they repeated themselves in her mind, deep and thrilling. Oh, Elizabeth, you are in love. How wonderful and terrible it is. She closed her eyes dreamily and thought about it. In love. It was such an enormous thing to think that it frightened her. But you must face the facts, Elizabeth. Even though it's hopeless, even though others would laugh if they knew, you can be brave enough to admit to yourself that you are in love. It is a far, far braver thing that I do now. . . .

A figure brushed by her and she jumped, startled. "Oh, hello, Elizabeth," he said.

"Why . . . hello, Robert." My hair! Does it look all right? Is he going to stop? Will he walk with me? If I could only think of something to say, something to make him laugh or something.

He hesitated only a moment and then rushed on, mumbling about being late. Elizabeth kept smiling stiffly until he had disappeared around a corner, and then her muscles went slack. Her hands were cold and perspiring.

I hate him, she thought passionately. I hate all men. He couldn't stop to talk to me—not even for a minute. She plunged ahead with set jaw. Finally she realized that she had reached Vernay Park. She had walked with head down, unseeing, and now the green turf stretched on either side of the walk, cool and inviting. Her feet were hot. She stepped into the grass and went toward the trees, still trembling inwardly in a queer way. I'd like to lie down on the grass and pull out handfuls of it, she thought savagely; I'd like to grab the ugly old roots of that elm tree and pull them up and hear them tearing loose from the ground. Perspiration trickled down her scalp and wet the roots of her hair. She walked aimlessly among the trees, looking for a place to sit down.

"Why, Elizabeth Kane!" a voice said archly behind her. "What are *you* doing here?"

Elizabeth avoided the light, sliding eyes. Sophie Turner, she had forgotten about Sophie Turner. She doesn't have a date either, thought Elizabeth drearily. That makes two of us. *They are as sisters*. She gagged on the thought. "Going for a walk," she said shortly.

"Well, then," said Sophie brightly, tucking her arm in Elizabeth's, "why don't we walk together?"

If I'm to die, I choose to die alone. "No," said Elizabeth, bending down to tie a shoe that was not untied, freeing her arm. "I can't. I'm meeting somebody."

"I *bet!* A girl or a boy?"

"Well, so long."

"Stuck up!" Her voice followed Elizabeth. "Anyway, if you want to know, all the fellas are over by the tennis court." Elizabeth felt her face grow red. Can those eyes pierce the sacred fortress of my mind? *Those* eyes?

Bitter with humiliation, she took another direction through the park. Who is this creature all forlorn, unloved, unwanted and forsworn? I am a marked woman. A poor bony thing who walks through parks on Sunday afternoon, hoping a boy will look at her. Ah, no, I am not like that.

Or am I? Maybe I'm just a coward. Sophie admits it, but I won't. Does that make me any better? Face the facts, Elizabeth. Always face the facts.

It's hot, she thought. She fished a dime from her pocket and went toward the concession, debating whether to buy ice cream or a cold drink. Under the trees a fair maiden passed. She allowed herself a silent snort of cynical laughter. Ah, yes. Ah, yes. Floating like a zephyr on the soft summer air.

At the door of the concession she drew a quick breath and walked quickly away. Robert was inside, drinking a soda. The plate glass windows reflected her image as she rushed by. I'm ugly! she thought in terror. The curl is coming out of my hair, my dress is wrinkled, my nose is too big. They are in there now, saying, "Look at that big, ugly girl." Look at me, my knuckles are too big and my neck looks scrawny and the bone in my wrist sticks out like a doorknob.

I never knew before what I really looked like. My arms . . . I saw my arms, long as an ape's. It is only when you see yourself unexpectedly in a plate glass window that you know what you really look like. I saw myself, myself now and myself as I shall be when I am older, an old maid with a jutting profile and big feet and cotton stockings. It was all there.

I shall never be happy, I shall never be loved.

She sat down on a stone bench beside the little fish pond, clutching at the rough edge with her hands. If only I were old now. About thirty, thin and tall and dressed in printed lavender cotton that covered my feet. My big, ugly feet. Away, far away from people. I will have a damp, sweet, dark old house at the bottom of a hill, and I shall flit among the shadows, never speaking. If I wear long, full sleeves, nobody will notice my long ape arms. People will wonder about me, but never dare to ask. I shall be remote and gentle and mysterious.

With those big feet?

The sun beat down. Freckles, she thought. While I sit here the freckles pop out on my great big nose and my hair gets stringy. I'm sweating. I don't perspire. I sweat. Not for me the dainty corner of a handkerchief. Rivers of sweat. "Rivers of sweat," she said aloud, wading in it.

An old woman, her face the color of sandpaper, walked by and glanced at her. She knows, thought Elizabeth. As Sophie knew. When that old woman was a girl, no man ever looked at her, either. We recognized each other. We are kin. Sisters. Horrified, she averted her eyes and flopped down on the grass.

"Well, gee whiz," said Robert, above her. "I was hoping I'd find you here."

She lay quite still and looked at the matted grass. She could see a black ant hauling a bread crumb through the moist corridors among the roots. It's nothing, she told herself. He just wants to know whether I've seen Joe Zilch or something. She tilted her head upward and squinted through the sun.

"Well, hi," she said.

He sat down on the bench and began whittling on a twig. His foot almost touched her elbow. She saw that one shoelace was broken and tied in a knot. A little cascade of shavings began to fall on the grass.

"Do you know what's on at the Lyric?" he asked.

"No." Her heart began to thud and she swerved her head around to look at the fish pond. A snake doctor was winging around in circles and she watched it very closely. You think he'll ask you to go to the Lyric with him? Ha.

"It's one of those Bergman pictures. You like her?"

"Oh . . . sure." She had to repress a gust of nervous laughter. I love you, Robert.

"Well, why don't we get together? I mean, would you like to see it? I mean, I'd like to take you, if you want to go, I mean . . ."

Why, he *is* shy! she thought. She felt a casualness, a delightful sense of ease and discovery. "Why, yes, thank you. I'd love to go, Robert." She got to her feet and pushed back her damp hair. "I was just about ready to go home. Coming?" As easy as that.

"Sure."

And they were walking across the park together. It was no dream. It was real. He asked me, she thought. *He asked me!* She wanted to grab all the trees and shake them and bring the leaves down over her hair. She felt like yelling and singing and running in all directions at once; at the same time something sweet and sluggish crept through her veins, dragging at her footsteps. They passed the concession again, and the windows reflected their passage. Why, I'm very pretty! thought Elizabeth. I'm almost beautiful. Surreptitiously she gripped one wrist between her fingers and felt the bone and thought how delicate it is, how small.

When they came to Robert's corner he continued to walk down Vernay Street beside her. With slanted eyes she looked at him. Bergman and I, she thought, and she began to laugh. Her laughter rang out clearly in the gathering dusk, and Robert looked at her questioningly, the corners of his mouth beginning to twitch.

"What are you laughing about?"

"Nothing. I just happened to think of something."

She liked the way he began to laugh with her, his eyes curious but friendly. She liked his long, loose-jointed stride as he ranged along beside her. She liked everything about him; she was having a good time and she was not at all in love.

Willie Kline's roadster came boiling past and stopped in front of Rossiters'. Benevolently, Elizabeth waved at Rose Marie. We'll have to double-date sometime.

"Hello, Mrs. Sprunt," she called gently as they passed the old woman, still sitting on her front porch. How serene and kind she looks, thought Elizabeth. And, I wish that I had brought her some ice cream from the concession.

Her own front porch was empty now. Probably her mother had gone inside to get supper on the table. "I'll be back in about an hour," said Robert. "Will you be ready?"

"Mmm-hmm." She watched him go a little way down the street and then went quietly into the house. She was suddenly very hungry, and the clatter of dishes from the kitchen was a reassuring and welcome sound. It was good to be home.

There was no sunlight now to reflect her image from the glass pane in the door. But Elizabeth did not even stop to see. She looked just the same, she knew. Everything was just the same. And entirely different.

About the Author

Lucile Vaughan Payne wrote "Sunday Afternoon" to express "as truly as I could the feelings of many young girls just as they are beginning to turn into women. The main character is not described in the usual sense—I wanted to make the girl reading the story see *herself* in the role of Elizabeth."

Born in Bicknell, Indiana, Lucile Vaughan Payne attended Indiana State University. She now lives in Eugene, Oregon, where she and her husband both attended the University of Oregon graduate school. She is the author of a volume of short stories, *The Boy Upstairs and Other Stories,* and a textbook, *The Lively Art of Writing.* She is now serving as editor of *Old Oregon,* the University of Oregon alumni magazine.

A HUNDRED YEARS FROM NOW

Nancy Cardozo

Lucy rubbed the smudge of her breath from the window of the day coach in which she was traveling. The fog that all afternoon had spread its patina across the countryside had lifted to show low hills and arabesques of twigs and wires against a colorless sky. It was impossible to lose herself in that humdrum landscape, and she longed for the trip to be over. Once, she saw a boy move along a row of sycamores, his yellow dog following, slack-tongued, stepping from hummock to hummock, but most of the time, trees and telephone poles and houses slid slantwise away interminably. She had to blink to keep from being dragged off with them.

Five seats down the aisle, she could see two other girls from Briarwood Hall, just the tops of their heads, their tan hair ruffled as they leaned together whenever anyone went through the coach. When they had passed her earlier, their camel's hair coats slung from their shoulders, Lucy had hidden her face. She would have liked to have them sit with her, but it was embarrassing to be as vague as she had to be about her vacation, to have to say: "I don't know just where I'll be staying—I'd love to come, but you see, my mother . . ." For Thanksgiving, she had stayed in school with Theresa, whose parents were divorced. They had eaten tinned turkey and cranberry and cold brussels sprouts off the thick white plates. After dinner they had walked around the hockey field, telling each other great tales of feasts and families.

If the girls from school should see her getting off the train, it would be all right, Lucy told herself, because Roger would be at the station to meet her. She would introduce them: "I want you to meet . . . this is my brother . . ." and Roger would bow, perhaps no more than tilt his head and smile, and they would go off dazzled as if many invitations to tea dances and parties had been exchanged.

Roger was seventeen, three years older than she, and he was going to Amherst next year. They were supposed to be the image of each other, though he was fair like Laura, their mother, his hair the color of brass and curly. In less than an hour she would know how many shows he had tickets for, how much allowance they would have for gifts, and most important, what kind of place they would live in this time. Oh, not a house, thought Lucy, while the train rattled its bones over a bridge and hurried itself past a dismal depot, a house would be too much to hope for, but perhaps it could be a two bedroom apartment with a kitchenette and a sofa that opened in case they should have a guest.

She would have the walls green and a real fireplace and a radio in a mahogany cabinet with a small Christmas tree on it. But now as she tried to enter this make-believe room, it faded, and she saw instead the living room of the house that she had loved in California, where they had lived until her father was killed. That room had been white, its furniture dark oak with faded slipcovers, and it had opened on a patio where the shade was spattered with mimosa, and, early on Christmas morning, with the cries of doves.

After that house had been sold there had been nothing but furnished rooms. She and Roger and Laura had slept in sanitized motor courts on the desert. (That was before Laura stopped driving.) One winter they had lived in Louisville with a great aunt. Summers they went to the mountains and boarded in mammoth wooden castles where no other children played on the long porches among the creaking rattan chairs. During winter vacations when Laura was away, she and Roger went down on Long Island to Grandmother Ransome's house with its tetherball pole and spruces bristling on the lawn, but the last two Christmases they had all spent in what she was aware of as respectable residential hotels in mid-Manhattan. Wherever they went, the paraphernalia of home (what was left of it) came too. Photographs of them all at different ages in shagreen and silver frames came out of Laura's trunk, with the hot water bottle and the supplies for the medicine shelf. Lucy had a collection of fairy-size soap cakes which would not lather and were embossed with coats of arms and mottoes like *sic transit gloria.* This fall, Laura had promised to take a real apartment for them. But she had promised before.

The sound of the wheels going along the tracks where now the darkness was running too became the voice of Lucy's apprehension. Somewhere within the swaying frame of the coach it seemed as if frightened canaries were chirping. Her eyes closed. Her head fell forward into her dream. Roger was coming to meet her under the golden dome of Grand Central Station, that was not the station but the beach in Coronado with its line of palms waving their arms above their heads. And she, crouched on the sand, watched through those fronds the long white house crystallize and dissolve again and again.

Lucy woke as the train hurtled into the tunnel. Lights were on and all about her people gathered up their coats and bags. The girls from school were singing: *Deck the halls with boughs of holly*. She felt an excitement, quite voluptuous, kin to the frenzy long ago when she and Roger had hidden gifts in the enormous wardrobes, and scents of peppermint and oranges had filled the rooms at home.

She hunched her shoulders into her reversible raincoat, the collar up against her cheeks, her hair caught in it, and swung her big rawhide suitcase off the rack and into the aisle. She was swept out of the coach by the crowd of passengers. Faster and faster they moved along the dusky concrete platforms, until it seemed to Lucy that at any moment they might all begin to run.

Then she saw Roger, his gold-crested head searching above the other heads at the top of the ramp. She wanted to call to him, but it was impossible to raise her voice above the subterranean echoes that roared like sea shells held against her ears.

They met finally in a muffled embrace of overcoats. Roger stepped back. "You've grown taller again," he said, and his grey eyes would not meet hers. There was no hope. "What do they feed you on up there anyway?" he asked, and she knew there was no apartment for them this time either.

He took her suitcase, and staggered on purpose. "What have you got in here? Rocks?"

Lucy giggled. "Books, silly, and shoes and galoshes."

Suddenly she was aware of someone else. A girl in a

dark fur coat with a gardenia was watching them. And Roger had turned and was smiling at her. She came forward slowly to where they stood.

Her name was Andrea. It seemed to Lucy, as Roger spoke it, to be one of the most beautiful names she had ever heard. Andrea's small, black-gloved hand came out of her big fur sleeve. "Roger's told me so much about you," she said with a faraway smile.

Lucy shook her hand and said hello. She had never heard of Andrea before. There was nothing familiar about her sweet, rather flat face. I am taller than she is, thought Lucy with some satisfaction, as they walked abreast through the sea of travelers. But while they waited in the arcade for a cab, Andrea whispered to Roger, and Lucy, lost, out of hearing, listened to the hiss of tires against the curb, and felt that they both were much bigger than she; they seemed somehow larger than life.

"Is Andrea coming with us?" she asked. But although she thought she shouted, they did not hear, and there was a green cab waiting for them, the driver opening the door with his black arm stretched backward. Andrea tossed her hair about as she stepped inside. Her hair was light brown and straight till the bleached ends mingled with the fur of her coat. She seated herself against the window and her face shone white and pink out of its soft hood of hair. Lucy took her place in the opposite corner. Roger sat down between them. They drew their knees tightly together, not touching one another. Her suitcase balanced and bounced at their toes and they were off.

Roger leaned toward the driver. "Prince Albert Hotel," he said. Lucy knotted her fingers in her lap. She had lost her gloves in the ladies' room in Boston.

"You never told me what a beautiful little sister you had," said Andrea.

"Hush," said Roger gravely, "We mustn't spoil her."

"Roger," said Lucy. "We're going to give *Twelfth Night* next term and I'm to be Viola."

"Oh, I can remember when we did that at St. Agatha's," said Andrea, as if it had been centuries ago. Gradually the air in the cab was being stricken by the odor of gardenias.

"I think Mother will be pleased," said Lucy.

Roger chose not to answer. He was staring at the lighted shopfronts where mannequins bedecked with tinsel snow postured under the imponderable stone night.

After a while he said, "Mother's in Philadelphia. She's supposed to come back tomorrow."

"What's she doing there?" asked Andrea.

"A wedding," said Roger, and Lucy could not tell if he were being truthful. His lips were always smiling somehow, even when he frowned. Bands of illumination whipped across their faces, as they sped through the streets, lighting an ear, a closed eyelid. At night on the island, Lucy remembered, the light rose off the water so that playing on the seawall their faces had been oddly foreshortened. "When we grow up; when we are older . . ." they had whispered, and out on the Pacific the ships had winked at them.

Now Roger and Andrea were talking softly to each other, but this time she could hear. They were going to a party. "You're coming with us," said Roger. "Andrea asked her sister and she said to bring you along by all means."

"I don't know," said Lucy. "How old is Andrea's sister?"

"Twenty-two," said Andrea. "There are three of us, not counting Mother and Dad of course, and I'm the youngest. Margaret made her debut in sixty-three. Her parties are divine." She waved one hand, as if to summon a genie in the dark shell of the cab. "Champagne. This is for Charlie who's going back in the Army."

"Margaret is married to Charlie," said Roger, as if that settled everything.

She did not want to go to their party. Everyone there would be strange. She had never known anyone who had made a real debut, or known any girls who went to St. Agatha's. But Roger must have. She saw their two profiles superimposed like heads on an antique coin.

"All right," said Lucy. "I'll come, if you promise . . ."

"Promise what?" asked Roger and Andrea together.

But the cab had pulled up in front of the Prince Albert. The orange light shone through the iron-worked glass doors, and two holly wreaths like eyes flapped their ribbons in the wind.

"Oh nothing," she said. "Never mind."

Always, it was the smell in the lobby which assailed her first and here it was cigar ash and nickel polish. And the maroon carpeting hushing their footfalls made her feel that she could only whisper. Voices and glasses sounded faintly on their left. Above a curtained doorway Lucy saw a license plate that read "Tables for Ladies." She glanced at Andrea, but her shallow almond eyes were inscrutable.

Roger went to the desk, where a fat woman in black pressed her large bosom against the counter, guarding the honeycomb for mail. Suddenly, Andrea nudged her with an elbow. Lucy followed her gaze to an armchair, beside a prickly plastered pillar, where an old gentleman sat, staring at them. His head trembled with a palsy. Lucy turned away, clenching her chilled fingers in her pockets to warm them.

Roger came back with the key lying in the palm of his hand. "Do you want to wait for us down here?" he asked Andrea.

"I don't think it would be safe," she said loudly. "Do you?"

"Naturally not," said Roger. "I only thought . . ." Then the two of them burst into laughter.

The old man still watched them over the edge of his evening paper which fluttered terribly in his hands. Lucy hoped he might be deaf.

They went up in the elevator slowly past the shelves of two landings. Andrea bit the fingers of her gloves but she could not stop her laughter. Roger leaned helplessly against the iron grill. "Oh, for heaven's sake," sighed Lucy. The elevator boy's neck was flaming, but when he slid back the gate to let them pass, she saw that his bony face was quite austere.

They went single file along the corridor, Roger leading, past all the doors that hid their unimaginable occupants. Lucy always prayed that none might open as she passed. Andrea's laughter had subsided, but there was no way of telling from behind whether her lips were still in awe or scorn. Roger stopped at number 435, fitted the key in the lock and opened the door. Home safe.

"Voilà!" He lit a bridge lamp. Shadows leapt across the room. "The dame downstairs calls it a suite."

"Oh, Roger," Lucy's cry escaped her. "Why must it always be so hideous?" Each piece of furniture wore a shawl, or a crocheted doily. On the desk was a green blotter with edges picked away by mouse-like fingers;

and all about were scattered ties and balls of socks, and magazines and crushed cigarette packs.

As if in apology, Roger tossed a few things into a dripping valise on the radiator. Andrea curled up on the couch away from the pile of bedclothes. Lucy, sitting on the edge of her suitcase, saw how Andrea's furs fell back revealing her round throat with that line called the collar of Venus on it, and her black velveteen dress.

"Maybe I'd better not go to this party," said Lucy. "I don't know what to wear."

"Don't be silly," Andrea said. "It's only for poor old Charlie. A farewell party. It doesn't matter what you wear."

"That's right, Sis," said Roger.

Lucy carried her suitcase into the bedroom. She felt along the wall and found the light switch. On the dresser, Laura's *flaçons,* jars of cream and lotion, caught the light and doubled themselves in the mirror. She sensed the potpourri of odors hidden there, jasmine and the clear water scent of roses, and she missed her mother, although she had come to accept the fact that Laura could not be relied upon for greetings or farewells. In the top drawer, stockings and gloves curled limply over a black Gideon Bible. Lucy looked at herself in the mirror. She was dark and solemn like the Ransomes. Laura was blonde, and suddenly Lucy thought how her incandescent fairness could be embarrassing at times, like a lamp left burning in the daylight.

A rush of water came down the pipes behind her. She threw her coat over the bedpost and pulled her good red silk (for matinees and teas in the headmistress' office) from her suitcase. The skirt was creased, and as she tried to smooth it, she listened, as really all along she had been listening, for a sign of those two in the other room. But all she could hear was the wash of city noise against the outer walls of the hotel.

Lucy drew her sweater off and remembered a game they had played at night on the wharfs at home. They had called it King of the Mountain, and Roger nearly always would be king, lording it on top of a heap of nets, while she and Candy and Edward (the only other children allowed up so late) would try to unseat him. Once when Candy had reached the top, Roger had rolled down with her in his arms, shouting, I love you. She and Edward had watched spellbound, until, unable to bear it longer, she had thrown herself painfully into the phosphorescent water.

She stepped out of her skirt and with her slip fallen around her hips went to the basin in the corner. She had wanted to tell on Roger that night, but when she had stamped into the kitchen, strands of her long hair plastered to her cheeks and wrapped around her neck, she had been told that the Captain and the Madam were at the Officers' Club, and it had seemed quite pointless to betray Roger to the cook.

Andrea came into the bedroom, closing the door after her. "What a heavenly dress!" she said. Lucy did not turn to look at her. She took the stiff, rough towel from its glass rod and dried her neck and arms. She rubbed hard but the lardy smell of soap would not come off.

"I adore that shade of red," said Andrea.

"Roger helped me choose it," said Lucy.

"He does have such good taste. It's really surprising, considering . . ." She paused.

Lucy swung around with the towel clutched to her small breasts, and saw Andrea take one of Laura's lipsticks from the dresser. "Considering what?" she asked. Roger would not have dared to give away their secret.

Andrea lifted her eyebrows and colored her lips that were thrust toward the mirror, half opened, fishlike. Lucy shivered; goose bumps broke out on her arms. She had forgotten to pull the shade, so that the whole world could see her through the window.

"You must have had a glorious time in California," said Andrea. She dabbed Laura's powder puff against her nose, just as if the room were hers, too. "I mean," she continued, "when you and Roger were kids and left to run quite wild. He told me how you used to do all kinds of things by yourself. I wasn't even allowed to cross streets alone till I was eleven."

"We fixed our own meals sometimes when the cook was off, if that's what you mean," said Lucy. She stood with her back to the window and adjusted her slip. "Mother never bothered much about meals and such, after Daddy was killed." Perhaps that would shut her up.

"He was killed in Korea, wasn't he?" said Andrea.

"Yes—his plane was lost," said Lucy. But Andrea knew everything.

"It must be odd," she said, gazing at Lucy in the mirror with level, knowing eyes, "to grow up with so little family . . ."

Lucy pulled on the red silk dress and bent her head to find the gold buttons that marched from collar to waist. Until now she had always liked Roger's friends, the pink-cheeked, or freckled or sallow, pimply-faced boys. There hadn't been any girls.

"Red is stunning on you," said Andrea. "It's your color really, with all that black hair. Very gypsy."

Roger was weak. She, at least, would not be taken in

by flattery. "I had a Spanish costume one time," said Lucy. They had had a birthday party in the patio, the white wall lined with children in fancy dress under a green and scarlet swag of bougainvillaea. Roger had been a matador, the tricorne low over his light eyes; and there was someone with long blue-trousered legs, head under the black cowl of a camera, but she could not remember who. There had been so few grownups around them in those days; they had been reserved like special treats for holidays and fireworks on the Fourth.

Roger pounded on the door.

"All right, darling," called Andrea. "Good old Charles," she said softly to Lucy, as if they had been sharing confidences for years, "I had a fierce crush on him once, before he married Margaret, of course. We shouldn't be too late for his last party. Thank God it isn't Roger's."

Lucy picked up her coat and followed Andrea out of the room. At the door, she looked back almost regretfully. A red eye of a cigarette left burning on a table glowed balefully at her.

"Come on, Sis," called Roger down the hall.

"Stop ordering me as if I were an infant," she said, and shut the door on the darkness.

At every party Lucy had ever attended, even when Roger stood beside her, there was at least one moment when fate hesitated, the question undecided whether she would be within the party or outside it, wallflower or belle.

They had left their wraps in a bedroom on the other side of the foyer, and had been led by Andrea's sister's cold, bare arms into the immense living room. Actually, it was two rooms, the folding doors between having been pushed aside. Just as Lucy had feared, Roger and Andrea had been caught in a flurry of voices and outstretched hands, while she had been swept, by a tide of people and unfamiliar names, against a small veneered table that stood between two windows.

All about were drifts of skirts, party skirts of net and taffeta and velvet, spread upon the chairs and sofas, swaying around the dark bodies of the men. Everyone talked, everyone laughed. Only she was silent and her silence was more conspicuous than a scream.

She repeated to herself the charm that she and Roger had used so many times to ward off unhappiness. In a hundred years, she told herself, what difference will this make a hundred years from now? There was still some comfort in those receding arches of time that left her alone in her red dress between the windows, forgotten.

The walls of the room were putty green, the green she would have chosen for her own. There was a fireplace, too. And on the mantel was a Christmas tree, small, green and hung with silver balls, her own, the very one she would have bought herself. Beside her now a woman pulled a tall Navy man down by the lapels of his jacket, and shouted in his ear: "The answer is that we don't have a set of values. How can anyone be satisfied?"

"Only successful people," said the man.

"Success!" the woman hissed at him. "What's that? Now tell me, whom do you know that's really first rate?"

The Navy man leaned across the woman's grey shoulder and winked at Lucy. "My name is Edgar," he said. He had red hair. She smiled. The party still might claim her. "Edgar," he repeated. "You must call me Edgar."

He left the hissing woman and came to stand beside her. Shyly, she looked down at the table, where a gold clock sat, its cogs and weights exposed under a glass bell. "It never runs down," said the man.

She could think of no answer to his remark. Innumerable quotations (the kind that Roger put over so well) marked time on the threshold of her memory. Meanwhile the golden minutes ran down in the clock and something would have to be said or she might be left alone again. She took a deep breath. "It doesn't seem much like Christmas, does it?"

He nodded his saturnine head approvingly. "Hasn't been Christmas for years. But that red dress of yours helps and we might pin some holly on it. You need a drink. Wait here for me," he said. "Promise not to disappear." To her dismay, he moved off. Roger (but where was he now?) would never allow her to drink cocktails, though they had sipped wine long ago when there had still been parties at home.

She found herself looking up at a young man with an old face whose close-cut yellow hair fitted his head like a cap. "I know you," he announced. "I am convinced of it. Where did we meet?"

"I don't know, I'm sure," said Lucy. "Perhaps you mean my brother."

"I beg your pardon," he gasped. "I never make mistakes like that."

She had put her foot in it. Blushing, she stared at the books that flanked the fireplace, behind a frieze of talking faces, like colored stones in a mosaic. At home, there had been only her father's sets of Kipling and Stevenson, tooled in gold on red, on top of the commode on the upstairs landing. Roger had read them all aloud to her before Laura had packed them away along with the uniforms and the medals and the shell collection, jewelled limpets and periwinkles and the chambered nautilus. (To keep them safe, she had claimed, and it was true that mildew filmed the bindings like the haze on red grapes.)

The young man was telling her a story about his life. "It's like a dream repeating itself," he was saying, watching someone at the far end of the room. "Over and over again and more intense—the kind you have before you go under ether."

Just then a group of people parted and Lucy saw Roger. A piano raised its great black wing behind him. She fastened her eyes on him, willing him to look at her. It had always been easy to accomplish, in church, in the sanatariums when they visited their mother, wherever it had been against the rules to talk. But this time Andrea seemed to float between them. Lucy gave up. The smoke and scent in the room oppressed her. A hundred years from now, she thought, everyone here will be dead.

Edgar was coming back to her with two long-stemmed glasses clutched above his head. "Couldn't find any holly," said Edgar, as if he had been hunting it all this time, and the young man shrugged his shoulders and moved off. "If it would snow, now, then it might seem like Christmas." He pulled back the drapes that covered the window, but when they pressed their faces to the glass there was only the black drop down to Fifth Avenue, and a few lamps lit in the snowless stretches of the park.

"Brought her amethysts from Chile," said a girl's voice behind them.

"Naturally, people who can afford their own bomb shelters . . ."

"The loveliest legs and the dirtiest neck . . ."

Someone had started to play the piano, an improvisation, a fox trot.

"Flights of angels," said the man whose name was Edgar. They sat on the floor. Her head rested against his shoulder. From here, she could see the matched legs of couples dancing beyond the folding doors, and faces floating above them, and right overhead, a maid's hands, like starfish, supporting a platter of canapés.

"I think it is very nice of you to be so young," Edgar said. "How did you manage it? Where did you come from?"

"I was born on the island of Oahu," she told him.

"Did you know that everyone who is young is beautiful?"

"I don't think so, really," said Lucy. "We lived mostly in Coronado, which is an island, also, you know. You have to take a ferry across the bay." There had been a trolley to cross the island, its overhead cable strung straight, between the palms and eucalyptus trees, from the ferry slip to the white hotel on the ocean side where the movie stars stayed. "In the wintertime my brother and I went to school together, and in the summer we played on the beaches." The ceiling loomed like an Arabian tent above the hooded lamps.

"I don't suppose I'll ever go back," she said. "I used to think that Roger and I would buy our house again, but that was a childish thing to believe, wasn't it?" It had been an island of flowers and crystalline mornings when she and Roger had looked out their dormer window before the fog rolled in; and all around it, perpetual and natural as humming birds among the vines, the roar of planes rose and fell from the air base. "You can't imagine," she said, "how very beautiful it was."

"I know not where His islands lift their fronded palms on air," Edgar intoned flatly. His big head sagged between his shoulders. *"I only know I cannot drift. . . ."* Lucy thought of a bee buzzing in the choir. Her dress was a red pool about her legs in the lamplight. A girl began to laugh.

"Roger and I never wanted to leave. But you see," she explained, no longer certain that he was listening to her. "After my father was killed in the war, my mother went to pieces." She had never spoken to anyone about her mother's trouble. Even she and Roger had kept it secret from each other. Each had known the other knew, but they had never spoken it aloud.

"Schizophrenia." She was not sure of the pronunciation. "We had it in mental hygiene and once I looked it up in the dictionary at school." She remembered the smell of ink and moldy leather, and her own hand hiding the minuscule schizo: plus heart and mind from the Greek. Now she had said it. Edgar looked sad. If he had not heard her, he must be sorry for himself. Perhaps he had been unhappy in love, or had lost a friend in the war.

She got to her feet and walked straight and steady, between the clumps of furniture and people, into the mirrored foyer where the glass held another room of dancers weaving in a waltz. Roger and Andrea were not among the dancers. They were nowhere to be seen. In which room had they left their things? All the doors were shut. The first one she tried opened noiselessly, but as the creamy light from the hall cut through the dark and roses blossomed on the wallpaper, she heard a girl moan, "Oh Lord, not again!" Quickly, Lucy shut the door, but not before she had seen the figure that was two people against the dusky, flowering wall.

She found her own coat on the enormous bed in the next room among the layers of wool and fur with here and there the spark of a white glove. No one saw her cross the foyer and go out the door.

Down on the street, the air congealed around her legs like ice water. Her cheeks were stones. She looked up at the apartment house with all its lighted windows. What floor was it on, the party with the music and the dancers, where Roger and Andrea hid? It was only a party, she told herself, and after a while it would be over and the lights would go out. But Roger had deserted her. She had betrayed their mother. These things would last forever.

And in the same eternal way, thought Lucy, ducking her head against the cold that streamed along the avenue, the days stretched out ahead. She would have to get through them somehow alone, before her own life could begin; facing the fat woman at the hotel desk, the meals wrapped in warm napkins, the matinees and sodas without Roger; and after New Year's dinner at Grandmother Ransome's, the train ride up to school where, beside the tracks, the boy and his dog might walk again; and midyears and the teas in the dorm smelling of coal gas, and in the spring, hockey on the muddy field.

A bus careened past her and all the colored lights on the avenue rose in triangular perspective to the height of a gigantic Christmas tree. How long would she have to wait? And would it wait for her, her life? It was as if she could see it, far ahead where the lights came together, hanging like the topmost star on the tree, infinitely desirable and remote.

About the Author

Nancy Cardozo is a poet as well as a short story writer, and has been published in *Atlantic Monthly, Harper's Bazaar, Mademoiselle, The New Yorker, Poetry,* and many other magazines.

Born in New York City, she is a graduate of Swarthmore College. She is married to artist Russell Cowles and the mother of two sons. Currently she divides her time between the family's homes in New Milford, Connecticut and New York City. She is now at work on a novel and a book of selected poems.

THE LEGACY
B. J. Chute

Irene said, "You're not being fair to the child, George You're only thinking of yourself."

George Ashe looked up to meet his sister's hard kindly stare and shook his head. "I don't think I'm that single-minded," he said. "I don't mean to be."

"Of course you don't mean to be," she told him. "Nobody ever *means* to be anything. But a man your age can't be expected to understand anything at all about a fourteen-year-old girl. It's a woman's job."

He didn't say anything. Marjorie's mother had died when Marjorie was eight, leaving him their small intrepid child as a reason for living. He had needed a reason very badly. In a moment Irene would say that it had been six years ago. After six years you were entitled to scars, but not to pain. He waited and she said it. "It's been six years, George."

He said shortly, "I know that."

Irene went on. "It's chiefly Marjorie I'm thinking of. The child has no real social life at all."

"Depends on what you call a social life," George said. "Marjorie has plenty of friends."

"You know very well what I mean by a social life." She shifted in her chair and replanted her feet. She was not so much stout as of a geometric persuasion, with solid cubed corners. "When other girls are going to proms, Marjorie's home with her nose in a book. She reads too much. She's a lot worse than you ever were."

"I survived it. Marjorie likes books."

"That's not the point. Really, George, you're much too detached about things. I suppose it's being a professor but when Eleanor was alive you were a lot more human."

His mind warned her silently, talk about anyone else.

Luckily she did. "You say Marjorie has plenty of friends and I don't doubt it at all. She's a nice child. But that's not what I'm talking about, George. I'm talking about the kind of thing any normal girl wants—you know, going to dances and having boys cut in all the time." She gave him a sharp look. "Marjorie doesn't even have a dance frock, does she?"

He shook his head. "She doesn't care for dances."

"You mean she never gets asked," his sister said. "She's shy, George, she always has been. That's why she needs help right now."

George frowned. This picture of his daughter gave him a sudden inward wrench for which he was not prepared and against which he had no defenses. It was true that Marjorie was a shy, solemn child but she had always been shy and solemn, even when her mother was alive, although she had been subject to abrupt personal fits of delight when she would stalk the house from basement to attic, filling it with her hoarse triumphant chants. He had assumed that now, at fourteen, she was as contented and well adjusted as she seemed to be. He preferred not to believe that her admirable and selective young mind was really bemused by a picture of herself in a frilly dress, stampeding the stag line.

He sighed. Perhaps he was too much the detached professor, impatient of all these meaningless social patterns. Perhaps, to Marjorie, they were not meaningless at all but very wonderful.

Irene went on, her voice suddenly more gentle. "If Eleanor were alive, George, I wouldn't say anything. Eleanor could give the child what she needs. It's hard for a man to see it."

She had caught him on his most vulnerable point and it was out of a sense of his own inadequacy that he said, "What do you suggest, Irene?"

She told him promptly. "Have a talk with Anita Marshall. That pretty little daughter of hers is a tremendous hit. The boys are crazy about Lee."

George stirred uneasily. He liked Anita very much and her husband was a good friend of his, but the idea of Lee as a butterfly example for his daughter irritated him. He hedged. "I don't think I ought to impose on Anita—"

"Nonsense. She'd be delighted. After all, Lee's about the same age as Marjorie and that makes everything so much simpler. She must have at least one extra boy on her string that she wouldn't mind lending."

It sounded like a friendly exchange of polo ponies and he almost choked on it.

"I could speak to Anita, I suppose," he said reluctantly.

Irene rose. "I already have. She'll be expecting to hear from you." She looked at him with approval. "I'm glad to see you getting some sense, George."

It seemed unanswerable.

After she had gone, he went out into the kitchen. Mrs. Dolan, his small sparrowlike housekeeper, was peeling apples at the sink, the waxy green spirals falling back from her knife. She glanced at him and went on with her work.

"Marjorie not home yet?" he asked.

"Any time now, Mr. Ashe."

"Apple cobbler?"

She nodded. He watched her hands moving deftly and wished he could ask her what she thought about Marjorie but of course he couldn't. At that moment the back door opened and Marjorie came in.

He looked at her with what he told himself was implacable objectivity, as if she were anybody's child. It was the first time that he had realized she wasn't pretty. She had a square pale face, given a Celtic look by the heavy black eyebrows drawn straight over gray eyes. Her dark hair was pulled back by a ribbon and wind-tangled so that the uncompromising bangs looked like a Shetland pony's. She had a rather stocky figure and her hands were exceedingly capable. He could not, for the life of him, imagine those hands patting a masculine coat sleeve.

Her sweater and skirt outfit seemed all right. He said, "Hello, darling."

Economical of words, she smiled at him and put her pile of books on the table. He picked up the top one and glanced at the title. *Madame Bovary*. Flaubert seemed an odd choice at fourteen. "Is this required reading?"

Marjorie shook her head.

"Isn't it rather heavy going for you?"

"No." The Shetland shake of the head again. "She was a stupid woman, wasn't she? It's awful the way he knows everything about her."

He agreed, rather pleased. A lot of adults encountered

Emma Bovary's pitiful vacancy without the faintest recognition of the awful brilliance (*awful* was exactly the word) that had created her.

Mrs. Dolan, speaking to the apples, said, "You read too much."

"I suppose." Marjorie accepted this as an apparently inescapable fact and picked up her books. George followed her out of the kitchen and she asked him over her shoulder about the plans for his lecture course.

"I finished the outline this morning."

"Daddy! That's the hardest part."

He would have like nothing better than to tell her all about it but there was his promise to Irene. He sat down on the sofa and pulled Marjorie down beside him. "I want to talk to you, honey," he said. "Your aunt was here a little while ago." He waited a moment, got no assistance and went on. "She's worried about you, Margie."

"Me?" She seemed surprised.

"Yes. She doesn't feel you're getting any social life."

She traced the pattern of a rose on the carpet with a scuffed toe. "You mean dances—and things?" she said carefully.

He nodded. "Dances and things."

There was quite a long silence and she did the rose counter-clockwise. She was, perhaps, too used to being honest with him so that he was very afraid of forcing her. When she finally got the words shaped up in her mind, they came out sounding as if they had been pushed. She said, "I don't get asked, Daddy."

He had not wanted this admission at all, since it confirmed what Irene told him. He had wanted to be assured that dances and things didn't interest his daughter, that she was independent. Now he had to admit with a pang of real discomfort that Irene was entirely right, that

Marjorie was missing something she really wanted. He waited unhappily for her to go on.

She made a funny little movement with her shoulders. "I never seem to know what to talk about, for one thing."

"Just what interests you, honey."

"Oh, no." She looked at him then. "I know that much about it, Daddy. You're supposed to talk about what interests *them* but that's part of the trouble. I don't know what does. And if they do want to talk about what I want to talk about, that means they're what the other girls call drips and it's really better not to go to a dance at all than to go with a drip."

This was a long speech for Marjorie and it opened up vistas that confounded him. He remembered Irene's dictum that this was a woman's job and, with a real effort, he committed himself. "Marjorie, your aunt suggested I have a talk with Mrs. Marshall."

"About me?"

He nodded and then, because this seemed a little crude, he added a stumbling statement about Aunt Irene's thinking Mrs. Marshall could help with, well, clothes and things.

There was no need for his earnest tact. Marjorie viewed the prospect with unexpected eagerness. "Do you really think she would, Daddy? She's awfully nice." She stared past him at the wall, her lips parted. "There's a big school dance next week. Maybe—"

He wanted her to be happy. He said, "Do you want me to—to talk with Mrs. Marshall, dear?"

For a moment he thought she was going to say no, that she was contented with things the way they were. Then she turned suddenly and buried her nose against the lapel of his coat, a small child trick of hers from years ago.

"Would you, Daddy?" she said, muffled. "Dresses and things?"

And things.

He said yes, he would.

He wanted nothing less the next day than to call Anita, but he had no morning lecture and consequently no excuse for putting off the inevitable. Prepared for his call, she had already made her plans and said she would drop in on him that afternoon. "That way I can see Marjorie at the same time," she said, "and we can fix everything up."

He was a little alarmed because she sounded so executive but she was being extremely kind and he made the suitable sounds of gratitude. When Anita came, everything went very smoothly. She talked to him before Marjorie came home and she stamped on the anxious retina of his mind an extremely clear picture of herself as a helpful and wise woman. She told him how necessary a real social life was to a young girl and she made it very plain how satisfyingly well her own daughter had done in this respect. "Of course, it's no credit to me," said Anita disarmingly.

"Lee has a better example than Marjorie, I'm afraid."

She smiled at him forgivingly. "You *are* rather a hermit, George, but after all you can't be expected to know what the child needs. She ought to be taking it for granted that she'll go to dances."

"She doesn't seem to get invited," he said with difficulty, feeling disloyal. "And I don't think she'd ever get around to just asking someone to take her. I suppose that wouldn't be protocol anyhow."

"Oh dear no!" She was amused by his innocence. "It's really just a matter of getting started. Men are such sheep about things like that and boys are even worse. If one asks a girl, the others will ask her."

"Well?" said George, not knowing how to set this desirable chain reaction going but anxious to be helpful.

Anita clasped her long-fingered hands together lightly. "I've arranged everything," she said reassuringly. "Lee has a cousin who'll be in town just in time for the dance. He's a charming boy and there's no reason on earth why Marjorie shouldn't have him. Lee will tell him she's fixed up a blind date and there you are." She smiled. "Mind you, George, it's very good of Lee. She had a picture of herself with two escorts, but we talked it over and I've promised her a new dress instead." The barter-and-trade quality of this transaction must have eluded her, because she went on serenely. "Marjorie will need a new dress too, of course. That's all right, isn't it?"

He said hastily that, of course, it was all right. And when Marjorie came in at last, everything was settled and all Anita had to do was tell her the plans.

He had thought his nice-mannered daughter would be suitably grateful but he had not expected her to glow. He was glad for her and he was also distressed. The occasion seemed too slight.

But the day Marjorie came home with her new dress, he knew that he was wrong and that a piece of happiness is a piece of happiness, whether for large cosmic reasons or small social ones. She came flying into the living room, clutching a shiny white box and chanting, "We bought it! We bought my dress." Her neat square hands wrestled with the string and she finally had to break it before she could lift the dress reverently out of its tissue-paper nest. "Lee's coming over tonight to see it. Daddy, isn't it lovely?"

It was a charming shade of blue and in obvious good taste. "It's beautiful," he said.

She sighed deeply. "I hope Lee likes it."

He was annoyed. If she liked it herself, what did Lee's opinion matter? But then he remembered that Lee's social success was assured and her judgment counted.

Fortunately, Lee did approve. She came over after dinner, melting with delicious charm for the benefit of Marjorie's quaint old daddy and making him feel every century of his forty-five years. "It's just sweet," she told Marjorie, stroking the delicate folds of blue, "and it's definitely your type. Can you manage the long skirt, honey?"

Marjorie said, too humbly, that she hoped she could. He looked at them, standing together, Lee graceful and cuddly and pretty as a kitten, Marjorie with her hands hanging at her sides, simply because her skirt had no pockets, and her face flushed with rather childish enthusiasm. He knew if he were a boy which one he would want to take to the dance, and he damned the whole race of males.

"Bob's a senior in high school, you know, Margie," Lee went on. "He's really sweet."

Marjorie said, "He sounds nice," and George saw she was stiff with foreknowledge of uncertainty and clumsiness and the agony of going out with a senior. But Bob was hers, for that night he was hers, and who knew what wonders might follow the first real dance, the first genuine escort?

He said heartily, "You'll have a fine time."

"I hope he'll like me," said Marjorie.

She spent so much of the next week taking her new dress out of its cover that George became concerned for its health, but she only laid it most tenderly on her bed or held it up to yearn over her mirrored reflection. She had new shoes too, with heels much higher than they should be, but twice he heard her talking to them on such a note of love that he never mentioned his conviction that they were unsuitable for a little girl.

Unused to prayer, he merely relayed a request to God to make it a happy evening for his daughter.

But the tragedy came anyway and it was a real tragedy, small only because it had no dignity. It was ignoble from the beginning, starting as a severe cold in the head of Lee's escort, Johnny Dayton. The Dayton doctor ordered the Dayton pride and joy to bed and Mrs. Dayton phoned Anita Marshall. Anita phoned George immediately.

She was terribly distressed, telling him about Johnny, much more distressed than the occasion seemed to warrant. There seemed to be no doubt of the young man's survival. "Lee's so upset," Anita said.

George said he was sorry and added, "Marjorie will be sorry too, but I'm sure she'll get along all right. Maybe it's better for her to be on her own."

There was a short silence. Then Anita's voice came over the wire again, and it had a curious, placating sound. "George, dear," she began, "I'm afraid—"

He waited, faintly uneasy.

He could almost hear her draw the long necessary breath. "I don't think we can ask Lee to be the one to stay home," she said.

He looked at the telephone in his hand. It was an excellent instrument, suitable for perfect communication. He had not heard wrongly. "But, Anita—"

"I know. It's a dreadful shame." He could imagine her smiling, expecting him to understand. "Your dear child's been looking forward to it so, the new dress and everything. But Lee's on the dance committee and of course

Bob's counted on having her there and—George, there'll be plenty of other times for Marjorie. I'll see that there are. It's just that—"

He said that he understood. He reassured her automatically because she was talking so fast, almost distractedly. It was embarrassing for her, he understood that, too. When he finally hung up she was still saying that she was so distressed, so really distressed . . .

Ahead of him was the task of telling Marjorie. All that morning his papers lay on his desk untouched.

In the end he didn't even try to explain. He just told her. Johnny Dayton was sick, Lee was going with Bob, there would be other dances. He looked at her anxiously, hoping that she wouldn't cry.

She didn't. She just stood quietly, accepting his words. After a while she said, "Well, I guess it's just one of those things. It's too bad about Johnny."

He looked at her helplessly, thinking that tears would almost have been a relief. After a moment, he thought he had better leave her alone.

It was just as he turned to go that he had his idea. It was the thought of the blue dress and the foolish little shoes that gave it to him. All she needed, surely, was an escort to take her to the dance. Once there, she could rely on Lee and the stag line and all the youngsters she must know.

Marjorie needed and escort and Marjorie's father had a perfectly good dinner jacket. He would take her himself. He turned back. "Darling, I've got an idea. How would it be if *I* took you to the dance?"

She looked startled. "Oh, Daddy, I don't think—I mean, nobody ever—"

She stopped.

He tried not to show his disappointment. It had

seemed such a good idea. A little stiffly, he said, "Well, I just thought–"

She flung herself suddenly into his arms and hugged him tight. "It would be wonderful," she said. "Would you really take me?"

He kissed the top of her head, feeling delightfully expansive. It was all going to work out fine in spite of everything. . . .

George looked down at his daughter. The blue dress was certainly very charming and suitable but they had been standing there glued to the wall for ten minutes now, watching the dancers move past in their intricate routines, faces smooth and absorbed. No one in the stag line had given Marjorie so much as a second glance. The bored young eyes rested on her father in faint surprise, then passed on.

It was ridiculous for a middle-aged man to feel so lost and awkward. In this small jungle he should be an amused explorer, and instead he felt like a rather backward monkey. This bit of self-criticism cheered him considerably. He told himself they were only children after all and pressed Marjorie's cold hand.

"Want to dance?"

She nodded dumbly and he took her in his arms. She was such a square little thing, he thought, so compact and somehow so nice. They moved out onto the floor.

He had never been a good dancer but he had always managed to get by without actual damage to his partners. This music, however, with its nervous beat was new to him, and it never seemed to be doing quite what he was doing. Marjorie was stiff in his arms and he couldn't say that he blamed her. What she needed was one of those tall young men with their relaxed and casual steps, half dance, half walk. He noticed the way the other girls, dancing past the stag line, smiled at the boys in it. He looked down at Marjorie and found she was staring at his lapel with dreadful earnestness.

"You know any of the boys in the stag line?" he said.

She gave them a quick sideways look and shook her head. "Just by sight," she said. "One or two. I don't know many of these boys."

He gave her a small playful hug and missed a step. "They might remember you—by sight—if you'd smile at them, sweetheart. They don't bite."

"No," said Marjorie.

He felt a mild prick of impatience. The stag line was only there to be danced with but he could see they would at least have to feel that a girl was willing. He could also see what Anita meant when she said Marjorie had a lot to learn. Poor kitten. He pulled her close to him and looked out over her head. "There's Lee," he said suddenly.

"Where?"

"Over by the orchestra." Lee was radiant and, although the palm of his hand itched to smack her for her annexation of Marjorie's partner, he was still very glad to see someone who knew all the ropes. If that was Bob dancing with her, he was a good-looking youngster.

Marjorie said, "I guess that's Bob."

"I guess it is," said George and steered their way toward the orchestra. He knew a few ropes himself, he thought indignantly. When they bumped into Lee and Bob it was not unintentional.

"Why, Mr. Ashe! Marjorie!" The Marshall poise seemed to have forsaken Lee for a moment but its passing was brief and, almost at once, her voice was exactly like her mother's. "Of all people!" she drawled enchantedly. "Mr. Ashe, this is my cousin, Bob Wheeler. And Marjorie Ashe, Bobby—" Her hand made the correct social wave.

"Sir," said Bob and nodded to Marjorie. She gave him a small uncertain smile and her father felt again that dim annoyance. Surely, with her quick mind, she could think of something to say to the boy.

George sighed inwardly. He had brought her to the dance but apparently that wasn't going to be enough. He turned to Lee, said heartily, "How about finishing this dance with me, young lady?" and took her hand. She was surprised but most embraceable. There was nothing for Bob to do but turn to Marjorie, and George felt intensely relieved. Entranced by his own finesse, he moved away with Lee in his arms and found that he was dancing much better. He couldn't understand why she was so deliciously light and Marjorie so unmaneuverable; they had gone to the same dancing class as children.

He looked around for Marjorie and Bob and saw them, moving grim and wooden, unspeaking, glued together. A wave of honest anger swept over him with the knowledge that Bob was frankly sulking. Whatever they taught the exalted seniors in that young man's school, it was certainly not manners.

On the other hand, it was no use pretending that Marjorie had Lee's light touch. He wondered if it could be learned.

Lee said, with just the right blending of deference and admiration, "It was really sweet of you to bring Marjorie, Mr. Ashe. I know you think I was awfully bad but I couldn't have been more upset. I just *couldn't.*"

"I'm afraid Marjorie isn't really socially minded," George said unhappily.

"Well, you were *sweet* to bring her," Lee said firmly. Someone tapped George's shoulder, and a tall boy said, "Sorry, sir."

George went back to the wall. He wasn't going to cut in on his own daughter. She had an official escort now and, whether she was happy or not, it looked all right from the sidelines.

Lee already had another change of partners. For the first time he understood the slight smugness in Anita's voice when she talked of her daughter. It would have been somehow so satisfying to see Marjorie whirl from one pair of arms to another. He only wanted it for her sake. If her mother were still alive, she would have known the things to tell Marjorie, the things a girl had to know for her own success and happiness. He sighed. Perhaps Anita—

The music ended in a crash. Marjorie and Bob stood in the middle of the floor, clapping. The orchestra leader lifted his baton for the next dance and, as the trumpet gave its first mewling wail, Bob took Marjorie by the elbow and steered her toward her father. Safe, stowing her within this paternal harbor, he muttered, "Lee'll be looking for me," and left them.

Marjorie said, "Thank you for the dance," to empty air. After a moment she said uncertainly, "I guess I was supposed to say that I enjoyed the dance, not thank him for it. The man is supposed to say thank you." She turned to her father. "I looked that up in an etiquette book at the library but then I forget which way it went."

She had been reading etiquette books these days, then, not *Madame Bovary*. "It doesn't matter," George said.

Side by side, they waited for something to happen, someone to come. Finally, George held out his arms. "Dance, dear?" She nodded and they started out again. He was troubled because she was so quiet and her hands were still so cold, and then he began to be exasperated again. If she would only make some effort to attract the boys! Everyone was staring at them, father and daughter dancing interminably together, or at least it felt as if everyone was staring. When he looked around no one seemed even interested. Eyes were following the girls like Lee, casual and lovable, pressed against one faultless tuxedo after another. It wasn't a jungle really; it was more like an exclusive club and he couldn't get his daughter into it.

"Margie," said George.

She looked up at him and they both missed a step. He felt infernally clumsy. "Sweetheart," he said hopefully, "if you dance with Bob again, try to find out what he likes to talk about. He probably plays fullback or short-stop or something."

"He plays center on the basketball team and he's captain of the baseball team," said Marjorie, "and he's president of the dramatic society."

This was cheering news. "He told you all that?"

"I found out from Lee."

"Oh," said George.

They passed Lee at that moment, arm in arm with her current escort in a strolling dance-step. Her dress frothed out around her, and she smiled when George caught her eye.

On an impulse, he spun Marjorie around so they were shoulder to shoulder.

"Having fun, Lee?" he said casually.

She looked at him in surprise. "Wonderful," she said.

Deliberately, weighing the words so she would be sure to get the point, he said, "I must remember to give your mother a report on you, my dear."

A very pretty archness overlaid a slight uneasiness. "I hope it's a good report, Mr. Ashe," said Anita's daughter.

"I hope so," said Marjorie's father and moved away. When the dance ended, Lee turned up, admirably prompt, with a boy in tow. George beamed upon her, gently congratulating himself on the success of his social blackmail.

"Margie," said Lee, with something of the efficient kindliness of a very worldly aunt, "this is Dick Peterson. He's on the refreshment committee so he hasn't danced a step tonight, but he's just dying to." She smiled at the pink-cheeked representative of refreshments, then looked to George for approval. See? her look said. Tell Mother how good I've been, bringing boys around.

She left them and Dick gazed after her with the melting eyes of a cocker spaniel, then turned to Marjorie. "I didn't plan to dance tonight," he said. "I'm not much good at it but if you'd like to—"

George's heart warmed toward him. The youngster was half a head shorter than Marjorie and looked as if he belonged in grade school but any partner was better than none.

Marjorie smiled anxiously and the two moved off together. George lost some of his good cheer. Dick had understated the case against his dancing. Their feet, moving, collided. They tried again but the music was sharp and exact and unsympathetic. An earnest dew appeared on Dick's forehead, and Marjorie's smile was starched.

Her father felt suddenly irritated with the child. Everyone was doing everything they could for her. He had brought her to the dance himself, Lee had found her a partner, poor young Dick was struggling along as best he could. If she got mixed up with the dance steps, the least she could do was to make an effort and be charming to the boy, say something gay and amusing.

The dance stumbled to a close. The couples stood, politely clapping, waiting for the music to start again. The orchestra leader lifted his baton, and Dick turned to Marjorie with a dreadful virtue. George's heart ached for him, martyr to his own good manners.

But unexpectedly, Marjorie was backing out of the reluctant grasp. "I have to powder my nose," she said fiercely, loud enough for George and nearly everyone else to hear and, picking up her long blue skirt, she fled across the floor.

Dick watched her go, relief and distress almost equal on his pink face.

George stayed where he was. He stayed there during the playing of two dances and he had just begun to be really worried when Marjorie reappeared. She looked very tidy and completely controlled, unlike the little girl who had run off the floor. She smiled at him and he drew her hand through the crook of his arm. "Want to go home, honey?"

"No, thank you," said Marjorie.

"Want to dance with me some more?"

"Please," said Marjorie.

They stayed on to the end and then Marjorie went and got her coat. Lee and Bob were on the steps outside and for a moment George thought of offering them a lift home, but reconsidered. He wasn't sure how Marjorie was feeling although she had seemed quite happy during the last dances with him. Maybe it hadn't been such a bad evening for her. After all, she had no previous standards to measure the dance by.

They drove home in silence. He wanted to ask her straight out, for his own reassurance, but all he could do was hope. When they got into the house he took off his coat and hat, laid them over a chair and then turned uncertainly to look at his daughter.

She was smiling, a really happy smile. It lit up her eyes. "Thank you for taking me," she said and suddenly she put her arms up and gave him a swift tight hug. "Oh, Daddy, I had the most *beautiful* time." She turned and ran up the stairs.

"Well!" said George. The whole dreadful weight of the evening rolled off him.

And that was the moment when the phone rang.

He almost didn't answer it because it was far too late to talk to anyone and then he hurried to it, realizing the call might be urgent.

"George?" said Anita's voice.

Good Lord, he thought, but he said, "Hello there," very cheerfully because here was someone who could share his relief and pleasure.

Anita said, "George, Lee just got home. She told me all about it—about your taking Marjorie." She sounded terribly wrought up. "George, how *could* you?"

"How could I what?"

"Take that child to a dance that way!" It was a moment before he realized she was accusing him. "Oh, I know you meant well but, good heavens—! Why didn't you phone first and ask me? I could have told you."

"But, Anita, I don't see what—"

"Lee said that everyone was laughing at her. Marjorie's not a fool, George, she must have known. A girl doesn't go to a dance like that. With her *father*. Like a baby. You might at least have considered her feelings." She must have realized that she sounded too sharp. Her voice smoothed out. "It's not that I'm blaming you, George. It's—"

"But, Anita— Marjorie said she had a beautiful time. She said—"

Suddenly his voice trailed off. He stood there, staring at the telephone in his hand. Dismay and a sense of shock held him for a moment, and then he did something he had never done to anyone before in his life. He hung up, without apology, without explanation.

He turned and walked upstairs and he was barely halfway up before the phone started ringing again. He let it ring.

He walked to Marjorie's room, and the door was closed. He leaned against it, listening, and he heard what he had known he would hear from the moment he hung up the telephone.

He heard his daughter crying.

She wasn't noisy. They were long deep slow sobs, muffled against the pillow. They had a controlled quality about them. If he knocked on the door, they would stop at once.

He turned very slowly and walked downstairs. The phone had stopped ringing. He went into the living room and stood, hands in pockets, staring at the furniture. He and Eleanor had planned the room together, a long time ago now, and he hadn't changed anything.

It was Eleanor's daughter who was crying upstairs on her bed.

George knew what he wanted to do. He wanted to turn and go back to Marjorie. He wanted to take her in his arms and stroke her hair and comfort her. He wanted to tell his daughter that none of this mattered, that the flimsy world of social success wasn't what counted, that there were other values, infinitely more important—

He stopped himself.

Marjorie already knew what was important, knew it better than he did. It was Eleanor's daughter who was crying upstairs on her bed, but it was also Eleanor's daughter who had put her arms around his neck and said, "Oh, Daddy, I had the most beautiful time."

The evening had hurt her. She would not let it hurt her father too.

Dismayed, he realized how completely he had failed her. He had wanted to see his daughter shine, he had been impatient with her inability to attract partners. He had wanted Marjorie to be successful as Lee was successful. He had admired Lee with her pretty ways, and he had been humiliatingly willing for Marjorie to learn from them.

He was ashamed of himself.

His daughter was crying upstairs now because she had been a failure in the world where Lee did everything so well. Eventually, he knew, she would stop her tears. She would blow her nose and go sensibly to bed. Tonight's world had been Lee's, not hers. Her enchanted hopes for it were all gone, and she would just accept that now, this grown-up child of his, and let them go. There were other worlds. In the end, she would possess something that Lee could never hope for.

Meantime, she was crying, and he would be very careful never to let her know that he had stood outside her door and listened.

He walked upstairs to his bedroom. It was a lonely place, but tonight it was not quite so lonely as usual. Eleanor was less far away than she had ever been, and George Ashe was thinking of the very lucky man who would, some day, marry Eleanor's daughter.

About the Author

B. J. Chute began her literary career as a writer of boys' sports stories. She sold her first adult short story in 1942, and since then her stories have appeared in nearly all major magazines. She has published four novels, as well as two collections of short stories. In 1960 her novel, *Greenwillow,* became a Broadway musical.

B. J. Chute is a past president of the American center of P.E.N., the international writers' organization. She was one of the fiction judges in the National Book Awards for 1960, and in 1964 became an Associate in English at Barnard College.

Born in Minneapolis, Minnesota, B. J. Chute grew up in the country. Now she and her sister Marchette, also a writer, share an apartment in New York City.

DOWN IN THE REEDS BY THE RIVER

Victoria Lincoln

Why are we never prepared, why do all the books and all the wisdom of our friends avail us nothing in the final event? How many deathbed scenes we have read, how many stories of young love, of marital infidelity, or cherished ambition fulfilled or defeated. There is nothing that can happen to us that has not happened again and again, that we have not read over a thousand times, closely, carefully, accurately recorded; before we are fully launched on life, the story of the human heart has been opened for us again and again with all the patience and skill of the human mind. But the event, when it comes, is never anything like the description; it is strange, infinitely strange and new, and we stand helpless before it and realize that the words of another convey nothing, nothing.

And still we cannot believe that personal life is, in its essence, incommunicable. We, too, having lived the moment, are impelled to convey it, to speak the words so honest in intent, so false in the final effect. Now, after so many years, I want to tell you about Mr. deRocca, although it is a queer story—not a story at all, really, only an incident in the life of a young girl—simply to show that it was not what you would have expected. It was not like the books or the whispered, ugly confidence that you remember from your school days; it was quite, quite different. I want to tell you, although I know from the outset that I shall fail, as we all fail.

But now that I come up to it, I hesitate. It should have been evil, frightening, all wrong; of course it should. It should have been the repellent accident that can queer an emotional development for years to come. And still, when it was happening, it was not like that at all.

I was fourteen, a wiry, red-headed, unimaginative little tomboy, fond of sand-lot baseball. My parents were dead, killed in an accident a year before, and I lived with an aunt and uncle in Braeburn Heights, a suburb of a small city in Kansas. Bereft, rudely transplanted from the life I had known—a happy-go-lucky life in the brown hills of California—I was lonely beyond words. I had grown up in the careless warmth of love, and for my Aunt Elsa's genuine, if worried, kindness I could feel nothing but ingratitude. The house was strange, the neighboring children were strange, with their neat, pretty bedrooms, their queer talk of dates, and formals, and going steady. I felt dry and hard and empty inside myself, day after day. I used to take my bicycle and ride out into the country, but the country was strange, too, and ugly to my eyes, all flat and dull.

And then, one day, I found White Creek Row. It was the town's Hooverville, a row of shanties between the creek and the railroad, little huts like the playhouse that I had built back in the hills with the children of our Mexican gardener—a tragic, shocking, sordid shantytown, as I see it now. But to my enchanted eyes it was romantic and delightful and, more than that, comprehensible, as my aunt's house in Braeburn Heights was not.

It was in White Creek Row that, unknown to Aunt Elsa, I made my first real friends in Kansas. The squatters in the row were shy of me at first, as I was shy of the people in Braeburn Heights. My decent clothes, my bicycle, made me alien, an object for suspicion and resentment. And still, somehow or other, I managed to scrape an acquaintance with Posy Moreno, an acquaintance that grew into love.

She was a gentle creature with a mop of soft black curls piled high on her head and a womanliness, at sixteen, that made me feel, for the first time, glad that I, too, was growing near to womanhood. She lived in the last shanty in the row with her little brother Manuel, and next door was Mrs. Grimes, her self-appointed duenna. She was very proud of Mrs. Grimes' watchfulness.

"Me, I'm never chasing with the feller," she used to say, "but if I was to chase with the feller, Mrs. Grimes she's knock me down, you bet. She's not let anybody get fresh with Posy Moreno."

"I wouldn't want anyone bossing me like that," I said once. And Posy, lifting her head in the pride of her womanhood, replied, "You not need. You just a kid." But as we became better acquainted she treated me less and less like a kid.

Through our long afternoons on the creek bank, listening to her conversation, I would sit spellbound, infinitely flattered that she considered me a girl and not a child, feeling within myself a new softening, a shy preening, a tremulousness delicious and unfamiliar.

Besides Posy and Manuel, the only other child on the row was Chuck Hansen, who was twelve. I liked him, too, and I used to let him ride my bicycle while Posy and I talked. I could never hear enough about life in the row, and the people who lived in it. They had everything, I used to tell myself, everything that anybody could want, for I was too young to understand the need for security, for dignity. They had everything, and they had got it all free—even a church.

Mrs. Grimes had wanted the church, and Mr. deRocca, who had been a carpenter in Italy, had built it for her, although he was a freethinker and had accompanied every hammer blow, so Posy told me, with a lot of bad talk about religion being made up by rich people to keep poor people quiet.

How I wished I might have been there to see him, sitting on the roof, pounding down the shingles that were made from flattened tin cans, with his delicate, hard little old hands, and shouting all the time, "Opium of the people. You getta pie in a sky when you die!" The church even had a piano, with a good many keys that still sounded nice and loud, if not true, and Mrs. Grimes played gospel hymns on it by ear.

Mr. deRocca would not go to the prayer meetings. He lived in the best shanty in the row, and in his front yard was a beautiful American flag laid out in bits of broken brick and slate and white stones. I admired it intensely and used to stop before his house, the better to enjoy it, but Posy would shy off and draw me away, throwing up her head with a sort of wild-pony elegance. "Better we're not hanging around here," she would say. "Mr. deRocca, he's liking the girl."

I did not understand. Would anyone so old want a wife as young as Posy, I wondered. It must be that, I decided, when Posy told me that Mrs. Grimes had not let Mr. deRocca help with the building of Posy's shack. I supposed they thought it would not be fair to encourage him. But I saw no reason why the caution should also apply to me. I was charmed by the little I had managed to see of Mr. deRocca. He seemed to be a very clever, very nice old man.

And now I come to my story, and it is hard to tell. It is hard to tell because I should have been so different. Perhaps there were undertones that I have forgotten. That is likely, for the memory has a curiously clear and classic air, quite unlike life as I have since found it—the nymph and the old satyr frozen in attitudes of timeless innocence under the box elders by the creek bank, the sacred grove where liquid Peneus was flowing and all dark Tempe lay. And still, still, I remember it like that. If there was fear, if there was guilt, they came later.

One afternoon, Chuck Hansen met me on the cinder track, looking wistful. "I don't guess you'll want to stay today, Connie," he said. "Mrs. Grimes and Posy, they went uptown." He rubbed the handlebars of my bicycle with his hands, hard, as if he were fondling a horse. "Guess you won't have much to stick around for," he said humbly.

How nice he was, I thought, never teasing.

"Well, listen, Chuck," I said. "I'm tired, a little. I'll go down and walk around a while and sit on the creek bank."

His grin made me feel warm and pleasant. I began to saunter along the front of the row. Mr. deRocca was sitting on a packing case by his door, eating an onion. His face, lifted to the sky, wore the blank, peaceful expression of one enjoying the quiet of a village street after a procession has passed, the look of remembering in quietness.

I came along very slowly, watching Mr. deRocca from the corners of my eyes. He wore a plaid flannel shirt, ragged and, of course, unironed, but fairly clean, and the neck was unbuttoned. I noticed how the flesh under his chin was firm and didn't hang down in wattles, and the cords in his neck didn't stick out. He looked harder and nicer than other old men.

How old was he, really? About fifty, I should guess now, looking back; maybe a little less. But if I had known it then, it would not have changed my picture of him at all. Fifty to eighty in those days were all of a piece in my mind. Mr. deRocca was an old man. And he was nice. As I came very close, I realized with a sudden throb of excitement that he had been watching me all along, just as I had been watching him. Watching me and waiting for the moment to speak, just as I had been, with him. I turned, pretending to have seen him for the first time. I smiled at him. The white teeth gleamed in the thin, brown face; the elegant, small, brown paw that held the onion described a vast semicircle of greeting. "Hi, kid," he said. "Looka for da Posy? She's a not home."

I did not answer. I had realized, quite abruptly, that it was the sight of him sitting down there below me, fully as much as Chuck's longing hands rubbing the handlebars, that made up my mind for me up there on the embankment, and I turned shy, hoping that he would not guess it.

"I always like to look at that flag, Mr. deRocca," I said.

"Come on in a yard," he said. "Looka good. It's a pretty, hey?"

We stood together, eying the charming sight in a sort of shared pride. He pulled out another packing case from the corner of the house and waved me to it with the flattering charm of a courtier.

"Please to sit," he said. "Scusa." He went in the house for a second and returned, extending his hand with the same grave courtesy. "You like-a onion?"

I looked at it dubiously. Father had disliked salads, saying firmly that hay was for God-damned Frenchmen, and Aunt Elsa's were of the pineapple, cream cheese, and mayonnaise school. Raw onions were new to me, and alarming. But it was so lovely, being treated like a lady, that I could not disappoint him.

I took it and bit into it gingerly. The sharp, pungent, biting juice ran over my tongue, the firm, fleshy layers crunched between my teeth in a stinging, breathtaking ecstasy of delicious pain.

"Oh!" I cried in sincere delight. "It's good!" Then, with the snobbery of the young guest who does not wish his host to think him ignorant of the wines he is offered, I added, "It's one of the best onions I ever ate."

"Sure," he said proudly. "Sure, you bet it's a good, it's a fine. I grow."

I regarded him happily, rejoicing in his kingly acceptance of the compliment, so unlike the mincing, genteel self-depreciation which, of all the mannered compulsions of the Heights, I found most unfamiliar and most dismal.

I went on with my compliments, sincerely, but also eager for the continuing pleasure of his openness. "You have a wonderful house," I said. "The church is wonderful, too. You're a fine carpenter."

His eyes glowed and he swayed his head from side to side, like someone keeping time to music. "You bet I'm a good," he replied. "I'm a learn in a Old Country, worka slow, take-a pain, think for the job, for looka pretty, not think for hurry up, getta money. I'm a good like nobody's business."

"I should think you'd get lots of jobs," I said, "and be rich."

He shrugged. "Bad a time," he said. "Everywhere bad a time. Smart a man everywhere hungry, no work. Someday come a good time." He finished the onion and wiped his thin lips on the backs of his neat little fingers. "Someday, different time, all be good, not graba, graba, be man and man together, not dog and dog. First a big fight, maybe, then all be good."

I remembered something we had studied in social science. I leaned forward, trying to look intelligent and grown up. "You mean a revolution?" I said. "Are you a Communist, Mr. deRocca?"

"Pah!" he replied. "Not!" He spat to one side, to emphasize his attitude. Then, with a flashing, all-embracing smile: "Lots good in de Comunista, lots smart. I read, I like, good. Only alla time boss, boss. Boss so bad like we got here, now. I'm a no like all a time boss. I am Anarchista, me."

"What's that?" I asked.

"Everyone's treat everyone else right. No push around, no boss. People no gotta lot of stuff, graba, graba. No law, no boss, everyone a same. Treata them right, they treata you right. All good."

It sounded lovely.

"What do you call that? Anarchista? I guess I'm Anarchista, too," I said.

He threw both arms wide, embracing me in the universal fellowship. "That's a fine. You smart a kid."

Master and disciple, we sat happily together in the blissful country of utopian anarchy, regarding the flag of America spread out at our feet with absent, gently admiring eyes. Gradually, the conversation took a personal turn.

"You name a Constansia?"

"Constance."

"Pretty name," he said. "Pretty name for pretty girl. Nice when a pretty girl have a pretty name."

No one had told me I was pretty since my mother died. I was grateful to him, but unbelieving. "I have awful red hair," I said.

"Pretty," he said. "Pretty hair, pretty eye, pretty shape. How old?"

"Going on fifteen."

He smiled, as if I could not possibly have been a nicer age, as if it were a peculiar grace and wisdom in me to be going on fifteen.

"Last year, da little kid," he said. "Next year, da woman, look at da fella, think for da fella. Now she not know what she think—that right?"

I was deeply struck with the truth of his words. It was what I had been feeling in my inarticulate way all the time I was sitting with Posy on the creek bank, admiring her womanly young beauty, listening to her sternly virtuous, so very sex-conscious conversation, hoping that she did not still think of me as just a little kid.

I looked earnestly at Mr. deRocca sitting on his packing case, as if I could discover in the glowing, friendly eyes the source of his remarkable understanding. He was old, but I thought suddenly that he was handsome, as handsome as my father had been. His features were so sharp and delicate, his body so fine-boned, the shoulders so narrow, compared with the Mexicans with whom I unconsciously classed him. A fleeting wonder passed through my mind if all Italians were like him, so little and handsome and wise.

He held out his hand toward me, palm up and slightly cupped, almost as if he were coaxing a tame bird with seed. "That right?" he said again, quite soft.

I was surprised at my voice when I answered. It was unfamiliar—low and a little unsteady. "That's right," I said.

He stood up, smiling more than ever. "Come on down a creek bank," he said. "I show you where I gotta good catfish net. Other guy wait to fish, watch, work. Me, I sit and they come."

Thinking back, remembering, I wonder for the first time if he spoke in any conscious analogy. I do not believe that he did.

I followed Mr. deRocca trustfully down the creek bank, under the box-elder trees. At the water's edge, he turned and looked at me, and I saw the changed look in his eyes. It was as if the door had opened and I were looking upon a landscape that was both strange and familiar. I glanced around me, and I saw that the box elders grew thick where we stood, that we were in a place that was private, sheltered from the eyes of the world. Suddenly, I understood everything that Posy had said. I knew what she meant when she said, "He's liking the girl."

"Show me the net," I said nervously.

His eyes smiled at me, reassuring, his voice quieted me. "Pretty soon," he said. "Right down here." But he made no move toward going on. Instead, he put out a lean, brown paw and touched my head. "Pretty," he said. "Pretty hair."

His hand slipped down my back and around my waist, the fingers firm and hard against me, warm through my cotton dress. And again he paused, his eyes still smiling with that same gentle reassurance.

He was old at the game, I see now, and grown wise in

method, wise and patient. If he had hurried, if he had let me see his eagerness, I should have been terribly frightened, I should have run away crying. I should have run away full of fear and hate, and the fear and hate would have lived in me a long time.

But he stood, smiling at me, until I was used to his arm, his hand, feeling it not as a sexual advance but as warm, human affection in my body that was aching for human affection, for the demonstrative love on which I had thrived through a warm, loving childhood. He was quiet until I felt my fear dissolve in gratitude for the kindness of his arm, his firm, affectionate hand.

It was easy, then, for him to turn me against him, to hold me firm and close, stroking my hair, firm and close against him, waiting till his accustomed, patient hands should tell him that I was ready for more.

I knew that I must be doing something bad, and still I could not feel that it was bad yet, not yet. And his slowness made me confident that I was free to decide if it was really bad, that he would let me go quickly the minute I thought it had begun to be bad. It still did not seem bad when he kissed me, or when his kissing changed and made me feel all soft and strange inside, or when his hands began to describe all the differences that the year had made in my body, and to tell me silently that they were beauties, richness, a bounty of which to be proud.

Once he made a little motion to draw me down in the thick grass, and I had the sense to be frightened, but he felt it at once and waited, and I waited, too, sure that I would know when I should run away, growing softer and stranger by the moment, forgetting everything outside me. I was wholly lost when I heard Posy's shrill voice calling my name, and heard her pushing through the branches down the creek bank.

Mr. deRocca let me go and dropped to his knees at the water's edge. "Like a this," he said. "I'm a tie right here, da fish swim right in. Some net, hey?"

He looked over his shoulder and saw Posy. She was white and out of breath. "Connie!" she cried. "I don't know where you are. I'm scaring." She snatched at my hand, too relieved, too wrought up, to look at my revealing face. "Come along outa here," she said. Then, remembering her manners, "Hello, Mr. deRocca."

She yanked me back to the row. "You crazy," she scolded me. "What you think, you go down there with deRocca? I'm telling you he's liking the girl."

"You said I was just a kid. That's what you said," I repeated.

"I know," she said. "Well, I'm crazy. Just as soon Chuck he tell me you down here, I'm knowing I'm crazy. You no kid, not for looks. No more. Was a little while ago, now no more. Mother of God, I'm scaring." She paused, momentarily suspicious. "What you going down in there with deRocca for?"

"He said he was going to show me his catfish net."

"Ha, I bet! You poor kid, you got no sense. What he say? He talk dirty?"

"No," I replied with perfect truth. "He talked just as nice as you and Mrs. Grimes."

"Thanks God," said Posy, over and over again. "Thanks God."

In the unpleasant shock of nearly being caught out, all the new feeling that I had learned—the lovely, soft, flowing, flowering openness—was driven back in me, and the present moment closed about it so completely that the afternoon might have been lived years before, or not at all, by anything I felt in myself. Instead, I was troubled by an unwilling anger against Posy, as if she were making a disproportionate fuss.

Something of this she must have felt, or perhaps she now decided that my unwary innocence had been scolded long enough, for she took my hand, smiling again, as if, for her, too, the incident had suddenly dropped away out of sight.

"Come now," she said. "Is early yet, you don't got to be going home, come now down to the house. We don't say nothing from this to Mrs. Grimes."

"No, Posy, no, I've got to get home," I said.

All the way home, I pedalled hard, as if I were very late—so hard that there was no room in me for anything else. Even before I saw the letters lying on the hall rug, where they had fallen from the mail slit in the door, I could tell from the silence that the house was empty. I stood in the sun that poured in at the open doorway, absorbing gratefully the quality of an empty house. I had not realized at all, as I forced myself home, faster and faster, how I would need, once I had got there, to be alone. I shut my eyes and sighed heavily, feeling the silence, the aloneness all through me like a merciful, unexpected blessing.

What had happened that afternoon, what had really happened? It wasn't only that I had let Mr. deRocca kiss me and touch me like that. It was something that had happened in me. There was something in me—and in the world, too—that I had never known was there before, something powerful and lovely, something powerful and new.

I stood there alone in the quiet house, in the sunshine, with my eyes closed. "I wish," I thought slowly, "that Posy hadn't come. I wish . . ."

Suddenly, I knew that I had begun to be bad right there in Mr. deRocca's front yard, before we had ever gone down to the creek. I knew that I had been bad all along, terribly bad. Fear and guilt rose in me like a storm, shaking my body until my teeth chattered and I had to sit on the bottom step of the stairs and lean against the wall to hold myself still.

"If Posy knew," I thought, "if she knew about me, if she knew what I did, I'd die. I should die, I'd die."

Aunt Elsa found me like that when she came in a few minutes later. "Why, Connie!" she cried. "What is it, dear? You're sick."

"I got a chill," I said. "Just right now."

"Let me hang up my coat, dear," she said, "and I'll get you right into bed. Why, you poor baby!"

I let her help me up the stairs. I clung to her motherly warmth all the way, hungry for it, like a child that has been lost and found again. "Oh, Aunt Elsa," I cried. "I'm so glad you're home." And her gentle voice soothed me again and again. "There, dear, there. You're going to be all right. There, poor little girl. Aunt Elsa'll put you to bed. Yes, she will. Of course she will."

In the complex agony of the moment, I was broken wide open. She's real, too, I thought in slow wonder; Aunt Elsa is real, too. She was my mother's sister.

I caught at her light, smooth dress, hiding my face in it. She smelled nice, clean and fresh with a light perfume. I let my head fall against her shoulder, and it was soft and firm, comforting, comforting.

"Oh, Aunt Elsa," I cried, wondering because it was true, because it had not been true before, at all, and now it was wholly true. "Aunt Elsa, I love you."

That is the story, and that is all. When I woke in the

morning, the ecstasy and the shame alike were gone. I had shut my mind upon them, as I had learned earlier to shut it upon grief and loss.

Oddly enough—for the defense mechanism seldom works that way—I still liked Mr. deRocca. Apparently, his attempted seduction had been quite impersonal, for, as I used to pass his yard, walking up the row to Posy's house in the warm, dusty August afternoons, he would always wave his little paw at me and say, "Hi ya, kid," amiably, but with no attempt to detain me.

For my own part, I always felt a tingling as I passed him; not enough to be unpleasant—just a sort of shy, quickening self-consciousness. It made me avoid his face as I replied, "Hello, Mr. deRocca." My voice, as I spoke, was always a trifle breathless. I told myself that it was funny how I hardly remembered that afternoon by the creek at all. But as I passed his house, I always stood up straight and moved slowly, and tried to look grown up.

About the Author

Victoria Lincoln, a native of Fall River, Massachusetts, graduated from Radcliffe College. She now lives outside of Baltimore when not traveling with her husband, a professor who teaches in this country and England. She is the mother of three grown children.

Victoria Lincoln's short stories have appeared in such magazines as *Harper's, The New Yorker, Atlantic Monthly, Cosmopolitan, Good Housekeeping,* and *Redbook.* She is the author of eight novels, among them *February Hill* and *A Dangerous Innocence.* Her most recent book is *Charles,* a novel of Charles Dickens.

BOTTLE NIGHT

Jean Fritz

My last year in China I was sent to an American board ing school where I was assigned to the drafty second floor of the girls' dormitory—specifically, to the shorter end of the floor reserved for the younger boarders, twelve- and thirteen-year-olds like myself. At the other end of our floor were the high school girls, glorious and grown up, from whom we were separated by a white door bisecting the hall. Since the door was never locked, it was evidently not intended as a barrier; it seemed to be there simply in recognition of the difference in the life being led at the two ends of the hall. On our side of the door we went to bed earlier and wore flat heels. We applied pomade instead of lipstick and, when we went to the movies, which was rare indeed, we went all together and sat in a long row with a teacher, straight as a bookend, at either side.

There was only one night of the year when, had we been given the choice, we on our side of the door would not have changed places with those on the other side. It was the one time when the door itself was important in more than just a symbolic way. We could never have done it if the door had not been there, providing us with a ready target. We threw at it. Once a year, on the night before Christmas vacation, the younger girls lined up at one end of the hall and threw empty milk bottles against the high school door. Each would hurl a bottle and shout out a dedication like a toast. To the end of some pet peeve, to the rise of a current hero, to the downfall of an enemy. All the accumulated frustrations and daydreams of months of dormitory living went flying down the hall with each of those bottles. I can remember liberations swelling within me as I awaited my turn, tingling in my arms as I picked up a bottle, and finally bursting all bounds as the bottle left my hand. We would stand, then, fascinated through the splintering and tinkling as the mound of broken glass at the bottom of the door grew higher; at the end we would cheer. When all the bottles were gone the high school door would be flung open, and we would be invited to the other side for ginger ale and cookies. That was, of course, a happy aftermath, but it was definitely an aftermath. The great thing about that night was the bottles.

Even now it seems wonderful that there could have been such a night, that teachers who all year long seemed ordinary enough could have had the humanity, Christmas after Christmas, to have overlooked the bottle breaking. I suppose it was the secrecy that made it possible. As long as the teachers officially knew nothing ahead of time, they could close their doors on the floor below and pretend not to hear. Sensing this, we took pains to wrap new bottles in newspaper before carrying them into the dormitory and once there, to hide them out of sight—in dirty-clothes hampers, desk drawers, empty suitcases. Even so, there was always the threat that this year some teacher might revert to type and come stamping up the steps to put an end to the whole business. This added a certain amount of zest to the proceeding; but fortunately the year that I was there even Madame Marchette, the French teacher who was able to smell lights burning after hours—even she kept out of our way.

Collecting bottles was the one thing we six girls in the younger hall had completely in common, although now as I think back, it seems an unlikely interest for us to have shared. Certainly no one would have expected the Graff sisters, Mary and Alice, to have been interested. They were plain, broad-faced girls whose thoughts and clothes both seemed to have been tailored by some well-meaning Ladies Aid Society in the Middle West. Daughters of missionaries stationed so far in the interior that they couldn't hope to go home for Christmas vacation, Mary and Alice had not even the same incentive for celebration the rest of us had. Still, they collected bottles and hid them, I remember, on a bookshelf the front of which they covered completely with a map of the Holy Land. It was the only impious thing they ever did and for that I forgave them their many moralistic stories. I almost, but not quite, forgave them the story of Uncle Howard.

The first time I heard the story I was sitting on Mary's narrow white bed under a framed quotation which in fantastically curled penmanship declared, "There is nothing either good or bad, but thinking makes it so." It was not until years later that I understood the quotation. Somehow at that time, instead of taking the quotation as a whole, I was carried away by the last part—"thinking makes it so." I interpreted it to mean that one's every casual thought might start off a chain of reactions for which he could be held accountable. It was an uncomfortable sentiment and I wondered that Mary and Alice could live with it. They sat that day on the other bed across the small, almost bare room, their feet tucked up under them as usual. Whenever they sat on a bed, I noticed, they pulled their feet up off the floor, but they never looked comfortable. They looked awkward. The rest of their bodies hunched forward in dark cotton dresses that were always a little too big at the shoulder seams and their faces, headlighted by thick tortoise-shell glasses, looked disproportionately large.

We were talking about Tamara, the Russian girl in the next room whose unsavory character was a rich source of conversation. Tamara had told another lie and in the course of her righteous indignation, Alice was reminded of her Uncle Howard. Uncle Howard, she explained, was her mother's younger brother who as a boy had indulged in small untruths from time to time—only, however, as the need arose and so was not to be compared to Tamara and her more vicious deceptions. Yet even he received his Punishment. Alice shivered under her brown shoulder seams and hugged her knees closer; still, she didn't try to name the source of Uncle Howard's punishment. It was clear that even through many repetitions she had never dared look that closely at the story. From the very beginning, her voice contained the frightening knowledge of something unnamable.

One summer night, it seemed, Uncle Howard had eaten a large bowl of strawberries reserved for the hired man. In itself, that wasn't so bad, but when asked, he had lied about it. And it was a fatal lie. Afterward, he had gone upstairs and as usual turned off the light at the switch near his door and walked across the dark room to his bed. I could picture him in oversize pajamas, stumbling innocently across the cool floorboards of that

Indiana farmhouse, his head thrust forward in the same nearsighted attitude of his nieces. It must have been a moonless night, dark enough to have lulled Uncle Howard into a false sense of security that the day and its misdeeds were both over.

He stopped beside the bed to pull the spread away from the pillow. He was leaning over, feeling for the far side of the spread when suddenly a hand shot out from under the bed and grabbed him by the ankle. It didn't hold him; it just grabbed and let go. The terrifying thing about it was that *there was no one under the bed.* The lights were turned on, the family aroused, but no one was found. But it did happen. There was a mysterious swirl on Uncle Howard's ankle to prove it. It looked like the partial imprint of an enormous finger or thumb and it stayed on Uncle Howard's ankle to haunt him the rest of his life.

The trouble was, it haunted me too. Generally I took little stock in the stories the Graff sisters had inherited from their God-fearing parents, yet after this one I found myself at night jumping into my bed from the middle of my room. I would turn out the light and give myself a running start so that my feet would not need to touch the floor within three feet of the bed. Each night I was determined I would cover the distance soberly (after all, *I* had not told a lie), but once the room was dark, the space under the bed gaped so ominously that I had to leap clear of it. I got so I hated Uncle Howard, and I decided, when the time came, to dedicate one of my bottles specifically to his downfall. I thought of Mary and Alice, their feet pulled up onto their beds, and I hoped they would do the same.

My roommate, Nancy Stockwell, was unmoved by Uncle Howard, but that was not surprising. In many ways Nancy didn't really belong on our side of the door at all. She was one of those girls one so often found those days in the Orient who matured early, ready at thirteen or fourteen not just for boy-girl relationships but for something on a much more complicated level which she referred to grandly as Life, which, it was clear, took place, far away from the American School and bore little resemblance to life as I had known it in the lower case. I adored Nancy. For one thing, she had a black velvet dress and two white satin blouses. She had a Victrola that wound up slowly with almost a sensuous movement and it played only the latest numbers. Through Nancy I learned how important it was to know the latest music, the latest fashions, the latest slang from the States. She never called it America the way I did; she always spoke of "the States" and, somehow, the way she said it, it didn't sound like the same country. I thought of my grandmother in Pennsylvania and the way I remembered her flapping her white apron at a chicken trespassing on her porch, and I knew for a certainty that my grandmother lived in *America.* "The States," like Life, was something altogether different, out of my range of experience.

Still, I could pretend. I could make tentative, imaginary little excursions into the world that Nancy lived in, and in order to do so I, too, began talking about "the States." I learned all the words of "Yes, Sir, That's My Baby." I said, "And how!" whenever remotely appropriate. That phrase, as I remember, had just drifted across the Pacific and I used it intemperately. It was beautiful. So simple, but it *implied* so much.

Most important of all, however, I fell in love with Jack Barron, a freshman in the day school who was supposed to smile like Clark Gable. I did not hope for anything from Jack in return; it was enough that he existed (even in the distance), that he smiled like a movie star (even a little), and that he gave me something to talk about. When I planned to dedicate half my supply of bottles to Jack and the prayer that he look my way, it was an extravagant gesture in what I believed was the direction of sophistication.

Gundred was the only one of us who did not seem to be collecting. When I said that all the younger girls collected bottles, I forgot about Gundred. In the beginning of the year we could forget about her and we often did. She was a frail, wraithlike Swedish girl whose relatives were all so far away that she had not seen anyone who really loved her for over two years. During this time, according to those who had known her longest, she had withdrawn further and further into herself; her body had become thinner and her skin more transparent. The only thing sturdy now about Gundred was the sound of her name. I remember her standing at the bathroom door with her faded pink Japanese kimono wrapped anxiously about her. She would look inside to see if anyone else was there and unless she could be alone with all six washbasins, she would flutter back to her room and close her door.

There was no reaching Gundred. The Graffs and Nancy and I all tried half-heartedly from time to time but she only trembled and withdrew further. Somehow I felt that if I could ever interest her in the bottles, it would be her salvation, and later when I was blaming myself for so much, I was sorry that I had not tried harder. It was her lips that stopped us. Whenever you talked to her for any length of time, her lips would begin to turn blue, the way a swimmer's do when he stays too long in the water. So we left her alone and sometimes even tried to find ways of blaming her for her own suffering so that we would not need to feel the burden of pity. Just once in the beginning we took up for her in her first encounter with Tamara.

The morning bell had just rung and we were all shuffling sleepily into the hall in our pajamas, clutching our towels and toothbrushes, when we saw Tamara. She was squatting stark naked in the hall, peering through the keyhole of Gundred's door. We were well enough accustomed to the sight of the nude Tamara. She was too pleased over her maturing figure to cover it more than necessary, but today there was something different about her. Every line of her short, square body was taut with a purpose we could not imagine. A line of sunlight, sifting in through the window at the end of the hall, turned white as it hit her and flickered across her back as if it had become charged with tension it found there. We, too, seemed to have been caught in the same current. We stopped behind Tamara and we waited—we didn't know for what.

Suddenly Tamara jumped to her feet and threw open the door. She stepped forward a pace into Gundred's room and threw back her head and laughed, a shrill laugh shot with venom. In front of her stood Gundred exposed at exactly the right moment. Her pink Japanese kimono lay still across her bed; her thin white cotton nightgown lay in a useless pool around her feet. I shall never forget the look that passed over Gundred—not just over her face but over her entire body as she crumbled to her knees in an effort to hide herself. But Gundred without clothes was more naked than I believed it possible for anyone to be. Cowering on the floor, she looked almost as if she had been turned inside out. Blue veins ran down the surface of her back; her ribs seemed about to break through thin spots in her skin. I had the feeling that if I stepped any closer, I would hear her heart beat.

We managed to get Gundred's door closed and Tamara, hissing with insults, into her own room. We stood, then, for a moment and looked at each other. Alice was the first to recover. She shook her toothbrush at Tamara's door.

"She needs to be taught the fear of the Lord!" She spoke with such authority that suddenly, as if the clouds had parted, we knew what we had to do.

Five minutes later we were dressed and gathered beside Tamara's door, waiting for her to come out. When she did, she was dressed in her bright red silk, her patent leather belt swung low on her hips. Her three black spit-curls lay in graduating sizes across her forehead, and her arms rattled with multicolored bracelets. In one beautifully coordinated movement we fell upon her. Nancy and I each took a leg; Mary and Alice, strong in the knowledge they were agents of the Lord, took her arms. Together we carried her into the bathroom and held her under the cold shower until her red silk dress dripped pink, until her three spit-curls were washed into her eyes, until she had divested herself of every oath in all three languages—Russian, Chinese, and English. Then we left her and went to breakfast. I believe we really thought that justice having been done, the episode was ended.

When we came back upstairs, we found Tamara in bed and Madame Marchette in attendance. Tamara in pink pajamas, her spit-curls in place, was sitting upright, her fingers pointed at us as we started past her door.

"Stop them!" she screamed. "They are the ones."

We were the ones, we were the ones, she repeated. We had kicked her and scratched her and called her foul names. We had held her under freezing water until she had caught pneumonia. She pulled the covers up and coughed into her pillow. In the end we had ripped her clothes so that she had to go back to her room part-naked. And for no reason. For no reason at all.

Tamara's voice came out scratchily as if, in order to reach us, it had to be dragged painfully over rough surfaces. To further this impression, she began then to use the stilted phraseology of the White Russian, fumbling so pathetically for words that her handicap seemed more than a language handicap. Madame Marchette patted her hand.

"And it is impossible to believe. Who was the one who commenced all this? All this devilness." Tamara broke her sentences into smaller and smaller fragments so that she could enjoy them longer. "This girl looks so weak. So poor in her body. Ah. She is not. She deceives. She is strong. Like a coolie." She looked slyly at her open door where we stood, transfixed. "The largest punishment would go to the leader. I think. She is not here. She still hides. The wicked girl who thought this in her head. Who turned on—what do you say—the water opener. To Gundred." She dipped her finger into her mouth and plastered saliva onto her forehead of curls.

The Graffs, Nancy, and I were each restricted to our room except for classes and meals for a week. Gundred was restricted for two weeks. After that I tampered no further with either justice or Tamara and I saved my feelings for Bottle Night.

By the middle of November I had seven bottles, a pathetically inadequate supply to take care of the suppressed resentments and desires I was rapidly accumulating. Bottles, usually acquired in infrequent off-campus excursions or begged from day students, were hard to come by. But not emotions. They were bred at incubator speed under the red brick walls of the American School. All institutions have in common a thick, shell-like quality that encases and isolates the life within it as carefully as an egg, propelling it in the same inevitable way to the fulfillment of its destiny. Were it not for the shell, an egg might conceivably turn out to be different and, I have often thought, were it not for the American School, things might have turned out differently for us in the younger girls' dormitory. As it was, each of us was hastened at an unnatural speed and without deflection down whatever path we happened to be on at the time we were separated from the world outside. Even from this vantage point, I cannot see myself clearly but I can see the others, each one becoming more rigidly Herself. Our days were laced with the same negligible threads of American history and mathematics, served up to us in the same thin brew of soup, yet it was not the sameness in us that the American School nurtured except in the most superficial ways; it was our inescapable differences.

I can see Nancy in her velvet dress growing persistently sleeker. The day she had lunch with a friend of her father's who was in the city on business, she borrowed lipstick and blue eye shadow, and when she came back, she reported snatches of conversation so startling that even she seemed unprepared for it. I can see Mary and Alice covertly watching Tamara, as if their faith hung in the balance, for signs that the Lord was doing the job on her that we had failed to do. And Tamara pursued her course more ruthlessly than ever. Her legs bulged with muscles; the hall rang with her poisonous laughter. She pinned pictures of nude women on Gundred's door and when she ran out of these, she drew nasty caricatures of Gundred picked bare as a chicken. In the morning as soon as the bell rang, she would shout to Gundred. "Gundred," she would call—only she always mangled the pronunciation. "Goondred," sometimes it would be, or

"Grundred," or even "Gunniedred." "It is time to take off the nightgown."

As for Gundred, poor thing, there was only one way for her to go. She became frailer and frailer until one morning when Tamara pushed open her door, she was not there and I had the feeling that perhaps she had simply melted away. At breakfast Madame Marchette told us that Gundred had been taken to the infirmary and that afternoon I went to see her—I suppose because in spite of myself Gundred scraped at my conscience in much the same way as Uncle Howard did.

The infirmary was a long, thin room closed off from everything I had ever known before. There must have been windows in it, although I can't place them now. A row of white iron beds protruded like teeth from one wall almost completely across to the other wall where the room ended abruptly. That wall was the one I remember. It stood, an unrelieved stretch of Arctic whiteness, and after a while it moved. I was once in one of those beds with a sore throat and I watched that wall creep up to me while Mrs. Murphy, who presided over that terrible room, went from bed to bed, treating the covers as if they were made of the same iron framework as the beds, locking the edges in place under the mattresses. Mrs. Murphy did not just reproduce the atmosphere of a hospital; she outdid it, and the sense of hopelessness that always possessed me as I walked into that room I know now was because, under Mrs. Murphy's stranglehold, the infirmary was no longer a segment of an institution. It was an institution in its own right, hiding subversively under cover of another institution. If one was sped to one's personal destiny in the larger institution of the school, one was accosted with it here. It lay, unavoidable before you, in the long white wall and it smelled like Lysol.

The afternoon that I went to see Gundred, I found Mrs. Murphy at her desk just outside the infirmary proper.

"I've come to see Gundred Nielson," I announced to Mrs. Murphy's starched white back. Back or front, it made no difference which side of Mrs. Murphy you addressed. She was all Nurse from all angles, so much so that the fact that she had anything as individual as a name came almost as a shock.

"I've come to see Gundred Nielson," I repeated.

Mrs. Murphy turned her other side. "Go right in," she said, but I didn't.

"Is she bad?" I asked.

"Oh, NO. Gundred is FINE." Mrs. Murphy spoke with an inflexible cheerfulness that built up to a climax in every sentence. "She'll be up and around again in a couple of days, as right as RAIN."

Gundred is FINE, I told myself as I looked down the long room and saw her, an almost imperceptible rise on the last bed.

As right as RAIN, I repeated as I pulled up a chair and sat down beside her, trying not to notice that her hands, limp on the blanket, were as white and useless-looking as the hands of the little paste figures that Chinese entertainers used to model at my birthday parties.

"Gundred," I said, "I've come to visit you. How are you feeling?"

Gundred was staring at the wall and she didn't look at me. "I don't hurt," she whispered tonelessly.

"You're going to be all right soon," I said and immediately I hated myself. I sounded just like Mrs. Murphy.

"Nancy has a new box of chocolates. They're the good kind with cherries in the middle. We'll save some for you. You'll be back in a couple of days."

I hitched my chair around so that the wall was more completely at my back. I talked and talked, dredging up silly irrelevancies, scooping out reassurances, and all the time the wall loomed up white behind me and Gundred, defenseless, lay before me.

I didn't want to look at Gundred. Her face, always pale, had faded to something even more colorless than it had been before. No, it had gone further than that. It looked wilted like a flower ready to have its head pinched off. I remembered how my mother would drop two aspirin tablets into a vase of drooping flowers and how I would watch them revive, standing straighter and straighter until they looked almost fresh again. Oh, I used to enjoy this little reprieve she gave them. Now, I thought, if I could only say something that was important enough, it might work on Gundred like the aspirin tablets. If I could just lean across her bed and say something important. Perhaps I could have talked to her about the bottles then, but I didn't. I just chattered.

Finally, in despair over the sickening sound of my own voice, I stood up.

"Gundred," I said, "you are going to be FINE." And I walked out of the room, past Mrs. Murphy's white back, into the sunshine.

I took a deep breath and I was surprised at how cold and clean the air was, free of all the cooking smells that in warmer weather rise from China in a vast mist. Only three more weeks until Christmas vacation, I reminded myself. Tomorrow I will take Gundred one of my bottles. Tomorrow I will do better.

I was so busy trying to blow my breath out into different shapes and watching it condense (always in the same shape) that I didn't hear footsteps behind me. I was not aware that anyone was there at all, not aware that anything was about to happen, aware only of the breath in my own body, when all at once someone came along beside me and instead of passing, fell into step with me.

"Hello," he said.

It was Jack Barron, and I was not ready for him. He had never spoken to me before and now I was not ready at all.

"Hello," I echoed.

"I saw you coming out of the infirmary. Been taking some of Mother Murphy's pink pills for pale people?" In those days at the American School this was considered amusing. Clearly it called for a rejoinder, but there I was in my brown oxfords. What could I say?

"No, I was visiting."

"You mean you got out of there without even having your temperature taken?" Here was another cue.

By this time we had walked out of the passageway and were at the football field. I was silent. The only sound was the click of the hockey sticks. They clicked with such assurance. Beneath me my feet spread out like two sleeping turtles.

"I went to see Gundred Nielson," I said.

On the far side of the football field, across the clicking hockey sticks, the main gate opened. Dick Carmichael, another day student and Jack's best friend, walked in, heading around the field toward us. I looked anxiously at Jack; yes, he had seen him. In another minute he would leave me and join Dick. Unless I could say something interesting and hold him here. Unless I could think of something startling to say.

"They say that Gundred Nielson is going to die," I said.

Click went the hockey sticks. Click-click-click. Jack dropped his eyes until they were fixed directly on my feet.

"Who says?" he asked.

"Mrs. Murphy," I lied.

Jack continued to stare at my shoes. "Gosh," he said, "that's too bad. Gosh." Dick Carmichael rounded the football field and went into the classroom building.

Suddenly Jack looked up and gave me a Clark Gable smile, both unsettling and undeserved. "Say, how are you doing on your bottle supply? If I brought some from home, could you use a few?"

I did not even have the presence of mind to say, "And how!" "Oh, yes, yes," I said, foolish as any second-grader.

That evening I sat on the edge of my bed and sorted out the afternoon, piece by piece—the ups and downs, the failings, and the one triumph—the one glorious triumph that somehow in spite of my inadequacies had really happened. Nothing else mattered, I told myself. The rest I could shuffle out of my mind. Jack Barron had spoken to me and would speak to me again. I got up and looked at myself in the mirror with awe. At my boyish bob falling over my forehead, yet retreating so hastily from the rest of my head that my ears were set adrift like two sea shells on either side of my face. Maybe I am like America, I thought hopefully; I look different ways to different people. Maybe it didn't matter how I looked to myself. Nothing mattered, I told my reflection. As long as it happened, I could forget everything else. Even the lie.

As soon as the lights were out, I knew, of course, that I had been wrong. In the dark Jack Barron wasn't important at all. Uncle Howard was the one. He moved in under my bed, and while I was able at the outset to leap free of him, I could not, no matter how deeply I burrowed under the covers, shut out his voice. If he had only talked like an Indiana farmer who had once lied about a bowl of strawberries, perhaps I could have handled him, but somehow the Uncle Howard who had received the punishment became confused with the nameless one who had done the punishing. He spoke in the hollow voice of The Hand.

"Gundred is FINE," he said. "As right as RAIN." The words, once loosed, rolled around the room slowly.

I turned over in bed. I had told other lies before, I told myself. Everybody had, sometime.

Not about life and death, Uncle Howard reminded me from the darkness. Not about death. Not even Tamara had done that.

I stared into space, into the direction of the wall across from my bed. I couldn't see it but I tried to re-create it in detail as if it were daylight. The red and white triangular school banner pinned in the middle, Nancy's framed picture of Gary Cooper, the crooked little crack which combined with the smudge just below it looked in the half light of the early morning like a squatting rabbit. When it was all there safely, I let myself answer Uncle Howard.

Tamara's lies hurt people, I told him. This lie couldn't hurt anyone.

For a moment I thought I had silenced him. All I could hear was the even breathing of Nancy across the room and on the table beside me my Big Ben alarm clock clicking like a hockey game. Then, it seemed to me, there was a rustle under the bed like a hand running over the surface of silk.

"And if Gundred dies?" Uncle Howard whispered. The whisper faded away and when it returned, Uncle Howard spoke slowly, picking his words, one by one, from Alice's framed quotation. "There is nothing either good or bad," he said, "but thinking makes it so. Thinking makes it so."

I buried my head under my pillow, feeling the white softness of it billow about my face. This is what a cloud feels like, I thought. The middle of a cloud is dark, not white. And Gundred is not going to die. Mrs. Murphy said so. Somehow I must have finally fallen asleep for I remember that when the knock came on the door before the morning bell, I awoke feeling untroubled and for a moment I thought Uncle Howard must have gone.

Madame Marchette stood at the door. Her hair, usually in precise, landscaped ridges, was tumbled under a dark net. She was wrapped in a wrinkled tan pongee robe, the color of package paper, gathered hastily around the waist with a black silk dress belt. On her feet were her everyday suede shoes, the laces not tied. Looking at her so jumbled, so out of character, I had a sudden, intimate picture of the way she must have jumped out of bed and grabbed whatever was at hand, and I was frightened.

She ran her hands in and out of her wide Japanese sleeves. "Ah, *mes pauvres enfants,*" she said, "are you awake? I have something I must tell you. Oh, how shall I say it?"

I sat up in bed, my feet safely off the floor. I knew what Madame Marchette was going to say. The knowledge settled in my stomach like a cold stone while Madame Marchette ran her hands in and out of her sleeves, in and out.

"Gundred died last night," she said.

That day Uncle Howard came out from under the bed and followed me about in the broad daylight. He wasn't always there but I never knew when to expect him. Without warning he would lean over my shoulder. "Gundred is DEAD," he would say, pressing down hard on the last word in the manner of Mrs. Murphy. During the next week he was there both times that Jack Barron stopped me on the campus to give me a promised milk bottle. I tried to shake him off and give the moment its wholehearted due, but I couldn't.

At Gundred's funeral, in a drab little parlor whose ceilings and walls were covered with old, brown-edged water stains, Uncle Howard sat on a straight chair directly behind me. It was a bright day. The sun poured in through long uncurtained windows and lay without mercy on Gundred's closed casket, on the lonely lily plant beside it, on the rows of empty chairs, and on us—Madame Marchette and the five remaining younger girls, the only mourners. At the doorway two black-frocked priests held pocket watches in their hands and argued as to which would conduct the service. The loser, a short, well-fed balding man, walked to the lectern at the front of the room, still nursing his watch and his ill temper, and began to read at top speed from the Bible already opened (and always opened, I suppose, at the same place). In front of me Tamara wept noisily, whether in remorse or not I could not tell, but Alice nudged Mary and she nodded her head. I moved up to the next row into an empty seat beside Mary. Uncle Howard moved up a row too.

After that Uncle Howard came and went, leaving me alone for days at a time. But on the evening of Bottle Night as I was lining up my bottles and waiting with the others for nine o'clock and crashing time, he came back. Nancy was holding up a bottle, showing us how she planned to do it.

"I am going to slam it down the hall like this," she said, "and with the first one I am going to say, 'Down with French lessons, down with tutti frutti and *s'il vous plaît,* and hurray for the States!' "

I picked up a bottle. "And I'm going to say," I started, but just then as unmistakably as if the door had opened and the maid announced him, Uncle Howard walked in. I put the bottle down. "I don't know yet what I'm going to say."

At eight o'clock, disappointed and disgusted, I invented an errand, put on my red leather jacket, walked outside and sat down alone on a bench beside the football field. I reminded myself of the time when I was seven and all at once I had become terrified that the verse all the children chanted was true. "Step on a crack, break your mother's back." For two weeks I had stepped so carefully in such a torment of fear—not that I really believed the silly verse, but just in case, oh, just in case.

Suddenly I hated the American School and Mrs. Murphy and Tamara and Uncle Howard and I hated Gundred's parents for leaving her alone too long. It was a wordless kind of hatred—nothing I could put a name to for crashing a bottle about. It went off into too many directions, like a firecracker rising within me and exploding into skyrocket splinters. All I could do was to sit within the half-circular embrace of the red brick buildings and watch it.

I suppose I sat there on the bench in my red leather jacket for thirty minutes before the door to the classroom reopened, letting out a flat square of light onto the football field and a group of Boy Scouts jostling and pushing each other around. I suppose I sat there for another thirty minutes after the door opened—an hour altogether. . . . Yet how can it be that when whole months slide away, leaving nothing behind, I should remember this hour so vividly, the two halves of the hour rounded like a fruit, the one half so bitter, the other sweet?

Jack Barron emerged from the lighted square and as the other boys, all day students, disappeared through the main gate, he walked toward me, tossing a tennis ball lightly in the air. He sat down on the other end of my bench.

"Hey," he said, "I thought this was Bottle Night. Aren't you going to crash?"

I had never seen him before in his Boy Scout uniform, his knee socks folded so carefully over the band of his khaki knickers. He put the ball in his pocket, and I noticed that his sleeves were short. His hands had left his cuffs far behind and now they lay on his knees, large and awkward and obviously strange to him. All at once I forgot about my brown oxfords. I forgot that I ever wanted to be clever.

"I'm going up to Bottle Night," I said. "When it's time. When the nine o'clock bell rings."

"I'd like to crash a couple of bottles like that once," he said. He half laughed, fumbling in his pocket for his ball again and began to bounce it up and down on the ground between his knees.

"What would you crash your bottles to?" I asked. "What would you wish?"

"Well, I'd crash one down to the end of Latin grammar, but that wouldn't be my first one." He bent forward and concentrated on the ball between his knees, hitting it faster and faster. "On the first one I'd wish that a certain girl, a certain girl with a red jacket, would like me."

The bench that Jack and I were sitting on suddenly seemed to swing off into the December sky where stars were hanging like a Chinese New Year parade. I knew that if I looked down toward the ground I would see the American School, just tiny red buildings, after all, becoming smaller and smaller until, if I looked again, they would be lost and instead, spread out below me would be the whole lovely land of China, swaying with rice fields and willow trees and tiger lilies.

"You might be wasting your bottle," I whispered. "Maybe she already likes you."

"I don't know." He put his ball away and locked his hands around his knees. "I gave her a couple of bottles recently. She didn't act as if she liked me much."

The bench straightened out. Sounds of the city drifted over the walls of the American School, separating themselves from the general hum of busyness, one by one, almost as if they were intended to mark the moment: the rhythmic flat padding of a ricksha coolie's feet, the honking of a distant horn, the many raised voices that dominate a Chinese city—a high complaining chant of a beggar, an angry coolie argument, the eternally shrill shrew. All at once I knew that I could talk to Jack Barron and he would understand. His understanding might have grown faster than the words to say it with, like his hands had grown faster than his arms, but no matter what he said, he would understand. So I told him. About Gundred and the funeral and Uncle Howard, and I told him about the lie.

When I had finished, he reached into his pocket for

his ball again. "I know how you feel," he said. "But you really know that your lie had nothing to do with it, don't you? Gundred would have died anyway."

"Yes, I know," I said and for the first time I did know. "But it's more than that. I wish I could turn time back. I wish we could begin the year all over again and maybe then if I'd been different, somehow it wouldn't have happened."

"I think it would have." He held the ball loosely in his right hand—gently, and looked at it. "Once when I was little, a bird fell out of a tree, a baby bird. He couldn't fly. He was so soft and small. I was going to put him back in the tree. I wanted to do it quickly before he could be frightened and I wanted to feel his softness and I was in a hurry because I didn't want him to drop. And I didn't mean to; I was just dumb. I held him too tightly and he died." Jack let the ball roll around the palm of his hand. "That was worse than your lie. I really killed him. Of course I was little and I haven't thought about it for a long time, but I wished that I could turn time back too. I wished that I could find that baby bird under the tree all over again."

We sat there quietly, suspended on the bench in the night. Never had the world been so sad and happy and lovely a place before.

After a while Jack looked at his watch. "It's almost nine," he said. He rammed his hands into his pockets. "Say, have you ever—" he spoke quickly and carefully as if he had practiced in his mind just what he was going to say, yet was not sure how it would sound out loud. "Have you ever kissed a boy?"

The bench rocked slowly back and forth. "No," I admitted, "I haven't."

He dug his hands deeper into his pockets so that his bare wrists and arms were buried up to the cuffs of his sleeves. "I've never kissed a girl either."

Suddenly behind us the American School asserted itself. The nine o'clock bell split the night into a thousand quivering pieces. Jack and I stood up.

"Before you go," he said, "I'd like to. If it's all right."

"It's all right."

He took his hands out of his pockets and placed them lightly on my shoulders. He leaned down and kissed me quickly on the mouth.

"Merry Christmas," he whispered. "I'll see you when you get back."

"Merry Christmas," I answered. *"Merry* Christmas!" And I turned and ran into the dormitory.

As soon as I opened the door, I remembered, as if I had just come from another country, that it was Bottle Night. I could hear the lights snapping off, all but the one red bulb at the head of the stairs; I could hear muffled giggles and the unmistakable clink of glass. I took the steps two at a time. At the top the girls were gathered —Alice and Mary, Nancy, Tamara—surrounded by empty milk bottles.

"We brought yours out," Alice said, "and we're all ready. Nancy's first and then you." She waved a bottle in the air—happily, carelessly, and she looked different than I had seen her before. Younger, somehow—like a little girl thinking only about the very moment and expecting the best from it.

They all looked different under the red bulb in the hallway. Even Tamara, her hair pushed off her forehead, had a kind of innocence about her. Perhaps it was the excitement that colored the hallway, but no, it was more than that. I didn't know the word then for what I felt had come to life among us, but I do now. There was a sense of deliverance.

Nancy crashed her bottle, saying just what she had planned to say. I picked up a bottle, hesitating a moment. Everything I had ever wanted to crash a bottle about belonged to some distant and unrecognizable past. As for Uncle Howard, I could barely remember the sound of his voice. I raised the bottle.

"Here's to Life!" I cried. Under my breath I added, "And how!"

About the Author

Jean Fritz was born in China and came to the United States when she was thirteen. "There were all kinds of wonders to be discovered," she recalls. "Maybe that's why I never did quite get over them, and why I like now to write about them."

She has been a children's librarian, and currently conducts a workshop in juvenile writing. Among her many books for children are *I, Adam; Magic to Burn;* and *Early Thunder.* Married and the mother of two grown children, she lives in Dobbs Ferry, New York.